Soviet and East European Studies

SOVIET ECONOMISTS OF THE TWENTIES

NAMES TO BE REMEMBERED

SOVIET ECONOMISTS OF THE TWENTIES

NAMES TO BE REMEMBERED

BY

NAUM JASNY

CAMBRIDGE

AT THE UNIVERSITY PRESS

1972

Published by the Syndics of the Cambridge University Press
Bentley House, 200 Euston Road, London NW1 2DB
American Branch: 32 East 57th Street, New York, N.Y.10022

© Cambridge University Press 1972

Library of Congress Catalogue Card Number: 77–168894

ISBN: 0 521 08302 8

Printed in Great Britain
at the University Printing House, Cambridge
(Brooke Crutchley, University Printer)

CONTENTS

Contents

PUBLISHER'S NOTE

Naum Jasny had completed the draft manuscript of this book before his death but some clarification and systematisation were needed before publication. The major work on the first task was undertaken by Paul Stevenson; George Garvy and Constantine Brancovan gave much assistance in the second task. Max Hayward and George Katkov were valued consultants. The editorial work was carried out by Michael Kaser on the authority of Dr Jasny's daughters, Mrs Natascha Brunswick and Mrs Tatyana Moss.

Acknowledgement should also be made to the American Council of Learned Societies for a grant made to the author, and to R. W. Davies, Philip Hanson and Alec Nove for comments when the book was submitted to the Press.

INTRODUCTION

This book deals with the nonconformists in the Soviet economic field during the 1920s. I am proud that it has fallen to me to honour the narodniks and others who did all they could, first to help Russia recover from the catastrophe caused by Lenin's mad decision to raise a backward agricultural country, weakened by war, revolution and civil war, instantaneously into the paradise of Communism, and then to counteract Stalin's efforts to collectivise and industrialise.

In due course the Soviet economy, industry in particular, grew for some years at rapid, one might say super-rapid rates. So it may seem that Stalin was right. But between the years of rapid growth (almost exclusively after World War II) and the drive initiated in the late twenties lies a whole decade (if the years of World War II are disregarded) of violent upheaval. The economic development started by Stalin in the late twenties did not lead directly to the high rates of growth in the thirties; its immediate effect was the decline of the early thirties which culminated in the disaster of the winter of 1932–3. If Stalin foresaw this disaster and accepted it as the price of progress, the secret went with him into his grave.

It seems certain in fact that Stalin foresaw the developments of the early thirties as much or as little as Lenin foresaw that his attempt to introduce Communism almost overnight (the so-called War Communism) in 1919–20 would lead to the disaster of 1920–1, which was even greater than that of the early thirties.

What happened on the economic front in the early thirties could have been attained only by a dictatorship of unprecedented scope and ruthlessness. The peasants did not submit to full-scale collectivisation until half their livestock was dead, and they themselves died of starvation in immense numbers during the winter of 1932–3. Every intelligent man in the economic field who believed in persuasion rather than force, every man with a conscience in the non-Communist camp, was put out of circulation in 1930–1. The

Mensheviks were condemned in a show trial,[1] which ended with jail sentences ranging from five to ten years. Uncounted thousands, perhaps tens of thousands, went into exile, where they were later joined by those with jail sentences.

The years in jail meted out to Groman at the show trial seem at first sight a trifle compared with the death sentences imposed on such stalwarts of Bolshevism as Rykov or Bukharin. (Murder was reserved by Stalin primarily for his party comrades, including even personal friends.) But from the point of view of the interests of the country, the results were the same. It was deprived of the services of a whole generation of the best of its intelligentsia. Those few who survived the more than twenty years of jail and/or exile to profit from the amnesty declared after Stalin's death (it is not known whether all of them have been rehabilitated) could not, of course, be of much use as economic leaders or teachers, even if there were room for this under Khrushchev.

The opposition of the twenties operated both inside and outside Russia. The positions of the two groups differed considerably. The opposition outside Russia was mainly interested in politics, the opposition inside operated mainly in the economic field. This book deals only with the opposition inside Russia, and specifically in the economic field.

The non-Communist opposition of the twenties inside Russia, prior to its annihilation, ranged from monarchists to socialists. However, if there was a monarchist opposition inside Russia operating in the economic field, it did not reveal itself clearly. The opposition in the economic field was in the main made up of bourgeois republican groups, various shades of narodniks (populists) – or neo-narodniks as they were called after the October Revolution, stretching from the so-called trudoviks (from the word *trud*, labour) to the Socialist-Revolutionaries – and finally of the Mensheviks, making up the extreme left but also containing different shades.

The original intention of this writer was to cover only the Mensheviks. There were, however, several reasons for adding the

---

[1] *Protsess kontr-revolyutsionnoi organizatsii Men'shevikov (mart 1931)*, (*The Trial of the Counter-revolutionary Organization of the Mensheviks (March 1931)*), Moscow, 1931, henceforth referred to as *Trial*.

neo-narodniks. The principal one was that both movements came close together in the most tragic period dealt with here, the years 1928–30. Moreover, if the socialist movement were ever reborn in Russia, sub-division into Mensheviks and other socialists would be extremely unlikely. Finally, it seemed unfair to cover one wing of the democratic intelligentsia and to neglect another which was so close to the first mentally and psychologically.[1]

Before continuing, we should be clear as to the meaning of the term Menshevik as used in this book. The term is generally used in two senses. The first involves formal membership in some Menshevik organisation. The second relates to a mode of thought: it primarily denotes Social-Democrats who objected to the dictatorship of a party and its leader, or to Lenin's Jacobinism. This writer, for example, did not for long periods formally belong to any Menshevik organisation, but he was always a Menshevik in his way of thinking.

In the Menshevik trial, Groman for example testified (*Trial*, p. 46) that he was a member of the RSDWP until 1922 and from 1926 to 1930. All such statements are disregarded here. Groman's political status was the same in 1924 as in 1921. All persons designated as Mensheviks in this book may be taken to have been such by reason of their mode of thought. Specifically the leaders, Groman, Bazarov and Ginzburg, must probably be classed as Mensheviks in outlook only. It is possible that very few were also formally members of a Menshevik organisation.

Part I of the book discusses developments in the Soviet economy from the October Revolution to 1931 and the activities of the opposition in 1922–31 as a whole. Part II is devoted to persons active in the opposition. There are separate chapters on those believed to have been the leaders – Groman, Bazarov, Ginzburg and Kondrat'ev; Ginzburg would probably not have received a chapter to himself if his draft of the Five-Year Plan (FYP) were not of special interest, but it might have been preferable to have

---

[1] However, the reasons for including persons other than the Mensheviks lost force as the work on the project progressed, since no one who could be definitely classed as socialist-revolutionary was discovered among those *prominent* in the economic field, including the teaching of economics. This was unexpected, in view of the predominance of the Socialist Revolutionaries in the Constituent Assembly.

discussed the Ginzburg draft plan in Part I and to have devoted the fourth special chapter to Sukhanov, a much more colourful and courageous figure than Ginzburg. The last two chapters contain short sketches of a large number of individuals. The selection is of course somewhat arbitrary, depending on personal acquaintance, the quantity of their published writings etc. For example, S. A. Pervushin, who is not discussed, was certainly a first-rank economist. He was removed from the list of permanent contributors to *Planovoe khozyaistvo* (*Planned Economy*) after issue No. 5 of 1930, and obviously was not approved of by those in power.[1]

For similar reasons S. A. Falkner is not discussed. He was a knowledgeable economist, speaking several foreign languages, who seems to have been for some time very close to Groman because of the interest of both men in the balance of the national economy. Falkner's name was dropped from the *Planovoe khozyaistvo* list after issue No. 6 of 1930.

Rybnikov, a neo-narodnik and a friend of Kondrat'ev, is not mentioned, although he probably should be. I am sorry for such omissions, because everybody in opposition falling within the broad definition of 'socialist' who held out for a considerable time, or who did not bow so low as to be admitted among the 'elect' but lost his normal occupation and perhaps died prematurely in exile, has a moral right to be remembered here at least in a few words.

The presentation in this book overlaps to a certain extent with some other publications of this writer, mainly Chapters II, III and IV of *Soviet Industrialization 1928–1952* (Chicago, 1961). Long-range and middle-range planning, especially Lenin's GOELRO and the first Five-Year Plan, were dealt with in some detail in 'Perspective Planning', one of the four papers in *Essays on the Soviet Economy* (New York, 1962). A note on Groman by this writer was published in the *Russian Review*, January 1954. Only on rare occasions, mainly in the case of GOELRO, was it thought sufficient to give merely a reference. Complete avoidance of repetitions would have made this book virtually unreadable.

[1] The listing of a given person as a regular contributor to *Planovoe khozyaistvo* is examined in Ch. 3 (pp. 55–6).

Personal contacts were important for the preparation of the book. The writer was well acquainted with Groman, one of the two principal leaders of the opposition on the economic front. He also knew N. D. Kondrat'ev, the second principal leader, N. N. Sukhanov, who, as will be shown, played a great role at one time, and F. A. Cherevanin. He occasionally met several others, including M. I. Teitelbaum, A. M. Ginzburg, L. B. Kafengauz, A. E. Lositsky, N. P. Makarov and A. V. Chayanov.

Extensive use (with due permission) is made of the memoirs of the late Nikolai Vladislavovich Valentinov, who from 1922 to 1928 was editor of *Torgovo-promyshlennaya gazeta* (*Trade-Industrial Gazette*), the daily organ of the All-Union Economic Council (VSNKh) in Moscow, and in this capacity and otherwise had wide contacts with people working in the field which is the subject of this book. In 1928 he was transferred to Paris, where he edited a Soviet journal until 1930. At the end of that year he severed his relations with the Soviet regime.[1]

No comments in general are needed so far as books and articles are concerned. The use of the official volume *Trial* needs some explanation. The trial was a farce. The accused and even the prosecution witnesses (there were no others) said what they were ordered to say.[2] The official designation of the published account of the trial as a 'stenographic report' is of course no guarantee of its accuracy (cf. Chapter 4 below).

Since the trial was primarily a show trial, it was not generally noticed that the published report contained also extremely valuable material, especially in the part dealing with the 'crimes' confessed by the accused. Disregarding such formulae as 'I confess to having

---

[1] The voluminous memoirs covering the period from 1922 to 1927 are available only in manuscript form at Columbia University. Access to this material was invaluable for this book, especially since the information in them was supplemented by the lively correspondence which Valentinov was good enough to have with this writer in spite of his age (he was 82 at the time) and bad health. I would add that Valentinov seemed to possess an excellent memory. He wrote to me about an article by Preobrazhensky published in 1923 in *Vestnik Kommunisticheskoi Akademii* (*Courier of the Communist Academy*). I found it in *Vestnik Kommunisticheskoi Akademii* for 1924. And yet he insisted that his memory was good only for conversations, not for dates.

[2] There may have been some exception. Kondrat'ev, who appeared as a prosecution witness, may have been promised that he would not be forced to name all members of his group – a case of the star performer enjoying a special concession.

committed the crime or treasonable actions, etc.', it is clear that the acts confessed really redounded to the credit of the accused. Again, the relation between the positions of the Mensheviks and neo-narodniks and the changes in these are nowhere so clearly defined as in the testimony of the defendant Groman and the prosecution witness Kondrat'ev. And, of course, evidence on the positions held and time of arrest, even data on age and the like has its value. The development of one who in 1923 applied for membership in the Communist party and finished as one of the accused in this trial seems nowhere so well brought out as in the testimony of Sukhanov.

It is of course realised that the source from which all this evidence is taken is untrustworthy. It is largely arbitrary when one decides that one piece of evidence is truthful and another is a lie. The reader must consider carefully for himself in each case whether acceptance of the evidence concerned is justified or not.

PART I. THE ECONOMY

I have the difficult task of outlining the development of the Soviet economy during the period of almost fifteen years from the October Revolution of 1917 to the trial of the Mensheviks in March 1931. This relatively short period saw many far-reaching and often violent changes in the Soviet Union. A greatly compressed description of the somewhat longer period from the October Revolution to the end of 1932 takes up almost four long chapters in this writer's *Soviet Industrialization, 1928–1952*.[1] Here the somewhat shorter period must be dealt with in a fraction of this space, although much ground not touched on in my earlier study must be covered.

In *Soviet Industrialization*, I subdivided the whole period into four stages, but here only three are distinguished. The first two in each case are the so-called War Communism (here called the pre-NEP period because the term 'War Communism' for this period is misleading – see p. 13 below) and NEP (New Economic Policy). The War Communism period extended from the October Revolution to 21 March 1921, when NEP was proclaimed. NEP lasted from then until December 1927, when the XV Party Congress announced a stepping-up of the campaign against the better-off peasants, the start of the industrialisation drive and hence, by implication, the end of NEP.

In my *Soviet Industrialization*, the NEP period is followed by the 'warming-up' period, which lasted until 7 November 1929, when Stalin announced the start of the full-scale collectivisation drive in a *Pravda* article entitled 'The Year of the Great Turning-Point'. The fourth period was that of the 'all-out drive', accompanied by an orgy of planning, to industrialise and collectivise. This period culminated in the catastrophe of the winter of 1932–3. It is considered to have ended at the plenary session of the Central Committee of the party on 10 January 1933, when a resolution was

[1] Naum Jasny, *Soviet Industrialization 1928–1952*, Chicago, 1961.

adopted entitled 'The Results of the First Five-Year Plan and the National Economic Plan for 1933' (1933 was the first year of the second Five-Year Plan).

In the present analysis the period from the end of NEP to the trial of the Mensheviks has not been subdivided, because the persons we are concerned with here spent little time out of jail after the publication of Stalin's article in November 1929.[1]

[1] The Socialist Revolutionary (S.R.) leaders were arrested earlier.

BEFORE NEP

WAR COMMUNISM

The unpreparedness of the Bolsheviks, after their seizure of power in October 1917, to organise the life of the country and specifically its economic life is best illustrated by some words of Lenin, who after all was by far the ablest of the Bolsheviks. As Lenin saw it: 'All will govern in turn under Socialism; soon they will get used to the idea that nobody governs.' Almost half a century has passed since then; socialism was officially declared to have been 'built' more than thirty years ago, but a situation in which 'nobody governs' seems to be as far away as ever.

However, Lenin was sensible enough to depart from the spirit of this dictum in the face of practical difficulties. One such difficulty was the fact that there were no Communists available for responsible tasks.

Valentinov[1] quotes a letter to Gorky in which Lenin said that if a man is seriously ill, Communist physicians should on no account be called in: they might be competent in politics, but knew nothing about medicine. Non-Communists, therefore, had to be used in large numbers in responsible positions even during the period of War Communism. When Lenin called for the GOELRO plan, those invited to draw it up were non-Communists to a man, except for Krzhizhanovsky, the chief, but his functions were mainly those of a supervisor.

In his article on planning published in *Pravda* on 22 February 1921 Lenin still showed great contempt for Communist planners.[2] This was reflected in the fact that when, in April 1921, the Gosplan was brought into being, the same non-Communist specialists were used who had worked on the GOELRO. The only Com-

---

[1] N. V. Valentinov, (*Memoirs*) (unpublished text, circulated privately), Vol. 1, p. 80.
[2] He called the articles by Kritsman in *Ekonomicheskaya zhizn'* empty chatter, and in his opinion the articles by Milyutin and Larin were not much better. But Kritsman, Milyutin and Larin were almost the only Communists involved in economic planning.

munist to be given a leading part in the work was a recent convert, Strumilin.

Lenin's basic idea during and after the October Revolution was that World War I must lead to 'drastic' social revolution. It was in pursuance of this idea that the October Revolution was followed by a wave of nationalisation. In accordance with a demand in the party programme of the Socialist Revolutionaries, now adopted by the Bolsheviks, the land was 'socialised'. (What a world of difference it would have made if this or a similar measure had been carried out – as would have been quite possible – a few months prior to October 1917.) In addition to the land, the banks and the greater part of industry were nationalised, as well as transport, wholesale trade, a large part of retail trade and so on. A state monopoly of foreign trade was established. Even small businesses with no more than one or two employees were nationalised. The work of registering these tiny concerns would have taken years. And all this in a country totally exhausted by the World War and a prolonged civil war.

Lenin attributed decisive importance to the nationalisation of the banks. In his opinion, banking had already been so highly developed before the Revolution that once certain abuses had been corrected the banks would be able to play a great role in the socialisation of the economy. The amalgamation of all banks in one gigantic State Bank with branches in every village and factory would, he thought, constitute nine-tenths of the socialist apparatus.[1]

From the first, attempts were made to control the management of the socialised land, and when the newly-nationalised land was made over to the peasants, Lenin warned that small lots only were to be permitted in the early stages. By a decree of 11 June 1918 the famous *kombedy* (committees of the poor) were organised in the villages. Their task was to combat the 'kulaks' (better-off peasants) and stimulate those elements who could be expected to help to achieve the goals of socialist revolution. Lenin took the *kombedy* very seriously. With their creation, he said, 'We move from unorganised socialism to real socialism.'[2]

[1] Lenin is here quoted from Friedrich Pollock, *Die planwirtschaftlichen Versuche in der Sowjetunion, 1917–1927*, Leipzig, 1929, p. 32.
[2] See Valentinov, *Memoirs*, Vol. I, pp. 17–19.

In reality the *kombedy* were like bandit organisations under the guise of which the peasants robbed each other, and they were abolished, little more than four months after their creation, by a decree published on 23 November 1918. After this disastrous experiment the idea of anything resembling 'forcible' collectivisation of agriculture was given up, and Lenin reconciled himself to individual peasant farming on socialised land. He now concentrated fully on introducing Communism in the towns with the help of farm products obtained without payment from the peasants.

The new programme adopted by the VIII Party Congress in March 1919 was an important stepping-stone towards Communism. As regards trade it demanded the replacement of retailing by the nationally-planned distribution of goods. By a decree of 11 October 1920, payment for telephones, water, sewage disposal, gas and electricity was abolished, and manual and white-collar workers were given free housing, fuel and transport. This decree was supplemented by one of 4 November 1920, according to which all consumer goods were to be distributed gratis to manual and white-collar workers.[1]

But Lenin was not able, by these decrees, to create a socialist, let alone a communist, economy. All he succeeded in doing was to stop the economic wheels turning, and he was forced to abandon the whole experiment only a few months after it had reached its peak.

The nationalisation of the banks, instead of fostering socialism, had simply led to the disruption of all banking operations. By 1920 the output of large-scale industry was down to 13 per cent of that in 1913. No pig iron or rolled steel was produced at all. The output of cotton fabrics by the textile factories went down to less than 4 per cent of the 1913 figure. By 1920 freight transport on the railways had declined, in terms of ton-kilometres, to 23 per cent of the 1913 level. This immense fall in output was accompanied by a corresponding decline in labour productivity. The 13 per cent of industrial output in 1920 as compared with 1913 required half as many workers as in the latter year. The labour force on the railways was 77 per cent larger in 1920 than in 1913.[2]

[1] Quoted in Pollock, *Die planwirtschaftlichen.*
[2] See *Planovoe khozyaistvo*, No. 11, 1927, pp. 258–9.

The calamitous state of socialist industry, in so far as it still managed to operate, is also clear from the fact that while wages (in terms of 1913 roubles) declined by 1920 to 59 per cent, production costs in the same terms went up by 69 per cent.[1] The money system was completely destroyed, the nominal value of the rouble having decreased trillions of times.

Agriculture, by comparison, showed up rather well as far as percentages go. Gross farm production reached 61 per cent of the 1913 level in 1920–1 and 52 per cent in 1921–2.[2] This output signified, however, just as great a catastrophe as in industry. The whole agricultural output was less than that needed for consumption by the peasants themselves. Almost all farm products supplied to the non-farm population were obtained by requisitioning. According to the calculations of the Central Statistical Office (CSO), total sales by farm producers in 1920 amounted to only 866 million pre-war roubles, of which 704 million were obtained by requisitioning – i.e. voluntary sales accounted for only 162 million roubles.[3]

Uneven distribution of available food supplies over the country's vast territory aggravated the situation, and deaths by starvation amounted to millions. According to Lorimer,[4] the Soviet population fell by 2.8 million in 1920 alone. The next two years brought further reductions of 368,000 and 406,000 respectively.[5]

THE END OF WAR COMMUNISM

Early in 1921, 'the first ambitious attempt to create a proletarian non-monetary economy',[6] an attempt introduced almost overnight, was abruptly discontinued and NEP was proclaimed.

The starving population had reacted to the grandiose experiment with revolts. The minutes of the X Party Congress, from 8 to 16 March 1921, describe a series of armed peasant uprisings in the

---

[1] See A. B. Gukhman, *Ekonomicheskoe obozrenie*, No. 9, 1928, p. 114.
[2] According to *Narodnoe kohzyaistvo SSSR v 1958g.* Moscow, 1959, p. 350, farm output in 1921 was 60 per cent of that in 1913.
[3] Quoted by V. G. Groman, *Sotsialisticheskoe khozyaistvo*, No. 1–2, 1923, p. 89.
[4] F. Lorimer, *The Population of the Soviet Union*, League of Nations, Geneva, 1946.
[5] But for the famine there would probably have been a substantial increase in population in 1920, despite the losses in the world war and the subsequent civil war.
[6] L. Kritsman, quoted by Pollock, *Die planwirtschaftlichen*, p. 77.

second half of 1920 and early 1921. It is noteworthy that the leaders of these uprisings were frequently Communists. Early in 1921, the workers also became restive and there were violent clashes between the government and workers in Petrograd.[1]

The abandonment of War Communism came at the same time as the great Kronstadt sailors' mutiny, from 28 February to 18 March 1921. The X Party Congress, in which Lenin announced the end of War Communism, took place on 8–16 March 1921. A session of the Central Committee of the Party approved the law on the replacement of requisitioning by a food tax on 18 March 1921.

In his great speech to the X Party Congress Lenin declared: 'Either we must appease the middle peasant (*serednyak*) economically and agree to liberalise trade turnover, or...it will be impossible to maintain the power of the proletariat in Russia. This must be stated clearly and frankly...' Lenin did not give his audience very much time to think the situation over: 'This very evening a message must go out all over the world that the Congress of the Ruling Party has replaced requisitioning by a tax...and in this way a firm relation between the proletariat and the peasantry is being established.'[2]

While Lenin, the ruler of a population dying from starvation, frankly recognised the immensity of his error,[3] the Party as such claimed that Communism had been forced on it by the conditions of war, and misleadingly described this period as that of War Communism.

NONCONFORMISTS UNDER 'WAR COMMUNISM'

The Whites continued to fight the Bolsheviks after the October Revolution, partly with the help of foreign powers. Most of the Mensheviks found it preferable to fight on the side of the Bolsheviks. However, not only the Socialist Revolutionaries but the Mensheviks

---

[1] See R. Abramovich, *The Soviet Revolution, 1917–1939*, New York, 1962, pp. 193–4.
[2] Pollock, *Die planwirtschaftlichen*, p. 116.
[3] In his speech on 17 October 1921, Lenin (*Sochineniya*, 5th edn., Vol. XVIII, Moscow, p. 370) said that the attempt to introduce Communism in the spring of 1921 had resulted in a defeat greater than those inflicted by Kolchak, Denikin or Pilsudski.

as well, and even such left-wingers as Sukhanov, were definitely opposed to the type of socialism Lenin was introducing.[1]

Valentinov in his memoirs says that: 'In the first years of the Soviet regime I did everything possible not to accept a government job.'[2] He was saved by his invaluable library: he exchanged his 84-volume Brockhaus and Efron Encyclopedia for 2 *puds* (about 72 pounds) of flour.[3] Valentinov's negative attitude to government jobs was, according to him, nothing out of the ordinary.

There was no reluctance, however, to accept work in food organisations. The consumers' co-operatives and particularly the Central Co-operative Union (*Tsentrosoyuz*) were flooded by non-Communists, including, for example, Groman and Ginzburg, who were later to become prominent planners. I myself was among those who sought refuge in Tsentrosoyuz. The only other outlet for people who disagreed with Lenin was in teaching.

Valentinov's memoirs throw interesting light on the attitude of people who did hold government jobs. Fedorov, an engineer and expert in the production of cotton fabrics, said to him. 'Why did we specialists work poorly before NEP? Not only because we were badly paid and looked upon as servants of capitalism, saboteurs and secret counter-revolutionaries. One went to work and felt like vomiting. At work it was as if one had to carry water in a sieve, to do things that did not make sense.'[4]

The engineer then went on to illustrate the futility of his work by describing how he had been ordered to calculate the exchange value of a certain kind of fabric not in money but in 'direct-work counting', but the people who gave him this order had not the faintest idea of what the phrase meant! Even more interesting is the story of I. A. Kalinnikov, a prominent member of GOELRO[5] and later of Gosplan, who was to figure as a defendant at the trial

---

[1] On the opposition of Sukhanov to War Communism, see the section devoted to him in Ch. 10 below, pp. 179–84.
[2] Some nominal job was needed to be entitled to a ration card and not to be treated as a 'bourgeois'.
[3] Valentinov, *Memoirs*, Vol. I, p. 2.
[4] *Ibid*. p. 2.
[5] For a detailed account of GOELRO see my *Essays on the Soviet Economy*, New York, 1962, pp. 185–93.

of the 'Industrial Party' (*Prompartiya*) in December 1930. Kalin-nikov told Valentinov:

In 1920 we had to work out a plan for the electrification of the country and simultaneously for its industrialisation [this is very illuminating: the plan for industrialisation was, as it were, incidental]; but this all-embracing plan had to be elaborated not for an abstract environment but for fully determined economic conditions. In the period of war communism, one had to hypnotise oneself into believing that this sense-less system was ideal and as such was being established for ever. I speak not of myself only, [continued Kalinnikov]. Many of us had the feeling that thanks to NEP, we had, thank God, jumped from the moon down to the earth.[1]

[1] Valentinov, *Memoirs*, Vol. I, p. 43.

2

DURING NEP

EARLY NEP

The fundamental reversal of economic policy implied by the proclamation of NEP is apparent from the fact that while the abolition of trade and its replacement by the free distribution of consumer goods was the basic feature of Lenin's Communism, NEP was summed up in the formula that 'the exchange of goods must be the prime lever of the new policy', the exchange to be in the first instance between the cities and the villages. This basic formula was not proclaimed until the party conference of 28 March 1921. NEP, however, is normally considered to have been launched at the X Party Congress of 8–16 March 1921, or, more precisely, on 21 March, the date of the decree by which the requisitioning of farm products was replaced by an agricultural tax and the possibility thus created for some exchange of goods between town and country.

Requisitioning was tantamount to the confiscation from the peasants of all surpluses, and even what they needed for their own subsistence. The single agricultural tax in kind, which replaced it, was still very harsh; while bringing in less than the amount obtained by requisitioning, it was nevertheless designed to cover the minimum requirements of the army, urban workers and the rest of the non-farm population. The regime felt it could now afford to take less from the peasants in direct taxation because the restoration of transport and industry would enable it to obtain farm products through normal channels, i.e. in exchange for the products of large and small-scale industry.[1] After the harvest of 1924, it was decided that the single agricultural tax must be paid in money rather than, as originally, in kind.[2] This measure obliterated every trace of Lenin's 'Communism'.

The abolition of requisitioning was accompanied by the elimina-

[1] X Party Congress (8–16 March 1921), *KPSS v resolyutsiyakh i resheniyakh s'ezdov, konferentsii i plenumov TsK*, Moscow, 7th edn. 1954, Vol. I, p. 563.
[2] XIII Party Congress (14–15 January 1924), *ibid.* p. 798.

tion of the other features of War Communism introduced in 1919–21. In 1919 it appeared that, come what might, the socialisation of the economy effected after the October Revolution would be maintained. But the decree of 17 March 1921 prohibited any further socialisation. A decree of 27 October 1921 went even further by ordering all enterprises which, as of 17 March, had not actually been put under state management but had only nominally been confiscated, to be returned to their owners.[1] Private small-scale industry was thus restored, and while large-scale industry in general remained state property, concerns which could not be operated by the state were to be leased to private entrepreneurs or even to foreign capitalists. Co-operatives, a form of management much less stringent than state management, were to be given every possible encouragement in cities and villages.

Though NEP was launched in the spring of 1921, Soviet agriculture suffered so much from drought in that year that no serious recovery took place for some time. Large-scale industrial production increased by 32 per cent in 1921–2 – an almost negligible recovery considering the amazingly low level of output in 1920–1 (less than 20 per cent of the 1913 level). Agriculture was badly hit by the drought. The sown acreage decreased, there was a fall in livestock, and the condition of the surviving stock deteriorated. The population continued to starve. Friedrich Pollock, a good observer,[2] in subdividing the NEP period into phases, described the first phase, from March 1921 to October 1923, as one of economic chaos.

The recovery brought about by NEP began with the 1922–3 harvest. The course of the recovery was anything but smooth. In his review of the 1922–3 fiscal year Groman wrote: 'The year 1922–3 was the first normal year of economic life after eight abnormal ones. The country was at peace internally and externally, enjoyed a satisfactory grain harvest, entered into relatively close

---

[1] Pollock, *Die planwirtschaftlichen*, p. 137.

[2] *Ibid.* In his study, apart from an exhaustive utilisation of published sources, Pollock draws on his personal observations made during a trip to the USSR in 1927. He was allowed to see scarcely anybody except Communists. Krzhizhanovsky is the only person in Gosplan whom he thanks for his help, apart from the Chairman, R. E. Vaisberg, who will be extensively quoted in Part II of this book on account of his role as the discoverer of Groman, Bazarov, Kondrat'ev and others. On his visit to Gosplan, Pollock apparently failed to see Groman or Bazarov, or even Strumilin.

Table 1. *Ratio of the price index of industrial goods to that of farm produce (retail price index of the Kondrat'ev Institute)*

Year	Month	Ratio	Year	Month	Ratio
1922	October	1.61	1924	January	1.78
	November	1.51		February	1.59
	December	1.67		March	1.60
1923	January	1.84		April	1.41
	February	1.80		May	1.27
	March	1.80		June	1.47
	April	2.21		July	1.37
	May	2.23		August	1.22
	June	2.19		September	1.29
	July	2.11		October	1.41
	August	1.87			
	September	2.80			
	October	2.97			
	November	2.49			
	December	2.02			

SOURCE: A. N. Malafeev, *Istoriya tsenoobrazovaniya v SSSR (1917–1963gg.)* (*History of Price-formation in the USSR*), Moscow, 1964, p. 386.

relations with the outside world, and achieved a basis for normal development.'

But the whole economic machinery was so stalled that it was not easy to get it to tick over again at a normal pace.[1] The output of large-scale industry, while increasing in 1922–3 by about 30 per cent, was by the end of the fiscal year still only little more than one-third of that of 1913. Actually Groman could have made his favourable statement on developments in 1922–3 only in a state of euphoria induced by the abandonment of the attempt to introduce Lenin-type Communism. While the features mentioned in his review had brought about a certain recovery, the price structure, not mentioned by him, was in bad shape in the year in question. This was the year in which an immense disparity between the prices of industrial and farm goods developed, a disparity which Trotsky aptly called 'scissors' (*nozhnitsy*) (see Table 1).

[1] *Narodnoe khozyaistvo SSSR na 1922/23g.* Moscow–Leningrad, 1924, p. 8.

If the price ratio was not favourable for farm products at the end of the 1921–2 fiscal year, by the end of 1922–3 the disparity had become immense. This disastrous situation was the result of unwise policies of VSNKh, and in particular of its deputy chairman Pyatakov. A famous order of the VSNKh (drafted by Pyatakov) of 16 July 1923, prescribed that 'The general guiding principle of the activities of enterprises as well as of the VSNKh for the coming period is profit as the aim, balance as the method',[1] and this directive was handled in the crudest possible manner. As a result there arose an absurd situation in which, at a time when the output of large-scale industry was only about 40 per cent of pre-war, the market was glutted with unsaleable industrial goods: in 1924 the rate of growth of output of large-scale industry was significantly reduced (see Table 2). The relationship between the prices of farm products and those of goods available for purchase by the peasants became considerably less unfavourable after the end of the fiscal year 1922–3, but at its very best the relationship under NEP never reached more than about three-quarters of the pre-war level.

ECONOMIC POLICIES

The most important changes during NEP were in the Party's attitude to the relation of agriculture to industry, i.e. of the villages to the towns, and to the different categories of peasants within the village. The resolution of the XII Party Congress (17–25 April 1923) declared that 'Agriculture, although it is still on a low technical level, plays the dominant role in the economy of the USSR. At the same time our party must not for a moment forget, or leave out of account in considering any of its moves, the virtual preponderance of the peasant economy'.[2]

The XII Party Congress resolution had in an earlier section stressed that 'agriculture will for a long time remain the basis of the economy of the USSR'.[3] One can see how unlikely a significant shift of emphasis from agriculture to industry appeared at that time from the fact that the resolution spoke of it as something

---

[1] See Valentinov, *Memoirs*, p. 166.
[2] *KPSS v resolyutsiyakh*, Vol. I, p. 687.   [3] *Ibid.* p. 682.

which could occur only when the work of electrification was nearing completion.[1] The same note was struck at the XIII Party Conference, 16–18 January 1924: 'The peasant economy is the basic foundation for the restoration of industry and consequently for the growth of the working class...Hence the greatest possible support of the peasant economy is required not only in the interest of the Soviet regime, but also in the interests of the speediest possible development of industry itself.'[2]

While the development of co-operatives in the village was favoured, it was to be 'gradual' and 'voluntary'.[3] At the same time the development of individual peasant farming was to be encouraged; moreover, the stronger peasant households were clearly designed to profit most from certain measures taken at that time. Thus, the decision of the Plenary session of the Central Committee of 23–30 April 1925 urged an energetic struggle against frequent redistribution of communal land – thus reflecting a standard demand of the stronger peasants. Furthermore, it was decided to make it easier for peasants to rent land, both communal and unused state land, and, last but not least, they were again permitted to hire labour. The freedom of peasant accumulation was emphasised repeatedly by Stalin himself. And Bukharin in a famous slogan urged the more well-to-do peasants to 'enrich yourselves'.[4]

By the next year, however, the tone had changed somewhat. The resolution of the Plenary session of 6–9 April 1926, stated:

The growth of productive forces in the countryside is taking place in conditions of a struggle among the various social groups of the peasantry. The inevitable strengthening of the kulaks at the present stage of NEP, and their struggle to become masters of the countryside, make it incumbent on the party to consolidate and expand the economic and political union (*smychka*) of the proletariat with the poorer peasantry.[5]

The resolution went on to speak of measures to curb the kulaks' appetites.[6]

---

[1] *Ibid.* p. 687. This statement is also indicative of great illusions or ignorance with regard to the probable tempo of electrification.
[2] *Ibid.* p. 789.   [3] *Ibid.*
[4] *Pravda*, 24 April 1925.
[5] *KPSS v resolyutsiakh*, Vol. II, p. 264.
[6] *Ibid.*

A few months later, at the XV Party Conference (26 October–3 November 1926), there was talk of giving priority to industry.[1] There was also mention, apparently for the first time, of the need 'to reach and then to exceed the level of industrial development in the advanced capitalist countries'.

Next, as NEP drew to a close, the Combined Plenary Session of the Central Committee and the Central Control Commission of 21–23 October 1927, having repeated in even more explicit terms the idea that socialist industry must be the dominant sector of the economy and that heavy industry was to have priority within industry as a whole, demanded 'a more determined attack on the kulaks, on the basis of the successes achieved in cementing the union of the proletariat and poor peasants with the middle peasants'.[2]

Less than two months later the XV Party Congress took place. Its main theme is evident from the fact that it was dubbed 'The Congress of Collectivisation'. The Congress decided on all-out collectivisation of agriculture as a matter of urgency, and formulated a plan for expanding and fostering the system of collective farms (*kolkhozy* and *sovkhozy*).[3] It proclaimed that: 'The proletariat, having overcome the bias in its own party against the middle peasant (*serednyak*), and having consolidated the worker–peasant bloc, is now in a position to embark on more systematic and more active restrictions on the kulaks and private entrepreneurs.'[4] 'It is necessary to give priority, on the basis of further co-operation of peasant enterprises, to the gradual transition of the peasantry to large-scale production (collective working of the land on the basis of intensification and mechanisation.'[5]

As already noted, according to the plenum of the Central Committee of April 1925, collectivisation was to proceed gradually and 'voluntarily'. The word 'gradually' still figured in the resolution of the XV Party Congress, but the word 'voluntarily' had disappeared from it. As regards policy towards the kulaks, while the April 1926 Plenum spoke of 'restrictions' on the kulaks, the XV Party Congress spoke of the need to bring about their 'definite economic elimination'.[6]

[1] *Ibid.* p. 294. [2] *Ibid.* pp. 414–16. [3] *Ibid.* p. 432.
[4] *Ibid.* p. 454. [5] *Ibid.* p. 437. [6] *Ibid.* p. 439.

This formula was already very close to the notorious call for 'annihilation of the kulaks as a class', which first made its appearance in Stalin's article 'The year of the great turning-point' in *Pravda*, 7 November 1929. This article also dropped the word 'gradual' in respect of the collectivisation of agriculture.

INDUSTRY

Table 2 shows the percentage growth by calendar year of the output of large-scale industry during NEP, as compared with the level of 1913; the prices are those of 1926–7.[1]

These figures show immense variations in the rates of growth from year to year. The variations were indeed so large that substantial differences in the rates of growth may be found between calendar and fiscal years. Thus while the figures in the table show a great drop in the rate of growth in 1924 (to 16.4 per cent), no such steep decline is observed for the fiscal year 1923–4.

The great decline in the rate of growth of large-scale industry in 1924 was obviously a result of the 'price-scissors' in 1922–3. By the end of 1924, i.e. almost four years after the end of 'War Communism', the output of large-scale industry was still not quite 50 per cent of the 1913 level, and it was only now that Soviet industry was in any position to make a big leap forward. According to Table 2, industry expanded in 1925 by fully two-thirds. Such an increase could obviously not be repeated in the following year. Nevertheless, the rise in 1926 was 43.2 per cent, so that over the two years 1925–7 there was a rise of almost 140 per cent. If the data in the table are correct, the 1913 level was thus exceeded in 1926, and this makes the increase of 43.2 per cent even more significant.

In retrospect, it is not difficult to account for the fact that the greatest rise in industrial output came only in the fifth year of NEP and in the penultimate year of the reconstruction period as a whole. But at the time there was no way of predicting this development. Groman, who, in his day, was the most outstanding student of

[1] *Sotsialisticheskoe stroitel'stvo, statistichesky sbornik*, Moscow, 1935, p. 3. Totals do not include the figures for forestry, fisheries and railway repair shops.

Table 2. *Output of large-scale industry in 1926–7 prices*

Year	Million roubles	Per cent of 1913	Annual increase
1913	10,251	100	...
1920	1,410	13.8	...
1921	2,004	19.5	42.1
1922	2,619	25.5	30.7
1923	4,005	39.1	52.9
1924	4,660	45.4	16.4
1925	7,739	75.5	66.1
1926	11,083	108.1	43.2
1927	12,679	123.7	14.2

economic trends, forecast for 1925–6 an increase of 20 per cent in both agricultural and industrial output. He was more certain that this level would be reached in agriculture than in industry.[1] While he turned out to be a fairly accurate prophet as regards the growth of agricultural output (which rose in 1925–6 by 18 per cent), his forecast was, as we see, very wide of the mark with regard to industry.

After the spectacular rise in industrial output in 1925 and 1926, the increment was reduced to some 15 per cent in 1927. The reasons for the high rates of growth of industry (and for that matter of the other sectors of the economy) up to and including 1926, as well as the reason for the great slowdown in 1927, are now clear. The high rates of growth up to 1926 were made possible by bringing many factories into operation, or by a great expansion of the operations of existing ones, which required relatively small inputs of fixed capital. The exploitation of unused capacities must indeed have continued even after industry as a whole had reached the pre-war level – at the expense of individual enterprises which had not yet reached this level.

This decline of the rate of growth from the high rates of the reconstruction period, from which there was still a residue of exploitable resources, to the much smaller rates of the following

[1] *Puti sel'skogo khozyaistva*, November 1925, p. 189. Groman made this prognosis in July 1925.

period and to more normal lower rates based on an expanding fixed capital, was called at the time the 'diminishing curve'. Nobody of course imagined that the rate might dwindle to nothing. The correct explanation of this phenomenon was first given by Groman early in 1925.[1] Bazarov elaborated on his hypothesis soon afterwards, and before long it was accepted by everybody. Here we are particularly interested in the fact that the explanation was also fully accepted by the Party.

The XV Conference of the Party (26 October to 3 November 1926) declared that:

With the termination of the reconstruction period the subsequent development of the national economy has to contend with the inadequacy and backwardness of the productive and technological means inherited from bourgeois society. The national economy is entering a phase in which the rate of growth is much slower than in preceding years.

There is no justification whatsoever for the defeatist ideology revealed in the opinions of the opposition, which has ascribed this slow-down to the discontinuance of industrialisation and a threat to the dictatorship of the proletariat...The development of industry on the basis of an expanding fixed capital never did and never could have proceeded as rapidly as industry was developing on the old basis in the recovery period in recent years.[2]

By way of consolation it added: 'But the specific conditions of the Soviet state ensure that industry will have a more speedy rate of growth than in capitalist countries.' That the favourable effect of the recovery process on the rates of growth would not stop after industry as a whole reached the 1913 output level was still recognised in 1928 and even in 1929, although some important qualifications to the theory of the 'diminishing curve' were made at a debate in the Communist Academy. For instance Strumilin, who was responsible for the first Five-Year Plan, said: 'We have entered this five-year period after the very high rates of the preceding recovery period. The residual effects of this recovery period will

[1] 'On Some Regularities Empirically Observed in Our National Economy', *Planovoe khozyaistvo*, No. 1, 1925, pp. 94–100.
[2] *KPSS v resolyutsiyakh*, Vol. II, pp. 294–5.

still be felt in the first years of the current five-year period, and then this growth will to some extent slow down.'[1]

Groman, in making his estimate of the rates of growth for 1925–6 (see above), may well have assumed that the year would come close to reaching the pre-war level and that the factors causing the 'diminishing curve' to operate would be effective already in 1925–6. He did not yet know that the current rates of growth were determined not so much by the level of pre-war output as by the higher level of pre-war productive capacity (see Chapter 7 below, on Bazarov). This fact may have made itself felt not only after but also before the level of pre-war output was reached. Specifically it may have operated with considerable force in 1925–6, the year with the most striking rise in industrial output. However, if this factor had a great effect on the rate of growth in 1925–6, it should also have had a significant effect on the rate of growth in 1926–7, so that the relatively low rise of output attained in this year becomes even more difficult to explain.[2]

The priority of industry over agriculture advocated by Preobrazhensky during the 'scissors' crisis meant preferential treatment for heavy industry. For this reason the rate of growth of large-scale industry, which averaged 52.4 per cent in 1923, was composed of a 63.8 per cent growth in heavy industry and 43.7 per cent in light industry (including in this case the food industry).[3] But after the restoration of more normal price conditions the rate of growth was larger in light than in heavy industry for three years in succession, though in the third year the difference was very small (see Table 3). The gap again increased somewhat in 1927, when heavy industry grew by 24.8 per cent and light by 11.8 per cent.

After the ruinous operation of the 'price scissors' in 1923, attempts to force heavy industry at the expense of light industry were soon resumed, but in a more sensible manner. In 1926–7 capital investments in heavy industry were planned to rise by

[1] The debate took place in 1928, and Strumilin published the passage quoted here early in 1929 (see *Planovoe khozyaistvo*, No. 1, 1929, p. 110). He obviously would not have done so if he had by then abandoned this view.

[2] According to *Kontrol'nye tsifry narodnogo khozyaistva SSSR na 1927/8g.* Moscow, 1928, p. 465, the output of large-scale industry increased by 15.1 per cent in 1926–7.

[3] *Narodnoe khozyaistvo SSSR : statistichesky spravochnik 1932*, Moscow–Leningrad, 1932, p. 4.

Table 3. *Percentage growth rates in large-scale industry*

Year	Heavy Industry	Light Industry
1924	9.7	22.8
1925	59.3	71.9
1926	37.9	38.4

53 per cent and those in light industry by only 23 per cent. In the next year the figures were 30 per cent and 7 per cent respectively. The drive for heavy industry gained greatly in momentum with the onset of the first Five-Year Plan in the autumn of 1928. Planned investments in heavy industry in 1928–9 were already 3.4 times as large as those in light industry.[1]

AGRICULTURE

The taxation of the peasants continued to be heavy under NEP. Despite this and an unfavourable price relationship between farm produce and consumer goods, agriculture recovered under NEP (see Table 4). The system of requisitioning under 'War Communism' had been an infinitely greater evil, so that its abolition led to a marked improvement, at least to the extent that production increased sufficiently to cover the needs of the farm population.

In 1920 agricultural output was nearly two-thirds that of 1913. The output of large-scale industry was only 14 per cent of this level. While the former was about half the 1913 level in 1921–2, the output of large-scale industry almost reached one-quarter of that of 1913. By 1925, the 1913 level was approached to about the same degree (close to 80 per cent) in agriculture as in large-scale industry. The 1913 level was exceeded by both in 1926. Considering the unfavourable price relationship between farm products and non-farm goods bought by the peasants, the level of output reached

[1] *Kontrol'nye tsifry narodnogo khozyaistva SSSR na 1929/30g.* Moscow, 1930, pp. 454–5.

Table 4. *Farm production index (1913 = 100) in constant prices*

Year	Statistical Yearbook, 1958 (a)	Groman (b)	Control Figures for 1927-8 (c)
1920	67	—	—
1921	60	—	—
1921-2	—	52	—
1922-3	—	71	—
1923-4	—	76	—
1924-5	—	79	79
1925-6	—	—	100
1926-7	—	—	104
1926	118	—	—
1927	121	—	—
1928	124	—	—

SOURCES: (a) 'Comparable' prices; *Narodnoe khozyaistvo SSSR v 1958g.* p. 350.
(b) Pre-World War I prices; V. Groman, *Planovoe khozyaistvo* No. 1, 1925, p. 94.
(c) Pre-World War I prices; *Kontrol'nye tsifry na 1927/8g.* p. 464.

by agriculture in 1926 must be regarded as good. From 1926-8, however, it increased scarcely at all – this was clearly due to the unsatisfactory price relationship.

Not much of the peasants' produce reached the markets, if we are to judge by the following figures for grain (in million *puds*) given by Stalin:[1]

Year	Output	Marketed
Pre-war	5,000	1,300
1926-7	4,749	630

While before the war somewhat more than a quarter of the grain crop was marketed, in 1926-7 the peasants disposed of only 13 per cent of the crop in this way. Instead of raising the procurement

[1] I. V. Stalin, *Voprosy leninizma* (*Problems of Leninism*), 11th edn. Moscow, 1947, p. 186. According to Oganovsky (*Sotsialisticheskoe khozyaistvo*, No. 2, 1927, p. 38) the marketing of grain *per capita* of the rural population was 32 per cent less in 1926-7 than in 1913.

prices the party resorted to 'extraordinary measures' (i.e. compulsory procurements) in the spring of 1928.

These 'extraordinary measures' remained in force only a few months.[1] But the decision to discontinue them and to raise the procurement prices for grain (the Party recognised the unfavourable price relationship as between grain and other farm produce, but not as between grain and the consumer goods available to the peasants) was made only by the plenary session of the Central Committee of 4–12 July, 1928, i.e. very close to harvest time, rather than before the sowing season.[2] Any favourable effect of the higher prices for grain would, consequently, only have made itself felt in subsequent years. But these new prices were, of course, adversely affected by the collectivisation drive.

RAILWAY TRANSPORT

The course of the economy as a whole during NEP is well demonstrated by the figures for freight carried by the railways[3] (see Table 5).

By 1918 shipments of freight had declined to little over a quarter of the pre-war figure, and there was not much sign of improvement till about 1922. But by the end of 1923 almost half the 1913 level had been reached. As in industry, 1925 and 1926 were the only two years to show substantial increases over the preceding year. The increase in 1927 was the smallest in five years, but it nevertheless finally brought the level above that of 1913.

THE ATTITUDE OF THE NONCONFORMISTS

The starvation, humiliation and other trials that the 'bourgeois specialists' had endured under War Communism meant that there was no immediate change in their attitude toward the Soviet regime after the introduction of the NEP. In the summer of 1922,

---

[1] *Narodnoe khozyaistvo SSSR v 1958g.* p. 350, put the increase in agricultural output in the two years from 1926 to 1928 at 5 per cent, but even this small increase is uncertain.
[2] *KPSS v resolyutsiyakh*, Vol. II, pp. 511–16.
[3] *Transport i svyaz' SSSR, statistichesky sbornik*, Moscow, 1957, p. 32.

Table 5. *Railway freight traffic*

Year	Millions of tons	Annual percentage change
1913	132.4	—
1918	37.2	—
1919	30.5	− 18.0
1920	31.9	9.6
1921	37.9	18.9
1922	44.6	17.7
1923	60.7	36.1
1924	70.7	16.5
1925	92.4	30.0
1926	122.2	31.2
1927	139.6	14.3

i.e. more than a year after the proclamation of the NEP, a survey was made among 270 engineers in Moscow, divided into those in high positions and those in medium ones. To the question whether they were in sympathy with the Soviet regime, only 9 per cent in group I and 13 per cent in group II answered yes. To the question whether the work they were doing was believed by them to be useful, 30 per cent of group I and 75 per cent of group II answered yes. Although the number of those questioned was small, the answers were thought to be representative of the vast majority of civilian engineers.[1] A somewhat different view is given by Valentinov: 'At a time when a substantial part of the intelligentsia was emigrating, *another part* started to work *with great enthusiasm* in different branches of the Soviet apparatus. This occurred not under compulsion but voluntarily, and the people in question were by no means of the kind who had thrown in their lot with the Communist Party...'[2]

It is of course easy to see why large numbers of intellectuals emigrated from Russia. It is much more difficult to understand why others stayed behind. In many cases the motive was of a more or less personal nature, such as uncertainty with regard to the possibilities of making a living abroad. Khinchuk, a prominent Menshevik,

[1] Pollock, *Die planwirtschaftlichen*, pp. 108–9.
[2] Valentinov, *Memoirs*, p. 4. The emphasis is in the original.

who went over to the Bolsheviks and held important positions, including that of Soviet ambassador in Berlin, replied to the question why had he changed sides, 'I could not become a nobody'. There may well have been others who feared that by giving up whatever positions they held in the USSR after the proclamation of the NEP and going abroad they would become 'nobodies'. In other cases it was simply a matter of not feeling able to live in any country but Russia. It would have been difficult to visualise Groman, for example, as an *émigré*. Life in exile was intolerable for A. Peshekhonov, a saintly man, who found it difficult to breathe any other air but that of Russia.[1]

Valentinov believed himself to be so much in disagreement with the Mensheviks abroad that on a visit to Berlin he could not bring himself to ask the editors of the *Sotsialistichesky vestnik* (*Socialist Courier*) for a set of the journal. Instead, he got Andreeva, a former actress of the Moscow Arts Theatre (later married to Gorky), who was for a time connected with the Soviet trade delegation in Berlin, to procure for him sets of the *Vestnik* for 1923 and 1924 from the library of that organisation. According to Valentinov, two others of those few members of the League of Observers who went on visits abroad agreed with him that encounters and talks with the editors of the *Sotsialistichesky vestnik* could only 'lead to mutual recriminations, accusations and bitter arguments', and that under such conditions it was best not to see them.[2]

Though Valentinov claims to give an idea of the feelings of the intelligentsia at large, it seems that at best he could speak only for the attitudes of a considerable number of his fellow Mensheviks. Unfortunately he is extremely brief when it comes to other groups. On p. 41 of his *Memoirs*, for example, he writes:

Did other groups, similar to ours, exist? It seems they did – one consisting of S.R.s, the other of Kadets. What is important is that, without any collective discussions, without forming any groups, a considerable proportion of the intelligentsia came in 1921–2, if not to such deeply thought out conceptions as those of the League of Observers, at least *to the same frame of mind* [*nastroyenie*].

[1] Peshekhonov, a minister in Kerensky's government, emigrated but later expressed his desire to return; he was, however, not granted permission to do so.
[2] Valentinov, *Memoirs*, p. 337.

It is not clear what fraction of Socialist-Revolutionaries Valentinov had in mind. 'Orthodox' Socialist-Revolutionaries are hardly mentioned in his *Memoirs*, and the persons involved could scarcely have been neo-narodniks, who were as important as the Mensheviks, or nearly so, at that time. Both Kondrat'ev, the leader of the neo-narodniks, and Groman insisted at their trial that until the end of 1927 there existed substantial disagreements between them. Groman said at the trial 'I was for the nationalisation of the land, for the retention not only of individual enterprises in the hands of the state, but for its leading role in large-scale industry and transport'.[1]

Kondrat'ev's attitude was quite different: in 1922 he declared that:

In accordance with the principles of freedom of economic activity and the guarantee of this freedom, the laws of land tenure, which have a very great significance for the development of agriculture, must be revised so as to establish a firmer connection of the entrepreneur with the land, greater freedom and flexibility in the change of ownership of land and methods of land utilisation.[2]

Kondrat'ev said furthermore in the Moscow Agricultural Society on 18 February 1922:[3] 'It is necessary to dot the i's, to raise the question of Russian capitalist enterprises, to welcome Russian capitalism, if we welcome the appearance of foreign capital.' He was also against the monopoly of foreign trade. He said in this connection: 'From the present restricted state of affairs, we must in one way or another switch to ordinary forms of international trade.'[4] To sum up, it can be said that Kondrat'ev went much further than Groman in his desire to undo the economic consequences of the October Revolution.[5]

The Kadets, for example L. N. Litoshenko, went even further than Kondrat'ev in this respect. Milyutin, in his article in *Pravda*

---

[1] *Trial*, p. 68.
[2] *Kondrat'evshchina (sbornik) : doklad V. P. Milyutina. Vystupleniya S. G. Uzhanskogo, A. S. Bondarenko, I. D. Lapteva i dr.* Moscow, 1930. Abbreviated: *Kondrat'evshchina*.
[3] Here quoted from V. Milyutin in *Pravda*, 20 October 1929.
[4] *Kondrat'evshchina*, p. 110.
[5] On the disagreements between Kondrat'ev and Groman before the end of 1927 see also Ch. 9 below.

already quoted, gives this categorical statement by Litoshenko:[1] 'The land will be in the hands of those who are stronger, who with hard work and love of property will be able to overcome all the disruptions brought about by the revolution. Our agrarian structure will be infinitely removed from all kinds of socialisation.'

Valentinov's talks with three high-ranking technicians are of great interest. The conversations with two of them, Fedorov and Kalinnikov, were mentioned in Chapter 1.[2] The third is of particular interest: it was with N. K. von Mekk, who before the revolution had been president of the board and chief shareholder of the Moscow–Kazan railway, in his political ideas one of the 'Black Hundreds'. Valentinov insists that von Mekk had absolutely no reason to lie to him and that 'he was entirely sincere'. Perhaps... Fedorov and Kalinnikov referred only to the immense advantages of the fact that the fetters of the War Communism period were over: the former said he felt as if he had left a morgue; the latter, that not only he but many felt as if they had jumped from the moon back to the earth. But von Mekk had much more to say. Incidentally Valentinov mentioned that 'for reasons unknown to me, he [von Mekk] apparently failed to cross the border like Guchkov, Konovalov and other industrialists and wealthy bourgeois'. This non-emigrant magnate said: 'After everything that we have gone through I am by no means frightened and embarrassed at the Soviet Government nationalising a huge proportion of the country's economy. Under the Tsarist régime, very large branches of the economy were owned by the state. Nationalisation does not seem to have been practised to such a large extent in any other country'...

The role of the nonconformists in the mid 1920s is best evidenced by what their enemies said about them. In his report to the Agrarian Institute of the Communist Academy on 1 October 1930, V. P. Milyutin, head of the Central Statistical Office, said:

These agents of world capitalism inside our country, agents of the internal bourgeoisie, chose special ways of struggle. They occupied responsible positions, a number of them occupied very important positions in our central state institutions. Groman was a member of the

[1] The quotation was unfortunately undated, but it seems to belong to about the same year as Kondrat'ev's statements quoted above, namely 1922.
[2] Valentinov, *Memoirs*, pp. 72–6. Editor's note: Fedorov may be Fedotov.

Presidium of Gosplan, Kondrat'ev for a long time played a great role in the Narkomzem [Commissariat of Agriculture] and Narkomfin [Commissariat of Finance]. Sukhanov for a long time did important work in Narkomtorg [Commissariat of Trade] and Narkomzem; Makarov had a responsible position in Narkomzem; Sadyrin was a member of the Central Executive Committee; Yurovsky played an exceptionally great role in Narkomfin and was a member of its collegium. So these persons occupied highly responsible positions in the USSR.[1]

Of the persons named, Groman and Sukhanov were Mensheviks, Kondrat'ev and Makarov were neo-narodniks (called the Worker–Peasant Party about 1930–1), Yurovsky was probably a left Constitutional Democrat (Kadet), and Sadyrin was of no discoverable party affiliation.

The evidence in *Kondrat'evshchina*, *Trial* and other publications, as well as Valentinov's *Memoirs*, indicates that the Mensheviks enjoyed a completely dominant position in the VSNKh, a very strong position in Gosplan and considerable influence in the Commissariats of Finance and Domestic Trade as well as in the State Bank. Their position in VSNKh and Gosplan is usually put on a comparable level, but this seems to be not quite exact. In the important years of NEP, VSNKh seems not to have had a single Communist in a responsible position, except for its head, Dzerzhinsky, and his deputy Pyatakov. When Ginzburg, Sokolovsky and Shtern of this organisation met for discussion (they usually reached agreement, according to Valentinov), it was not Mensheviks conspiring but a meeting of the heads of the most important departments of the organisation. And our important source, Valentinov, was the actual editor of *Torgovo-promyshlennaya gazeta*, the VSNKh daily newspaper. I. Bolshakov complained that the 'formation and development of the science known as "economics of industry" proceeds in the almost complete absence of Marxist cadres':[2] this was a reference to the pre-eminence in this field of the Menshevik Ginzburg.

The situation in Gosplan can be seen from the following. Referring to 1928, Vaisberg, who in the post-NEP period made a speci-

[1] *Kondrat'evshchina*, p. 7.
[2] *Puti industrializatsii* (*Ways of Industrialization*), 1931, No. 3–4, pp. 4–5.

ality of attacking Groman and Bazarov, wrote in 1931:[1] 'At that time, within Gosplan, the influence of the Communists had already somewhat increased', and this, in his opinion, compelled the 'wreckers' to make certain concessions in the wording of their recommendations. Still, he lamented the fact that young Communists joining the planning organisation were not given a chance to work and to learn.[2]

The principal role in Gosplan was played by the Mensheviks, although they were not as important there as they were in VSNKh. Of the fourteen members of the committee on the Control Figures for 1926–7, the political affiliation of three is not known to this writer. Only Groman, Bazarov and Gukhman were definitely non-Communists (they were Mensheviks or close to Menshevism). But the great personal influence of Groman made the first three sets of Control Figures (1925–6, 1926–7, 1927–8) a Menshevik product. While Bazarov and Groman had a great influence also on Gosplan's work on the Five-Year Plan, they were never mentioned in the relevant documents. However, along with Groman, Bazarov and the other Mensheviks or near-Mensheviks, Gosplan had Strumilin, a first-class man as Communists went, though no match for Groman or Bazarov. Gosplan also had a few Communists of the second rank, for example Mendelson or Vaisberg.

The non-Communist GOELRO engineers (none of them was a Menshevik), most of whom were moved to Gosplan in 1921, remained there for years and played a fairly important role there. The Mensheviks were furthermore prominent in some agencies other than VSNKh and Gosplan, for example in the consumer co-operatives. The teaching of Marxism in higher education was dominated by Rubin, one of the accused in the Menshevik trial.[3] And there were such good economists as the old Menshevik P. P. Maslov and those close to Groman, Pervushin, Falkner, etc.

The domination of the neo-narodniks was virtually complete in the Commissariat of Agriculture, especially in Zemplan (the plan-

---

[1] See *Planovoe khozyaistvo*, No. 2–3, 1931, p. 12.
[2] *Ibid.* p. 15.
[3] Finn-Enotaevsky, another defendant at the trial, was prominent in the teaching of international economics.

ning division of the RSFSR Commissariat of Agriculture).[1] The neo-narodniks and persons close to them also virtually dominated the teaching of agricultural economics. *Kondrat'evshchina* (pp. 26–7) says of their activities:

Everybody knows the place the Kondrat'evites occupied in agricultural colleges. For example, in Moscow the Scientific Research Institute of Agricultural Economics was called the 'Chayanov Institute'. The majority of the economic faculty of the former Timiryazev Agricultural Academy consisted of Kondrat'evites (Science of the Market Economy – Makarov; Organisation of the Agricultural Economy – Chayanov; Regional Agriculture – Chelintsev; Economic Geography – Rybnikov; Agronomic Service – Fabrikant; etc.). Thousands of students in higher and intermediate education were taught from the textbooks of Chayanov, Chelintsev, Makarov, etc.

The influence of the *Kondrat'evshchina* was great. The wreckers utilised all opportunities, creating strongholds and attempting to seize the commanding heights in government institutions. They had a great influence on the training of cadres and had their own cadres also. It is known for example that Chayanov gave courses in classes organised by Narkomzem for agronomists [in most cases former local agronomists and directors of farms], and enjoyed a great success.

In addition to their predominant position in Narkomzem and specifically their position in Zemplan, the neo-narodniks had a considerable influence in the Commissariat of Finance, of which the Kondrat'ev Konyunktur [current economic data] Institute was part.[2]

There were indeed very few exceptions to the domination of the neo-narodniks and persons close to them in official institutions concerned with agriculture. Vishnevsky, prominent in agricultural planning, was neither a neo-narodnik nor a Menshevik, but a Gromanite. Lositsky, engaged in work on consumption of farm products, was a Menshevik. L. N. Yurovsky was very prominent in work on public finance. He was not a socialist, but acknowledged his membership of the Peasant–Workers (Kondrat'ev) Party. For

[1] M. Kraev, 'Theory and Practice in the Perspective Plan of Agriculture', *Planovoe khozyaistvo*, No. 1, 1931, p. 129, complained: 'Such a central branch of the Commissariat as Zemplan was entirely in the hands of the bourgeois restorers [of capitalism].'
[2] Another contributor to *Kondrat'evshchina*, p. 33, also complained that the Institute was filled with Kondrat'evites.

that matter, extensive help on financial problems was accepted even from Kutler, who had been Finance Minister under the Tsar, in the industrial trial of December 1930.

It is worth emphasising that scarcely any of those mentioned had been engaged in government work, other than teaching, in Tsarist times. Groman and most of the Gromanites, such as Lositsky, Popov and many others, had been Zemstvo statisticians, the traditional province of the democratic intelligentsia (the Zemstvos were local government bodies which operated everywhere except in large cities). Ginzburg was a free-lance journalist, and Sukhanov largely so. The latter seems to have been the only one who performed any government service other than teaching before the Revolution, but he was employed by the Division of Statistics and Agricultural Economy of the Ministry of Agriculture, which for some reason happened to be a liberal institution.

3

AFTER NEP

The period following the New Economic Policy was marked by the rapid full-scale compulsory collectivisation of peasant farming, which led to a decline in farm output and culminated in the death of millions by starvation. It was, furthermore, the time of the drive to expand the quantity of industrial production, especially that of heavy industry, without regard to the quality of the goods produced, labour productivity or production costs. This drive culminated in such disorganisation that even the quantity of the output of industrial goods ceased to increase. The post-NEP was also marked by an orgy of largely unfulfillable planning with the 'big lie' doing duty, in most cases, for real fulfilment. Finally, this was the time of prosecution of all those who did not accept Stalin's General Line, a process which culminated in jail or exile for practically all nonconformists.

It seems odd to recall that at the time – many years ago – this writer was uncertain as to exactly when the NEP had ended. The combined plenary session of the Central Committee and Central Control Committee of April 1928 declared in the typical Stalin manner that 'the mischievous claims by kulaks, nepmen and their followers, to the effect that the NEP has been discontinued, must be decisively resisted by the Party'.[1]

The question regarding the termination of the NEP appeared to this writer to be settled by a reference in a book published in 1943 by Oscar Lange, then professor at the University of Chicago. The Professor, who was Polish Ambassador to the USA after 1945 and subsequently a prominent economist in Poland, may have had some inside information when still in Chicago. At all events, he related the end of the NEP to the decisions of the XV Party Congress (2–19 December 1927).[2] There were of course decisions, pronouncements and steps leading up to the decisions of the XV Congress,

---

[1] *KPSS v rezolyutsiyakh*, Vol. I, p. 497.
[2] *The Working Principles of the Soviet Economy*, New York, 1943, p. 16.

and the impact of its decisions became fully effective only somewhat later, but Lange's suggestion appeared more probable the longer one studied the history of those years. According to Valentinov, Groman had foreseen that the NEP would be terminated by the XV Party Congress, months before the Congress itself took place (see Chapter 6 below).[1]

The decisions of the XV Party Congress on items of interest for this book were summarised as follows: 'The XV Congress instructed the Central Committee to continue without respite the development of socialist industrialisation and the further attack on capitalist elements, with a view to their liquidation.'[2] The Congress gave first priority to the gradual transformation of small peasant enterprises into units of large-scale socialist production. Another part of the resolution embodied the decision to develop in every way the collectivisation of agriculture, including the working out of a plan for expanding and strengthening the kolkhozes and sovkhozes.

AGRICULTURE

The XV Congress was indeed officially proclaimed the 'Congress of Collectivisation'. In agricultural policy, increasingly harsh words, and actions had followed one another in rapid succession. Shortly before the end of the NEP, the task was 'liquidation of the kulaks'. Now the resolution of the XV Congress spoke of 'attack on capitalist elements with a view to their liquidation'.

But the term 'Congress of Collectivisation' was perhaps still somewhat premature. The joint plenum of the Central Committee and Central Control Committee of the Party on 21–3 October 1927 merely ordered a more energetic attack on the 'kulaks',[3] and probably meant only the kulaks proper rather than all peasants. More-

---

[1] A. Ciliga in *The Russian Enigma*, London, 1940, p. 94, states (unfortunately without any details) that Stalin said on 29 December 1929: 'To hell with the NEP'. But the decision of the VI Congress of Soviets of 12 March 1931, spoke of the time in question as that of the last stage of the NEP (see *Direktivy KPSS i Sovetskogo pravitel'stva po khozyaistvennym voprosam, 1917–57g.* (*Directives of the Communist Party and the Soviet Government on Economic Problems*), Moscow, 1957, Vol. II, p. 248); thus, according to the official version, NEP still existed as late as the beginning of 1931.
[2] *KPSS v rezolyutsiyakh*, Vol. I, p. 432.
[3] *Ibid.* Vol. II, p. 416.

over, in the decision of the XV Congress the transition of small peasant enterprises to large-scale organisation was still to be 'gradual'. Even according to the final draft of the first Five-Year Plan, approved more than a year after the XV Party Congress (Vol. I, p. 138), grain production was to be collectivised only as to 11.3 per cent by 1932–3; in the whole of socialised agriculture, i.e. kolkhozes and sovkhozes, the number of households collectivised was planned to reach 15.8 per cent.

The campaign for rapid full-scale collectivisation, with violent measures used openly and on a large scale, began a few days before Stalin's article 'The Year of the Great Turning-Point', the publication of which on 7 November 1929 may be taken as the starting point of the drive for full-scale collectivisation. This time, the drive was directed against *all* individual peasants. Every peasant who did not want to join a kolkhoz was considered a kulak, however small his private enterprise might be. Also at this very time, Stalin coined his famous formula 'annihilation of the kulaks as a class'.[1] More than half of all households were collectivised in a matter of weeks. Then came a temporary relaxation, but the Party did not rest. The number of peasant households collectivised was as follows (in thousands):[2]

1 June 1928	417
1 June 1929	1,008
1 May 1930	6,000[a]
1 July 1931	13,563

[a] In February 1930 collectivised peasant households numbered over 10 million.

A relaxation followed the publication in *Pravda* of 2 March 1930 of Stalin's cynical 'Dizzy with Success'. Two months after it appeared, the proportion of collectivised households in the RSFSR fell from 60 per cent of the total number to 23.4 per cent. However, the number soon started to grow again, although at a rate much smaller than before. By 1 June 1933, 64.4 per cent of all peasant households were collectivised,[3] instead of only 15.8 per cent as scheduled for this item by the first Five-Year Plan.

[1] *Voprosy leninizma*, 11th edn. 1947, p. 290.
[2] See *Sotsialisticheskoe stroitel'stvo, statistichesky ezhegodnik*, Moscow, 1932, pp. 170–1.
[3] *Sotsialisticheskoe stroitel'stvo, statistichesky sbornik (Socialist Construction)*, Moscow, 1935, p. 317.

The planning and operating of agriculture deteriorated to an immense extent in the post-NEP years. Gosplan's draft of the Five-Year Plan, completed in the spring of 1929, i.e. still during the NEP period, envisaged an increase of agricultural output of 22.8 per cent from 1925–6 to 1930–1.[1] Gosplan's targets for agricultural production in the draft of the Five-Year Plan as adopted in the spring of 1927 were thus far more than doubled in less than two years. According to the first Five-Year Plan, I, p. 133, agricultural output was to grow by 55 per cent between 1927–8 and 1932–3: crop production was to increase by 56 per cent and output of animal products by 54 per cent (excluding natural growth in herds, 50 per cent). The developments in agriculture in the interval of less than two years between the adoption of the Five-Year Plan in the spring of 1927 and the completion of the Five-Year Plan would actually have justified a reduction rather than a raising of the targets. It was quite unrealistic to set a target of 55 per cent for growth in agricultural output from 1927–8 to 1932–3 under the existing conditions, including full-scale collectivisation, very small appropriations for capital investments in agriculture, and so on.

Instead of actually rising by 55 per cent in the five years from 1927–8 to 1932–3, as provided in the approved version of the Five-Year Plan, total farm output declined by 14 per cent between 1928 and 1933.[2] The output of animal products went down by 48 per cent, instead of growing by 50 or 54 per cent: i.e. the target of the Five-Year Plan for them was fulfilled only by a little more than one third.

The yearly data for agricultural output in the period in question are given in Table 6.

In 1928 there was an almost negligible increase of 3 per cent in

---

[1] Gosplan USSR, *Perspektivy razvertyvaniya narodnogo khozyaistva SSSR na 1926/7–1930/1gg.* (Prospects of Developing the National Economy of the USSR from 1926/7–1930/1), henceforth referred to as *Perspektivy*, Moscow, 1927; Tables, p. 3. The total is for agriculture without forestry, fishing and hunting. The targets of Gosplan's Five-Year Plan accepted in the spring of 1927 for agriculture were in effect transferred to Ginzburg's draft. According to *Materialy k pyatiletnemy planu razvitiya promyshlennosti SSSR 1927/8–1931/2gg.* (Materials on the Five-Year Development Plan for the Industry of the USSR, 1927/8–1931/2), Moscow, 1927, henceforth referred to as *Materialy*, p. 17, the target was an increase of 23.3 per cent.

[2] *Narodnoe khozyaistvo SSSR v 1958g, statistichesky ezhegodnik*, p. 350.

Table 6. *Index numbers of farm output* (*1927 = 100*)

Year	Total gross product	Crops	Animal husbandry
1927	100	100	100
1928	103	104	103
1929	100	102	96
1930	96	111	75
1931	94	111	69
1932	88	110	56
1933	83	107	50

agricultural production. Starting later in 1928, i.e. after the approval of the first Five-Year Plan, the decline proceeded from year to year both for the total agricultural output and especially for the animal industry separately.

The decline in output of farm products, especially the great fall in output of animal products, spelled disaster, particularly in view of the great rise in urban population, an uneven regional distribution of the decline in output, and other factors. Millions died from starvation in the last years of the first Five-Year Plan, and starvation continued in the second Five-Year Plan period.

INDUSTRY

While with reference to farming the emphasis was on full-scale collectivisation, with output relegated to secondary or even less importance, in industry the drive for output was paramount, with everything else neglected. This different attitude was, *inter alia*, reflected in the stepping up of targets. The raising of targets for farm output after the end of the NEP was very large, but it appears small compared with that of industrial targets.

The target for increase in the output of the large-scale state industry, according to the draft of the Five-Year Plan completed by Gosplan in the spring of 1927, was 79.0 per cent,[1] and that of the Ginzburg draft of the Five-Year Plan of the VSNKh for the

[1] Gosplan's *Perspektivy*, tabular section, p. 3.

industry controlled by the VSNKh was 82.1 per cent.[1] The optimum variant of the first Five-Year Plan demanded a rise of the same industry by 179 per cent, i.e. the scheduled increase was more than doubled in less than the two years which expired between the early and the final draft of the Plan. Further increases for some important individual industries were ordered soon after the adoption of the Five-Year Plan, especially in the resolution of the XVI Party Congress (June–July 1930).[2] The unrestrained planning drive was crowned with the decision of the VI Congress of Soviets (8–18 March 1931), according to which the approved targets of the Five-Year Plan were to be fulfilled in four years and those for the basic and critical industries in three years.[3] Thus the targets of the two Five-Year Plans drawn up in the first half of 1927 were more than doubled, in some cases nearly trebled.

Thus far we have considered the targets for the total large-scale state industry or that controlled by the VSNKh. This is the category of industrial enterprises with the greatest rise in output targets, and it occupied the foreground of official statistics for the years involved. Less data were provided on the output of industry as a whole and that of large-scale industry. The least amount of evidence was available on the output of small-scale industry. The statistics of the output of small-scale industry incidentally have their own history, which is worth some attention. The year 1927 was still one of honest statistics. Consequently both Five-Year Plans approved in that year, that of Gosplan and that of the VSNKh, contained some data on small-scale industry. The data on the output of small-scale industry are however missing from the first Five-Year Plan, although this was in general much more detailed than the Gosplan 1927 draft. Statements on the output of small-scale industry are indeed missing from most collections of statistics since 1929.[4] Of course, so far as data for both total and large-scale

---

[1] *Materialy*, p. 403. The difference in coverage between the Gosplan and VSNKh drafts of the Five-Year Plans completed in 1927 was negligible. The drafts here cited were the second for each organisation. The first drafts, disregarded here, provided for still smaller rises than those shown here.

[2] *Direktivy KPSS*, Vol. II, Moscow, 1957, pp. 192–6.

[3] *Ibid.* p. 248.

[4] See, for example, *Narodnoe khozyaistvo SSSR v 1957g., statistichesky spravochnik*, Moscow, 1957, or the same for 1964.

Table 7. *Comparison of percentage increments in various drafts of the first Five-Year Plan*

Total industry	
Ginzburg draft, 1927–8 to 1931–2[a]	73.0
Gosplan, spring 1927, 1926–7 to 1930–1[b]	70.4
Gosplan Five-Year Plan, optimum variant, 1927–8 to 1932–3[c]	136
Large-scale industry	
Ginzburg draft, 1927–8 to 1931–2[d]	82.1
Gosplan, spring 1927, 1926–7 to 1930–1[e]	76.7
Gosplan Five-Year Plan, optimum variant, 1928–9 to 1932–3[c]	164

SOURCES: [a] VSNKh, *Materialy*, p. 17.
[b] Gosplan, *Perspektivy*, tabular section, p. 3.
[c] Text, Vol. I, p. 131.
[d] VSNKh, *Materialy*, tabular section, p. 403: large-scale industry controlled by the VSNKh.
[e] Gosplan, *Perspektivy*, p. 23.

industrial production are available, the data for small-scale industry may be obtained by subtraction.[1] The handling of these data in the official statistics released after 1928 is certainly dishonest.

The targets for rise in output of total and large-scale industry in the sources used here are given in Table 7.

As stated, the term 'small-scale industry' disappeared during the period analysed, but an estimate for it can be obtained by subtracting the output of large-scale industry from that of total industry. The data, available and calculated, on the planned growth in output of small-scale industry are as follows (in percentage of the output in the last year before the Plan):

Ginzburg draft, 1927–8 to 1931–2[a]	29.2
Gosplan, spring 1927, 1926–7 to 1930–1[b]	36.2
Gosplan, first Five-Year Plan, optimum variant, 1928–9 to 1932–3[c]	50.0

SOURCES: [a] VSNKh, *Materialy*, tabular section, p. 698.
[b] Gosplan, *Perspektivy*, text, p. 23.

[1] *Promyshlennost' SSSR, statistichesky sbornik (Industry of the USSR: Statistical Compendium)*, Moscow, 1964, does not have data even for large-scale industry.

43

The avoidance of reference to small-scale industry was partly due to the smaller amount of data and the lesser realism of what there was, but this was not the only reason. The targets for the output of small-scale industry were the lowest, and it was therefore desirable not to make them conspicuous.

Actual output

Let us turn to fulfilments. The relevant resolution of the Combined Plenum of the Central Committee and Central Control Committee of 10 January 1933 stated that 'Fulfilment of the Five-Year Plan in the USSR not in five, but in four years [more exactly in four years and three months], is almost without parallel in contemporary history.'[1] This and many other assertions relating to that time were of course made without the smallest regard to reality.

According to official statistical sources, industrial output increased in the four years 1928–32 by 101 per cent (total industry) and 132 per cent (large-scale industry), while the output of small-scale industry declined by 2 per cent.[2] These percentages compared with the scheduled rises of 136 per cent (total industry), 164 per cent (large-scale industry) and 50 per cent (small-scale industry).

The figures for the growth of industrial output, as given in regular official statistics, fall short of the targets even if the whole year 1933 is added to the plan period. In this case, the regular statistics show a growth of 114 per cent (total industry) and 151 per cent

[1] *Direktivy KPSS, op. cit.* II, p. 363. The text of the decision is a falsification. It is worded as if the targets of the Five-Year Plan remained unamended until the end of the Five-Year Plan period, thereby ignoring all revisions of those targets, including those at the XVI Party Congress and the VI Congress of Soviets. This treatment of the data then became part of the Party's history: *Istoriya Kommunisticheskoi Partii Sovetskogo Soyuza* (History of the Communist Party of the Soviet Union), 2nd edn. Moscow, 1963, p. 467, says, for example, 'At the beginning of 1933 the happy news swept over the country that the First FYP had been fulfilled before its time, in four years and 3 months'.

[2] *Promyshlennost SSSR, statistichesky sbornik* (Industry of the USSR, Statistical Handbook), Moscow, 1957, p. 31. The same figures are repeated in *Narodnoe khozyaistvo SSSR v 1958g.* (National economy of the USSR in 1958), p. 135. The figure for small industry was calculated from those for total and large-scale industry.

(large-scale industry), as against the rates foreseen in the Five-Year Plan of 136 per cent (total industry) and 164 per cent (large-scale industry). The discrepancy between plan and fulfilment remained largest for small-scale industry. The discrepancies between the targets and fulfilments as recorded in official statistics, substantial as they are, are significant in comparison with those revealed by the actual fulfilments data.

Nutter quotes seven private indices of Soviet industrial output.[1] Not one of these even roughly approaches the official target. The highest private estimate for the rate of growth of all industry in 1928–32 (81 per cent) is by Seton. But his index is derived as a regression from growth patterns in countries other than the USSR and may hence be not strictly relevant; the other indices are all rather close together. It will suffice here to discuss those of Hodgman and Nutter. At first glance there is a substantial difference between them, but this is fully, perhaps more than fully, accounted for by the differences in coverage.

According to Hodgman, the output of large-scale industry increased by 72 per cent from 1927–8 to 1932. Hodgman's index for this period, which is used as the Five-Year Plan period in official sources, is almost as high as the target set in the 1927 Five-Year Plan, but it is less than half of what was scheduled in the Five-Year Plan, and even smaller if the enlargements of the targets of this Five-Year Plan made in 1930 and 1931 are taken into account.[2] Nutter's calculations indicate a growth of 40 per cent in total industrial output from 1928 to 1932.[3] In his table 53 on p. 252, Nutter has annual data which show rates of growth of 44 per cent for 1928–32 and of 53 per cent for 1928–33.

The factor causing the difference between the estimates of Hodgman and Nutter is even greater than the difference itself. This factor, as already mentioned, consists in an immense decline in the output of small-scale industry. Discussing the period of the

---

[1] Warren Nutter, *The Growth of Industrial Production in the USSR*, Princeton, N.J., 1962, p. 158.

[2] The percentage rise in Donald Hodgman, *Soviet Industrial Production, 1928–51*, Cambridge, Mass., 1954, for the period 1927–8 to 1932 would fully coincide with the targets set in 1927, or even exceed them moderately, if an adjustment were made for the fact that the targets of the 1927 Five-Year Plans were for a period of 5 years.

[3] Nutter, *Growth of Industrial Production*, p. 158.

first two Five-Year Plans, Nutter (pp. 187 ff) rightly uses the heading 'Disappearance of Small-Scale Industry'. The data on small-scale industry used by Nutter are those calculated by Adam Kaufman, according to whom the output of small-scale industry was in 1933 equal to only 37 per cent of that in 1927-8.[1]

Great credit is due to Kaufman for performing the extremely difficult task of producing this study on small-scale industry. The statistical evidence was greatly deficient even for the early years, 1913 to 1928-9, and its condition is deplorable for the early 1930s, the decisive period in the history of this industry. Kaufman writes (p. 53): 'The output record one must work from is, to say the least, highly deficient in many important respects.' Kaufman quotes no fewer than 96 different sources (pp. 92-5), and yet 'some important activities of the small-scale sector involving diversified and custom-made products, like tailoring and dress-making, are not covered because of insoluble problems in measuring physical output'. But even with reference to items for which evidence is included by Kaufman, some estimates are difficult to accept. The fish catch by small-scale industry, for example, is given for 1933 (p. 84) at 1.5 per cent of the catch in 1927-8, thus coming close to zero. Meat slaughtering in small-scale industry in 1933 is taken to have been equal to 1.6 per cent of that in 1927-8; the smallness of the figure in this case was due to the fact that only the state industry was considered (p. 83).

All that Kaufman hopes for is that 'his index can be accepted as more or less correct' (p. 59). One thing speaks in his favour: the discovery even of very crude errors would not deprive his analysis and findings of great value. Even if it were to turn out, for example, that his index for the decline in the output of small-scale industry from 1927-8 to 1933 by 63 per cent needs to be adjusted upwards by, say, 50 per cent, the knowledge that there was a decline in the output of this industry in these years by 45 per cent would still be very valuable.

Data in Kaufman show (p. 89) that the immense decline in the output of small-scale industry was largely, but not wholly, caused

[1] Adam Kaufman, *Small-Scale Industry in the Soviet Union* (National Bureau of Economic Research), New York, 1962, p. 54.

Table 8. *Planned percentage increments in output of large-scale industry*

Year	Perspectivy of Spring 1927	VSNKh draft of mid-1927	Five-Year Plan as approved
1926–7	19.1	—	—
1927–8	13.2	16.3	—
1928–9	10.6	13.1	21.4
1929–30	9.9	13.7	21.5
1930–1	9.2	10.5	22.1
1931–2	—	10.0	23.2
1932–3	—	—	25.2
1925–6 to 1930–1	79.5	—	—
1926–7 to 1931–2	—	82.0	—
1927–8 to 1932–3	—	—	179

SOURCES: As cited in Jasny, *Soviet Industrialization*, p. 57.

by the fact that potential output was not realised owing to shortage of raw materials. Again according to Kaufman (p. 54), the output of large-scale industry increased from 1927–8 to 1933 by 74 per cent. With the figure calculated by him for the output of small-scale industry during the same period (viz. a decline by 63 per cent), he obtains a 37 per cent rate of increase in the output of total industry. While his figure for large-scale industry is only slightly smaller than the Ginzburg target, his figure for the growth of total industry is a good deal smaller than the Ginzburg one.

Actually Kaufman's figures hardly need drastic upward revision, and small revisions are unimportant under conditions when plans and fulfilments diverge as immensely as they did in those years.

Output, yearly data

An important indication of the ultimate immense disorganisation of the economy is the great difference between the pattern of year-to-year changes in industrial output in the drafts of the Five-Year Plan, and the curve of the actual changes in it. The targets of the Five-Year Plan drafts for the output of planned industry drawn up in the first half of 1927, and of the draft of the Five-Year Plan as finally approved, are given in Table 8, with actual changes shown in Table 9.

47

Table 9. *Estimated actual percentage increments in industrial output*

Year	Official[a]	Hodgman,[b] large-scale industry	Nutter,[c] total industry
1928	19	No data	No data
1929	20	20 (1928–9)	14
1930	22	16 (1929–30)	15
1931	20	18[d]	7
1932	15	5	1
1933[e]	5	12	6
1928–32	101	72 (1927–8 to 1932)	42
1927–33	114	92 (1927–8 to 1933)	51

SOURCES: [a] *Promyshlennost' SSSR; statistichesky sbornik*, Moscow, 1957, pp. 34 and 31.
[b] Hodgman, *Soviet Industrial Production*, p. 89.
[c] Nutter, *Growth of Industrial Production*, p. 196.
[d] Year and a quarter.
[e] According to Raymond Powell (see his article in A. Bergson and S. Kuznets (eds.), *Economic Trends in the Soviet Union*, Cambridge, Mass., 1963, p. 187), industrial output declined in 1933.

As the future growth of industrial output was visualised on a base of 1928, the rate of this growth was planned in accordance with the theory of the declining growth rate – smaller for example, in 1927–8 and 1928–9 than the rate attained in the respective preceding years. *Kontrol'nye tsifry...etc. na 1927/28g.* pp. 464–5, estimated the growth of output of large-scale industry in 1926–7 at 15.1 per cent. The target set in these figures for 1927–8, officially described (*op. cit.* p. 11) as demanding a vast effort to attain, was a growth of 14.1 per cent. For that matter, the target for growth of large-scale industry in 1928–9 was planned at a lower figure than that attained in 1927–8.[1] Then the planning orgy set in and the huge target of 32.1 per cent for growth of large-scale industry in 1929–30 was put on paper.[2]

All in all, it would seem that the rate of growth of industrial

[1] The 1928–9 target was 17 per cent according to G. F. Grinko ('Control Figures for 1928–9', *Planovoe khozyaistvo*, No. 9, 1928, p. 18). The preliminary figure for fulfilment in 1927–8 was a growth by 23.5 per cent (*Kontrol'nye tsifry...na 1929/30g.* pp. 422–3).
[2] *Ibid.* p. 423.

output showed a certain increase in 1926–7 to 1929–30 inclusive. There was then a decline in 1931, which became precipitous in 1932. The difference between the course of industrial development according to the drafts of the Five-Year Plan completed in the first half of 1927, and the course which it actually took, was due to two principal reasons. The first was in the operation of the 'declining growth-rate curve'. Incidentally, this curve has its own history. During the NEP the idea of the curve was accepted by everybody including the Party, as was shown in Chapter 2. In the early post-NEP (mainly before the show trial), 'the curve' figured among the crimes of which Bazarov, Groman and Ginzburg were accused.[1] I. Gladkov in his 'On the History of the First Five-Year National-Economic Plan', *Planovoe khozyaistvo*, No. 4, 1935, p. 139, spoke already of the destruction of the Trotskyist-right wing theory of 'the curve'. Thus, while originally it was no crime at all to believe in the idea, those whom it was desired to pillory were later accused of it. Groman and his associates were no longer a worthwhile object of attack in 1935, when Gladkov published his history. By then it was the turn of the Trotskyists and Bukharinists (right-wing Communists), in anticipation of their trial in 1936–8.

But to return to the rates of growth of industrial output in post-NEP years; as we have shown, industrial output grew considerably in 1927–8 rather than declining as expected by the planners. The fiscal year was not yet over when Bazarov offered a partial explanation of the phenomenon. According to him, the curve, rather than (as had been supposed) operating strongly once the pre-war *output* level had been reached, should, under conditions of nationalised industry, do so only when the higher pre-war *capacity* level was attained. This capacity level was, according to Bazarov, about 20–30 per cent higher than the output level.[2] The postponement of the operation of 'the curve' should, it would seem, have prevented a decline in the rate of growth of industrial output for some time after 1926–7. It should not presumably *per se* lead to an increase in the rate of this growth.

As was shown, according to *Kontrol'nye tsifry na 1927/28g.*

---

[1] See, for example, M. Rogal'sky, *op. cit.* pp. 82–3 and 92.
[2] For further details see Ch. 7, p. 132.

the target for the growth in the output of large-scale industry in 1927–8 was slightly smaller than the achievement in 1926–7. Even this somewhat lower target was declared impressive, great, hard to attain, etc. But the target was not to be reached at the expense of qualitative factors (quality of goods produced, labour productivity, production costs). *Kontrol'nye tsifry na 1927/28g.* emphasised this idea forcefully. Page 13 of the summary says: 'The qualitative growth of the socialised sector is the central theme of the national-economic plan for the coming year.' On p. 28 of the summary, the same idea is expressed with even more emphasis: 'It must be...stressed with all energy that for the coming year, an incomparably more important aspect than the scheduled increase in the share of the socialised sector is the solving of the extremely difficult task of improving the quality of the work of the whole socialised sector.'

In practice, far from emphasising qualitative factors as provided in *Kontrol'nye tsifry na 1927/28g.* there was a drive for output which wholly neglected them. This neglect may well have resulted, for a time, in a certain speeding-up in the rise of output. But the price was paid in the form of a rapidly growing disorganisation. By 1932, the economic apparatus was in pieces. In the winter of 1932–3, industrial output ran substantially lower than in the winter of 1931–2.[1]

How great the disorganisation was already by 1929–30 is apparent from the fact that in the two and a quarter years from 1929–30 to 1932 the output of steel increased by only 2.9 per cent. The output of rolled steel even declined by 4.8 per cent.[2] This occurred although Stalin had declared in his speech 'The year of the great turning-

---

[1] The rapidly growing disorganisation is apparent also, for example, from labour data. The labour force in large-scale industry was increasing moderately (by 6.4 per cent on average) in 1926–7 and 1927–8 (*Kontrol'nye tsifry...na 1929/30g.* p. 487). The increase in the year 1928–9 (8.7 per cent) can also perhaps be considered moderate, but then the labour force in large-scale industry jumped by 26.6 per cent in 1930 and by 28.8 per cent in 1931. Since the increases in output were smaller than these percentages, even ignoring the deterioration of the quality of the goods produced, there was a large decline in labour productivity. In 1932 it was impossible to achieve any increase in output, again irrespective of the declining quality of goods, yet the labour force grew by 21.6 per cent (*Sotsialisticheskoe stroitel'stvo*, Moscow, 1936, pp. 508–9).

[2] *Sotsialisticheskoe stroitel'stvo*, Moscow, 1935, p. 172.

Table 10. *Official percentage increases in*
first Five-Year Plan

	Targets[a] 1927–8 to 1932–3	Fulfilment[b] 1928 to 1933
Total industry	136	113
Producer goods	204	190
Consumer goods	103	63

SOURCES: [a] *Five-Year Plan*, text, Vol. I, p. 131.
[b] *Narodnoe khozyaistvo SSSR v 1958g.* p. 136.

point' (7 November 1929):[1] 'We are steaming at full speed towards industrialisation...We are becoming a country of metal, a country of the automobile, a country of the tractor.'

Noteworthy also are the data for building materials. In the three years from 1930 to 1933 the output of construction timber increased by 1.5 per cent, while output of bricks and cement declined by 20 and 9.9 per cent respectively.[2] 'The independent base of reconstruction of industry, construction and agriculture' which was 'created during the period of the first Five-Year Plan'[3] appears to have been actually created with even less building materials during a large part of the period.

Producer and consumer goods

While the target of the Five-Year Plan for industrial output was missed by a wide margin, there were important differences in the rates of growth of the two categories of industrial goods. The target for the rate of growth of output of producer goods was missed by less than that for the industry as a whole, while the much lower target for the rate of growth of consumer goods was missed to a still greater extent (see Table 10).

Even the very exaggerated official figure for actual growth in

[1] Stalin, *Voprosy leninizma*, p. 274.
[2] *Narodnoe khozyaistvo SSSR v 1958g.* pp. 251, 264 and 259.
[3] Resolution of the Joint Plenum of the Central Committee and Central Control Commission of the AUCP(b) on 'Results of the first Five-Year Plan'. See *Direktivy KPSS*, p. 363.

output of producer goods was greatly short of the target, but the output of consumer goods did not in practice increase at all. According to Nutter the increase in this output, which was scheduled in the Five-Year Plan as 103 per cent, in fact stood at only 3 per cent.[1]

The consumption of cotton in the textile industry, for example, increased by only 6.6 per cent in the four and a quarter years from 1928–9 to 1933.[2] In the face of the great deterioration in the quality of all industrial products, the figure for output of the textile industry must actually have meant a decline during the period. In agreement with this reasoning, we find in Nutter (p. 197) a decline of 7 per cent in 1928–32 for 'textiles and allied products'.

The absence of any rise in output of consumer goods during the period of the Five-Year Plan was of course tragic in view of the great increase in urban population in those years.[3]

Thus the targets of the Five-Year Plans adopted in 1927, even though low compared with those accepted late in 1928, were missed by substantial margins. There is in addition evidence of a great deterioration in the quality of industrial goods, of a decline in labour productivity and, in 1931 and 1932, a considerable rise in production costs, as well as the tragic repercussions outside industry, including the great mortality of the population. All in all, the conclusion must be that the modest results for industrial output, smaller even than those which would have been attained if the development of the NEP-years had continued after 1927, were reached at the cost of immense losses and sacrifices.

RAILWAY TRANSPORT

Transport data indicate that the operation of the 'curve' was postponed by fully three years. They also clearly point to the fact that during the operation of the first Five-Year Plan we face not only the effect of 'the diminishing curve', but one which had virtually flattened out. Only the disruption of the economy on an

---

[1] Nutter, *Growth of Industrial Production*, p. 193.
[2] *Sotsialisticheskoe stroitel'stvo*, 1935, p. 242.
[3] According to Warren Eason, the urban population of the USSR increased from 27.6 million in January 1928 to 41 million in January 1934. See Bergson and Kuznets, (eds.) *Economic Trends*, pp. 72–3.

Table 11. *Annual percentage increment in*
railway freight traffic

Year	Ton-kilometres	Tons
1926–7[a]	19	17
1927–8[a]	18	11
1929	21.0	20
1930	18.6	27
1931	13.6	8
1932	11.3	8
1933	0.1	0.4
1928–33	81.5	71

SOURCE: *Kontrol'nye tsifry...na 1929–30g.* pp. 438–9; Data from Holland Hunter, *Soviet Transportation Policies*, Cambridge, Mass., 1957, pp. 316 and 331.
[a] Fiscal years.

immense scale could have had the effect on railway transport shown in Table 11.

By 1933 the rate of growth of freight transportation fell to zero.

PRICES

The catastrophe in which the first Five-Year Plan period culminated, was, *inter alia*, clearly reflected in the development of prices. Malafeev's *Istoriya tsenoobrazovaniya*, in spite of some defects, contains illuminating data on this score. He shows an immense rise in prices of consumer goods and a great decline in the retail supply of these goods during the first Five-Year Plan period, especially its last two years, particularly if the calculation is made per head of urban population. According to Malafeev (p. 172), the supplies of food products in official retail trade declined from 7,367 million roubles in 1930 to 5,538 million roubles in 1932. Over the plan period the supply of retail goods other than food increased, but only by 1.5 per cent. During the same period, however, the prices[1] of both categories of goods rose by 62.4 per cent from 1930 to the first half of 1932 (*ibid.* p. 402), implying a decrease in the real volume of state trade to not much more than one half in the two years from 1930 to 1932.

[1] Current prices, not index numbers.

In the private markets, the increase in prices in the same short period was equivalent to 233 per cent (*loc. cit.*). The increase in retail prices in private trade was already very large before 1931. From 1927–8 to 1930 the rise was equivalent to 131 per cent (Malafeev, p. 402), and there was a total increase of almost eightfold from 1927–8 to the first half of 1932. There was a further huge rise of prices in retail trade in the second half of 1932.[1]

FINAL REMARKS

The topic 'Was Stalinism necessary?' is still alive. Quite recently it seems even to have acquired added popularity. So far as the period of the first Five-Year Plan is concerned, Stalinism did immense harm to the Soviet economy, and the only possible question is exactly how much. Industrial output did not grow even by the rates foreseen in the Five-Year Plans accepted in 1927, i.e. during the NEP period, at which time these targets were condemned as much too low. In addition, the quality of goods produced and labour productivity declined sharply and production costs rose, while agricultural output also declined. The situation deteriorated from year to year, and the period ended in catastrophe. Moral deterioration may be added to the charge-sheet.

The 'Great Purge' of the late thirties affected economic developments very adversely, not only in 1937–8, the years of the trials themselves: the repercussions of the removal of the most experienced directors, engineers and other technical staff were evident for many subsequent years. The disappearance of the ablest army commanders and a great many officers of lower rank, combined

---

[1] This is clear from the following data (given by Malafeev, p. 402):

With the prices of 1927–8 equal to 100, the indices of retail prices stood as follows in the first half of 1932:

Socialised sector 176.6

Private sector 760.3

Total 251.8.

The Index of retail prices in state and co-operative trade; was cited as 255 in 1932, 1928 = 100 (*ibid.* p. 407). Thus, the rise in retail prices of the socialised sector in the second half of 1932 was so large that the index which was valid for the socialised *and private trade* become applicable to the socialised trade alone, when the second half of 1932 had been added to the period of observation.

It was not exactly scholarly on Malafeev's part to avoid indicating the price rise in the second half of 1932.

with moral disintegration among the rank and file soldiers, had a very bad effect on the Soviet effort during World War II. This was recognised even by Isaac Deutscher in his *Stalin*.

THE NONCONFORMISTS

Grounds for criticism were growing rapidly, in volume and seriousness, immediately after the end of the NEP. At the same time, the possibility of criticising was diminishing even more rapidly and was soon to be fully eliminated.

The pressure from the top soon became intense. The neo-narodniks began to lay down their arms as early as the second half of 1928. By the end of 1929, when Makarov capitulated, all prominent neo-narodniks (Chayanov, Chelintsev, Kondrat'ev, Weinstein, Makarov and probably some others) had accepted Stalin's general line or made similar defeatist admissions.

At least some Mensheviks, notably Groman and Sukhanov, continued the struggle after the NEP had ended. The last act of opposition known to this writer is Groman's letter to Rykov of 10 October 1929 – see Chapter 7 below. Sukhanov's fighting participation in the debate of Kritsman's paper 'On Class Grouping in Peasant Economy'[1] did not precede this letter by very much.

The listing of a given individual as a regular contributor to *Planovoe khozyaistvo* is a very simple, yet accurate way of ascertaining how far the Mensheviks were allowed to publish their views. The list as a whole was very long in those years. Yet one does not find among contributors to the double issue No. 7–8 of 1930 a single name of anyone who would have been even under suspicion of unwillingness to accept the general Party (i.e. Stalin's) line. The names mentioned in this book disappeared from the *Planovoe khozyaistvo* list as follows after issue No. 2 of 1930:

> Vishnevsky (No. 3 of 1930)
> Shtern (No. 3 of 1930)
> Groman (No. 5 of 1930)
> Bazarov (No. 6 of 1930)
> Gukhman (No. 6 of 1930)

[1] See *Na agrarnom fronte* (On the Agrarian Front), No. 6–7, 1929, pp. 178 ff.

Pervushin (No. 6 of 1930)
Ginzburg (No. 7–8 of 1930)
Kafengauz (No. 7–8 of 1930)
Falkner (No. 7–8 of 1930)

The name of Shtern may have been taken off the list because of his death. But those of the rest were dropped for obvious reasons.[1] Actually the removal from the list of contributors occurred with a considerable delay. Not everybody on the editorial board of *Planovoe khozyaistvo* apparently showed the proper degree of hostility to the nonconformists.

Bazarov's speech at the conference on the General Plan early in 1930 (see Chapter 7) was the only regrettable action, before imprisonment, of a Menshevik or person close to the Mensheviks. Even this was a much milder concession to official pressure than the declarations of the neo-narodniks; it belongs indeed in another class.

There seems to be no explanation of why the neo-narodniks laid down their arms before – and in some cases long before – they were arrested. The only explanation I can see is that Groman, Bazarov, Ginzburg and possibly some others had been well acquainted with prison life since a long time before the Revolution, so it had less terror for them. Most neo-narodniks were just too young to have had this experience; in any case they were on the whole more moderate, and so less likely to have landed in jail under the Tsar.

Another difference between the Mensheviks and the neo-narodniks is that the latter were arrested months ahead of the former, and for some time it was expected that there would be an open trial of the neo-narodniks with only a sprinkling of Mensheviks. Again it must be said that no explanation of this phenomenon has been offered. It may be suggested by way of explanation that at the end of 1929 and early in 1930, the high point of full-scale collectivisation, the neo-narodniks, as experts in agriculture, may have appeared

---

[1] The test cannot be applied to other journals, because they succumbed even before the prosecution of undesirable contributors came into full swing. *Ekonomicheskoe obozrenie*, for example, was discontinued after the March issue. There was no need of many journals, since all that needed to be done was to extol the general (Stalin) Party line.

more dangerous than the Mensheviks. By mid-1930 the disorganisation of the economy reached such proportions that more general issues, in which the Mensheviks represented the principal opposition, were coming more and more to the centre of attention.[1]

Arrangements for an open trial of Mensheviks were apparently hastily made in late 1930 and early 1931. The trial took place in early March 1931; Kondrat'ev was the only neo-narodnik in it and no open trial of neo-narodniks was ever held. All the neo-narodniks, and those Mensheviks who did not appear in the open trial, were tried secretly or simply exiled (see Chapter 4).

[1] The disorganisation was strongly evidenced by the price development of which we spoke above. The price rise in the private sector of retail trade started directly after the end of the NEP and proceeded in a rapidly ascending line. In 1927-8 prices rose by 7.5 per cent. The rise in 1928-9 amounted to 23.4 per cent. Then came a jump of 83.1 per cent in one and a quarter years until 1930 (see Malafeev, p. 401).

PART II THE TRIAL

4

THE INDICTMENT

INTRODUCTION

Seen in perspective, the Menshevik trial, held on 1–8 March 1931, is an episode in the long chain of show trials which were part of Stalin's increasingly bitter fight for the dictatorship. These began in May 1928 with the trial of engineers known as the Shakhty trial. Next came the trial of the Industrial Party from 25 November to 7 December 1930, with L. K. Ramzin, the leading fuel expert, as the star defendant. The last trial to involve engineers, or non-Party men of any kind, was apparently that of the Vickers engineers in April 1933.[1]

Intensive prosecutions of Party members started at the XV Party Congress in December 1927 which put an end to NEP. At this time Zinoviev, Kamenev and some others were expelled from the Party. Several persons were exiled, notably Trotsky to Turkestan. Show-trials of party members began on a large scale in 1935; it does not seem possible to find out how many were held. The most celebrated were the three Moscow trials of Bolsheviks (Zinoviev, Kamenev and fourteen others in 1936; Pyatakov, Radek and fifteen others in 1937; and Bukharin, Rykov and nineteen others in 1938), and the secret trial of Marshal Tukhachevsky and others in 1937. As was unshakeably proven by Khrushchev's speeches at the XX Party Congress in 1956, the trials and convictions were fully and exclusively based on 'confessions' extorted by torture and similar means, which increased in severity as time went on.

The trials of 1935 ended in jail sentences (Zinoviev, 10 years; Kamenev, 5 years in January and 10 years in July). Some time between 27 July 1935 and the first big show trial in August 1936, murder replaced jail as the normal sentence. The much greater severity of the sentences and the tremendous number of trials held in 1936–8 lead some experts to distinguish these years as a unique

[1] DTV Dokumente, *Die Moskauer Schauprozesse, 1936–1938*, Munich, September 1963, pp. 55–6.

period, during which it is surmised that Stalin was afflicted with paranoia.

Lenin must be given credit for having foreseen the danger arising from Stalin's nature as early as 1923, when he wanted Stalin removed from the post of first secretary of the Party. Most prominent Party leaders had been murdered by the end of 1938, so a relaxation from the terrific rate of the two previous years was inevitable. But torture, death sentences and actual murders continued in less appalling numbers right through until Stalin's death in 1953. In 1950 Voznesensky, the gifted head of the USSR Gosplan, was condemned for 'treason' and murdered. Immediately before his own death, Stalin was preparing the doctors' trials, which are believed by many to have been intended to equal in scale the trials of the late 1930s.

The situation in the 1930s is now sufficiently clear. Any difficulties in analysing the Menshevik trial are due to the fact that it took place long before the peak of these murderous exhibitions was reached. Specifically the methods used, including the extent and severity of torture, were not quite as inhuman in 1930–1 as a few years later. According to the verdict in the Menshevik Show Trial (*Trial*,[1] pp. 465–6), defendants were:

1. V. G. Groman, 56 years old, former member of the Presidium of Gosplan;

2. V. V. Sher, 47, former member of the Board of the USSR State Bank;

3. N. N. Sukhanov, 48, journalist;

4. A. M. Ginzburg, 52, economist;

5. M. P. Yakubovich, 39, associate head of the Department of Supplies of the USSR Commissariat of Trade;

6. A. L. Sokolovsky, 47, economist;

7. L. B. Salkind, 45, economist;

8. V. G. Volkov, 47, former economist of the VSNKh;

---

[1] This is a volume of 476 large, double-column, small-type pages, badly printed. Perhaps a dozen pages of the photostat I had to use are stamped 'Reproduced from very poor material', and several pages not so stamped are also illegible. This large book has no index. Whether it is really a stenographic record without any changes or omissions cannot be known. It was difficult to carry out analysis on the basis of such material and absolutely impossible to utilise all major portions of the work. It is hoped that the writer will be excused for the inevitable shortcomings.

9. K. G. Petunin, 46, member of the Board of Tsentrosoyuz;
10. A. Yu. Finn-Enotaevsky, 58, professor of economics at the Polytechnical Institute in Leningrad;
11. B. M. Berlatsky, 41, former member of the Board of the State Bank, USSR;
12. V. K. Ikov, 49, journalist;
13. M. I. Teitelbaum, 54, former senior director on standardisation of export goods of the Commissariat of Trade;
14. I. I. Rubin, 45, professor of economics.

All fourteen accused were described in the verdict as having been at different periods members of the Russian Social Democratic Party (Menshevik). Salkind, Finn-Enotaevsky and Teitelbaum were said to have been members of the Bolshevik party in 1903–7, 1903–15 and 1900–7 respectively. Sokolovsky was stated to have been a member of the Central Committee of the Jewish Socialist Party from 1906 to 1920. Of the fourteen defendants, thirteen made a full 'confession' of the crimes ascribed to them. Finn-Enotaevesky, the fourteenth and incidentally the oldest, answered 'yes' to the question: 'Defendant Finn-Enotaevsky, are you guilty of the charges brought against you?' (*Trial*, p. 54), but later he disputed some of the accusations.

In addition to Groman, the star defendant, most other defendants had also been prominent in directing the national economy (Ginzburg, Sokolovsky, Sher, Salkind, etc.) or otherwise (Finn-Enotaevsky, Sukhanov, Rubin, etc.). But among the six called as witnesses by the prosecutor from the start (*Trial*, p. 53: the seventh witness, M. N. Ioffe, was called during the trial), five at least were as prominent as the Menshevik defendants. Chief of these was the star witness, Kondrat'ev, who was scheduled as a defendant in the proposed trial (which in fact never took place) of the counter-revolutionary kulak–Socialist Revolutionary organisation Kondrat'ev–Chayanov (*Trial*, pp. 194–210). Also highly prominent was Ramzin, the chief among those found guilty at the trial of the Industrial Party at the end of 1930 (*Trial*, pp. 172–83). V. A. Larichev, another witness, had been condemned in the same trial as Ramzin (*Trial*, pp. 183–6).

Also among the witnesses was K. A. Gvozdev (*Trial*, pp. 307–11).

He was one of the most prominent, if not the most prominent manual labourer engaged in politics before and during the February Revolution. In 1910–11, he was president of the Union of Metallurgists in Leningrad: in 1915–16 he was president of the workers' group in the Military–Industrial Committee (an important all-Russian organisation). In 1917 we find him as minister of labour in the Kerensky government.

Another prominent figure was N. V. Nekrasov, a member of the Provisional (Kerensky) Government (*Trial*, pp. 289–95). According to the declaration of the prosecutor (*Trial*, p. 53), the indictments of Nekrasov and Gvozdev were separate from the Menshevik trial. I. Z. Zheludkov was the sixth person called as a witness from the start (*Trial*, pp. 151–5). His role was a minor one.[1]

Hardly any difference was made between the defendants and the witnesses as regards their treatment by the Court. All witnesses appeared for the prosecution: the defence did not call any. No witness was asked his address; like the accused, they all came direct from jail. In contrast to the defendants, at least one of whom showed reluctance to 'confess' fully, all witnesses 'confessed' freely to practically the same crimes as the accused were alleged to have committed. Normally the witnesses were addressed by the court and the prosecutor alike simply by their surnames, rarely with the addition of the term 'witness', or even more rarely 'citizen'.

TRUTHS AND FALSEHOODS

The great difficulty in handling the 'stenographic report' is in separating lies from truth. After about 1928 tens of thousands of honourable men 'confessed' to crimes they had never committed. It may not be superfluous to touch here on this subject, since this particular trial was one of the early ones, and everything, including brutality and also the volume of lies, increased in those years by huge strides. To begin with, it was a gross error to fabricate the

---

[1] Zheludkov testified that for a fee of 2,000 roubles he permitted the use of his small house, gave lodging to the rare visitors from the provinces who belonged to the Menshevik organisation, and also stored and distributed *Sotsialistichesky vestnik* and other literature. Ioffe, testified on 'deliberate distortions' of plans for output and distribution of textiles (*Trial*, pp. 275–9).

lie that R. A. Abramovich, one of the most prominent Menshevik leaders abroad, visited Moscow in the summer of 1928 and had important conferences with the Russian Mensheviks. It did not occur to the prosecution that Abramovich would be in a position to have a German court nail down the lie. However, Abramovich prosecuted a Berlin Communist paper which published reports on the Moscow trial. The paper's attorney, a Communist member of the Reichstag named Löwenstein, had to concede that Abramovich could not possibly have visited Russia at the time specified in the indictment, because at that very time he was attending the Congress of the Labour and Socialist International. The Communist editor, adjudged guilty of libel, was ordered to publish prominently a notice of the verdict in his paper and to pay the court expenses.[1]

The lie regarding Abramovich's alleged visit to Moscow in the summer of 1928 suffices to prove that not a word of the trial can be accepted as definitely true. The more those in power were interested in proving something, the greater is the probability of lies. Everything said about foreign intervention, for example, must be ignored. But there are some other proofs of lies, though they are not so glaring as the one concerning the Abramovich visit.

Yakubovich testified (*Trial*, p. 45) on the literary contributions of the defendants to the *Sotsialistichesky vestnik*, the journal of the *émigré* Mensheviks published in Berlin: 'So far as I am aware, the following have written regularly [for the *S.v.*]: I. I. Rubin, A. M. Ginzburg, L. B. Salkind, V. A. Bazarov, V. V. Sher, V. G. Groman, F. A. Cherevanin and P. P. Maslov.' This all seems quite improbable. Groman would probably not have concealed from me such a fact as his having written for the *Sotsialistichesky vestnik*. As regards Ginzburg, Valentinov says of him: 'it is impossible not to mention his exceptional loyalty towards the Soviet power...He would not have had anything to do with activities of an anti-Soviet nature'. Valentinov goes on to describe how he offered to let Ginzburg read some issues of *Sotsialistichesky vestnik*, which he (Valentinov) had obtained by chance in connection with his job, 'He [Ginzburg] jumped away from me as if from boiling water. On his face was written fear and indignation'. Ginzburg also said,

[1] Abramovich, *op. cit.* p. 386.

according to Valentinov, 'I do not want to become familiar with this literature [he meant all the *émigré* press]. I do not need it. What is written in it does not interest me in the least...'[1]

Valentinov was an emotional man. 'Aversion' was one of his favourite words. In the *Memoirs* he uses it to describe his feelings towards Preobrazhensky, a Trotskyist economist, and towards so distinguished a person as Maslov. In the *Sotsialistichesky vestnik* he used it concerning his attitude to Groman. Valentinov disliked Ginzburg, but he could not have invented the incident described above. There is, moreover, other evidence that courage was not among Ginzburg's virtues in the later years of his known life.

Another obvious fable is the suggestion in the *Trial* that a small organisation like the Menshevik organisation in the USSR in the late twenties received subsidies to the extent of 480,000 roubles in one and a half years (see p. 80).

All accusations of sabotage on the part of the defendants in 1929 and 1930, specifically the sponsoring of foreign intervention, are simply unbelievable. With reference to the defendants in the Menshevik trial the accusations seem sufficiently absurd; but what can be said about the charge that Chayanov participated in meetings engaged in the organisation of foreign intervention in 1929 and 1930 (testimony of Ramzin in *Trial*, pp. 176–7), when already in 1928 he was declaiming under his own name that he accepted Stalin's general line? (See the section on Chayanov in Chapter 11 below.) Chayanov is also supposed to have said that the peasants should be driven into the kolkhozes with the help of armed force. Some statements of Makarov are as bad as those of Chayanov, the only difference being that Chayanov had printed his statements, while Makarov is only alleged to have made his during the purge of the Narkomzen (Commissariat for Agriculture) in December 1929. The statements seem nevertheless to have been reproduced correctly (see the section on Makarov in Chapter 11). According to Ramzin, Makarov participated in the same meetings, in 1929 and 1930, which were mentioned in connection with Chayanov.

According to Ramzin (*Trial*, p. 174), the loyal Ginzburg, who would not touch *Sotsialistichesky vestnik*, was very active in meet-

[1] Valentinov, *Memoirs*, pp. 226–7.

ings of nonconformists in 1928 and 1929, in which the question of organising foreign intervention played a great role.

It may not be superfluous to mention an issue which is very minor, indeed negligible, compared with others, but of which I can speak from personal experience. One of the Menshevik defendants, Teitelbaum, testified[1] that 'in 1925 in Berlin there existed a small organisation set up to propagandize the Mensheviks and their associates who might be coming from the USSR and returning there'. I myself, an alleged representative of the *Voukovspilka* (Union of Ukrainian consumer co-operatives), am supposed to have been a member of that group. I was perfectly safe abroad and there would have been no reason for me to deny this if it were true. But it was not, and Teitelbaum probably made his statement just because he knew I was abroad and safe. It was not I but he, Teitelbaum, who represented the *Voukovspilka* in Berlin, and at the time in question I was in Hamburg. I did not in fact know, until I read the minutes of the trial, that Teitelbaum was a Menshevik, my connection with him having been a strictly business one: in his capacity of representative of the Ukrainian Trade Commissariat he paid me for my articles for the Ukrainian weekly devoted to foreign trade. I learnt of his statement about me only in 1958, when I obtained a photostat of the minutes of the trial.[2]

When people start lying, contradictions are inevitable. In the written testimony of A. I. Lezhnev, who was not called as a witness because of sickness, we read: 'He [Brounstein] mentioned that hc had personal meetings with V. G. Groman...' (*Trial*, p. 232). Only three pages later (*Trial*, p. 235) we come to the testimony of Groman, who said: 'I personally did not meet Brounstein.' The prosecutor N. V. Krylenko probably hoped that Groman would change this portion of his testimony, and asked, 'You mean to say

---

[1] *Trial*, pp. 254–5.
[2] I hardly ever spent more than 10 minutes with Teitelbaum. Of the accused, I knew well personally only Groman (to a much lesser extent I knew Sukhanov). Groman I knew so well that in 1927, on his way back from Bad Nauheim to the USSR via Berlin, he made a detour to Hamburg to be my guest for a few days. One may wonder why Groman did not mention my name in the *Trial*. Of course I had no connection, or only a very loose connection, with the Menshevik organisation at that time. Any accusation he might have made would not have harmed me; but apparently he did not do even this on his own initiative, while those in the Cheka who handled his case and told him what to say cannot have known my name.

you did not meet him [Brounstein] personally?', but Groman did not take the hint.

Great efforts were made to prove that the Menshevik organisation, as well as the bloc which this organisation allegedly formed with the working peasants (TKP) and the industrial parties, had foreign intervention as their principal aim. Even Brounstein, a Menshevik *émigré* who came secretly from Berlin to the USSR in 1929, is supposed to have advocated intervention, although he was so far to the left of his party and close to the Bolsheviks that he is alleged to have said that the only reason he did not become a Bolshevik was that so many of his comrades were in jail.

While the mendacity of a great deal of the *Trial* is beyond doubt, the material in it is too interesting to be disregarded, altogether. The great role that the Mensheviks, and to some extent also the neo-narodniks and other nonconformists, had played in directing the national economy, specifically their role in preparing five-year and annual plans, is of course obvious from the literature. The violent attacks, the statements of Krylenko (the 'Comrade Abram' of 1905) who, to use a Russian expression, 'spoke as if he were God' in his denunciation, and the verdict on Groman, Bazarov, Kondrat'ev and others point to the same conclusion.

The main accusations, and the easiest to refute, are those involving alleged sabotage in the state organisations where the accused were employed, from relatively low positions to almost the top level, and concerning which official evidence is available.

'CRIMES' IN THE ECONOMIC FIELD

With reference to crimes in the economic field, the procedure pursued by the prosecution was very simple. Statements made by the defendants in all good faith, but which turned out to be erroneous, were branded as deliberate attempts to damage the Soviet economy, and the accused were forced to 'confess' to this interpretation.[1] Actually even actions which turned out to be correct were regularly made into crimes.

---

[1] The exact way in which the defendants were forced to 'confess' seems still to be unknown. That a great deal of force was used in many cases is of course beyond doubt.

The verdict ascribed to the defendants the following crimes, allegedly committed in the offices in which they were employed:

In *Gosplan*: The embodiment, in the Control Figures and annual reviews of the economy, of a plan structure which was deliberately at variance with official policy; defending in industry, agriculture and other branches of the national economy measures which were hampering, deliberately annihilating and disorganising these branches of the national economy (Groman) (*Trial*, p. 466).

In *VSNKh*: The growth of output in the Five-Year Plan was set absurdly low in order to disrupt socialist construction, especially in such decisive branches of the economy as metal, coal, petroleum, chemistry and electrotechnics, as well as the production of agricultural machinery and chemical fertilisers (Ginzburg) (*ibid.* p. 467). Working out and delivering conjuncture reports for industry which not only did not foster socialist construction, but confused the leading economic authorities (Ginzburg); obstruction of the realisation of the rates of growth decided on by the Soviet government for the metallurgical industry...(Ginzburg, Volkov) (*ibid.*). Drafting and achievement of minimal targets in the Five-Year Plan for raw materials, especially cotton (Sokolovsky) (*Trial*, p. 467).

Similar absurd accusations, but indicating (as in the case of Gosplan and VSNKh) the important and indeed decisive roles played by the defendants in their respective offices, were made in respect of the State Bank (Sher, Berlatsky), the Commissariat for Trade and Tsentrosoyuz (Salkind, Yakubovich, Petunin) etc.

In greater detail, the crimes which Groman, on behalf of himself and his collaborators, confessed to having committed in the USSR Gosplan were (*Trial*, pp. 36–7):

The damaging activities of the Mensheviks in the USSR Gosplan in the field of conjuncture observations, control figures and perspective plans, the last phase of which belongs to 1928, were carried out by me, Groman, and Bazarov, as well as the former Mensheviks associated with us – Zeilinger, Gukhman, Shub, Pistrak, Broitman – and the non-Party man Vishnevsky, who formed a counter-revolutionary sabotage group in the USSR Gosplan. These activities were prepared during the preceding five-year period (1923–7)...From 1928 on, the counter-revolutionary Gosplan group headed by me and Bazarov carried out directives of the new sabotage tactics of the C.C. of the RSDWP(m) abroad and the United Bureau of the C.C. of the RSDWP(m) organised inside the USSR.

These directives allegedly involved: incorporating in the Control Figures and conjuncture surveys plan decisions contrary to the general line of the Party and deliberately distorted conjuncture appraisals (curtailment of the rate of socialist construction; distortion of the class approach, exaggeration of difficulties, belittling of resources); stressing signs of approaching economic catastrophe (Groman) or, what is close to this, believing the chances for the realisation of the Party line, directed toward socialist attack, as negligible (Bazarov, Gukhman); giving priority, in constructing the perspective plans, to the genetic point of view over the teleological (Groman) or ascribing to them equal importance (Bazarov), instead of an active purposeful transformation of the historically given media; treating the agricultural problem, considered as a bottleneck in the national economy, on the basis of a two-year plan stressing the farm issue, which basically contradicted the plan for socialist reorganisation of conditions in the USSR. The indictment goes on to quote Groman's 'testimony' of 20 February 1931:[1]

...from 1928 I and my group (Zeilinger, Gukhman, Broitman, Shub, Pistrak, all former Mensheviks with whom were associated Bazarov and the non-Party man Vishnevsky) deliberately set up their own plans against those of the government and the general line of the Party with the object of distorting the class line in economic matters. This was done by tendentious interpretation of conjuncture processes, emphasising difficulties and pessimistic forecasts with the aim of diverting the Soviet power from the correct line...What was not successfully incorporated into the plans was effected in the course of their realisation, thanks to the authority of workers in high places; thus conditions were created for disruption of the supply situation, with consequent political dissatisfaction of the population.

Most of the statements in the above-quoted passages were basically true. Groman and the others certainly were against the general line of the Party. Groman, too, certainly wanted the genetic point of view to dominate in planning, and Bazarov wanted this

---

[1] *Trial*, p. 31. According to *Trial*, this part of the indictment is based on Groman's testimony of December 1930.

point of view to be seriously considered along with the teleological line. But neither Krylenko nor the court took seriously the accusations that Groman and the others acted with the deliberate intention of damaging the USSR. It is most significant that the warnings of the accused, made years before the trial, proved wholly correct. At the time of the trial the rates of growth of industry were already small, smaller than those foreseen by the Mensheviks, while agriculture had been brought close to catastrophe by mass slaughtering of livestock. After another year and a half, by the end of 1932, the catastrophe actually came, with millions dying of starvation. Indeed, matters turned out far worse than the defendants had forecast.

The 'confessed' sabotage activity of the 'counter-revolutionary' Mensheviks in the VSNKh was similar to that ascribed to Groman in Gosplan. Ginzburg 'confessed' responsibility for deliberately including too low rates of growth in the Five-Year Plan drawn up in 1927 and bearing his name.[1] At the beginning, the rates of growth had indeed turned out higher than those foreseen in the Ginzburg Five-Year Plan, but by 1931 they were already lower, at least if reliable statistics are used. As regards the forecasts in the Ginzburg Five-Year Plan, there is one item which would be decisive everywhere but in the 'real' democracy of Stalin. Simultaneously with the VSNKh Five-Year Plan worked out by Ginzburg, a Five-Year Plan for about the same period was worked out in the USSR Gosplan under the Communist S. Strumilin. Its targets were hardly different from those of the Ginzburg Plan, but nobody in the Menshevik trial or elsewhere in the USSR paid any attention to this fact, while Ginzburg himself, who certainly was fully aware of it was, no less certainly, forbidden to draw attention to it.

Note the following absurd testimony by Sher on sabotage activities in the State Bank (*Trial*, p. 36): 'The basic sabotage activity consisted in wrongful allocation of credits, curtailment [of them] for some branches and exaggeration of the needs of others. This was done by means of incorrect drafting of plans, complication of the methods of planning, refusal to assign credits for major needs...' and so on, with not a vestige of proof or even an example.

[1] *Trial*, p. 34.

5

ALLEGED GROUPINGS

THE UNITED BUREAU AND THE TWO OTHER 'SABOTAGE' CENTRES

It is much more difficult to reach conclusions where problems of organisation, political programmes etc. are involved. According to Ginzburg's testimony (*Trial*, p. 74), early in 1926 attempts were begun in order to renew the activities of the Menshevik party inside the USSR. According to *Trial*, Groman had apparently the chief hand in this activity, while Sher, at that time still in Gosbank, was also very interested. Later Ginzburg was allegedly drawn in.

The Menshevik 'United Bureau' is said to have been organised in February 1928 (*Trial*, p. 17). It was composed, according to the indictment, of ten persons: Groman, Sher, Shtern, Ginzburg, Sokolovsky, Volkov, Petunin, Yakubovich, Salkind and Finn-Enotaevsky. Early in 1929 Groman is said to have brought Sukhanov into the organisation. Rubin and Bazarov, while not members of the Bureau, were said to have frequently taken part in its meetings. A directing group of five was selected to take care of current business (*Trial*, p. 17). It consisted of Groman, Sukhanov, Sher, Ginzburg and Shtern. There was also a programme commission chaired by Bazarov and having as members Groman, Sukhanov, Ginzburg and Rubin, and a finance committee. Sher is alleged to have said (*Trial*, indictment, p. 25): 'I know of units [of the United Bureau] in the provinces at Nizhny-Novgorod, Orel, Tula, Astrakhan, Kharkov, Rostov-on-Don, Saratov etc.'

Early in 1929 Groman and Sukhanov negotiated with Kondrat'ev about forming a bloc of the Menshevik United Bureau with the TKP (Labour–Peasant Party) headed by Kondrat'ev. The negotiations soon led to the formation of such a bloc (*Trial*, pp. 22 and 24), replacing the looser connection which already existed.

Negotiations with the Industrial Party, alias the Engineer–Industrial Centre, were alleged to have started as early as the end of 1928, with Groman representing the Mensheviks, Kondrat'ev and Makarov the TKP, and Ramzin and somebody else (unnamed) the Industrial Party (*Trial*, p. 22). Here too an agreement was reached, but, as allegedly testified by Kondrat'ev (*Trial*, p. 196), not so close a one as between the other two organisations. On this point Kondrat'ev is said to have testified:

I insist on saying that the relation between the peasant party which I represented and Ramzin's organisation had a somewhat different nature from its relation with the organisation represented by Groman and Sukhanov, i.e. the Menshevik organisation. If the relations of my organisation with the Mensheviks were such as to constitute a bloc, our relations with Ramzin's organisation, later called the Industrial Party, were such that I would in honesty prefer to call them relations of agreement.

Kondrat'ev is said to have spoken, at the meeting of all three organisations at the end of 1928, of a possible agreement among them to fight against Soviet rule (*Trial*, indictment, p. 22). As objectives he indicated the liberalisation of economic relations, 'compensation' of capitalists and the establishment of a bourgeois-democratic republic: he emphasised probable support from outside in the form of an intervention. When he insisted on this point (*Trial*, pp. 170–80), Groman and possibly Ginzburg allegedly at first declared that they had no authority to give an answer, but later Groman is said to have accepted the plan for intervention. This position was affirmed (still according to Ramzin's alleged testimony) at a meeting in the spring of 1929 at which the following represented the Industrial Party: Ramzin, Larichev, Kalinnikov, Osadchy and Kogan-Bernshtein.[1] From the TKP were present Kondrat'ev, Makarov, Chayanov and Yurovsky; from the Menshevik side Groman and, it seems, Sukhanov (*Trial*, p. 176). At the beginning of 1930 a meeting took place to discuss the news that the intervention had been postponed from 1929 to 1930 (*Trial*, p. 177). It was attended by Ramzin, Larichev, Charnovsky, Osadchy and Stein for the Industrial Party; Kondrat'ev, Makarov and Chayanov for TKP, and Groman for the Mensheviks.

---

[1] Kalinnikov already played a leading role in preparing the GOELRO. The same is true of Osadchy, who in 1925–7 directed the work on the general plan.

As an amateur in politics, I can form no opinion on the likely attitude of such people as Groman and Kondrat'ev toward foreign intervention. In any case, I last saw Groman in the summer of 1927, when the NEP was not yet fully dead and the ferocities of 1929 and later years toward the peasants lay in the unforeseeable future. I did not see Kondrat'ev at any time after 1917. However, to a layman it seems quite possible that at a time when forced collectivisation was at its height, one or two nonconformists may have begun to favour any defence against Stalin's ferocities, even foreign intervention. What seems impossible is that an organisation with the membership described by Ramzin and the others in the *Trial* was in favour of an intervention, and that it was even the key point of their programme. Ginzburg, who even in 1925 was afraid to touch an *émigré* paper, would not have participated, in 1929 or even 1930, in an organisation favouring foreign intervention. Chayanov had already burned his boats in public in 1928. True, he was a somewhat unbalanced man and may somehow have found his 1928 articles compatible with advocating foreign intervention; but would the other persons who participated in the meetings in the spring of 1929, as described by Ramzin, have done so together with Chayanov? This seems very unlikely. All in all, I cannot believe that Groman or Kondrat'ev were in favour of an intervention themselves, still less that they formed an organisation for this purpose.

It is interesting that while, according to *Trial*, preparations for the intervention were in progress already in 1927,[1] the GPU did not know about them until quite late in 1930, or rather did not invent them until this late time. *Kondrat'evshchina*, published late in 1930, elaborated on the change of disorganisation of the economy (p. 8), specifying such crimes as wrecking machinery, preparing calculations which must have resulted in waste of raw materials, fuel etc. (p. 7), passing to foreign countries false evidence on the situation in the USSR (p. 9), etc. Similar charges figure in the articles of Vaisberg and Rogal'sky in issue No. 10–11 of *Planovoe khozyaistvo* for 1930, likewise published late in 1930; endless 'crimes' in planning and generally on the economic front were mentioned, but

---

[1] According to *Trial*, p. 86, Petunin talked with Dan, the Menshevik leader, about foreign intervention as early as October 1927, when they met in Berlin.

nothing about foreign intervention. Either the accusation did not yet exist or Milyutin and the other contributors to *Kondrat'evsh-china*, as well as Vaisberg and Rogal'sky, did not wish to put their names to such a thumping lie.

The late appearance and/or late invention of the tale about intervention is indicated also by the fact that some of the defendants who, according to *Trial*, knew of the intervention plan for years, for example Petunin, were not arrested till close to the end of 1930 (Petunin on 17 November).[1] Is it probable that the GPU would have let people who were engaged in preparing for a foreign intervention remain at liberty?

THE UNITED BUREAU AND THE MENSHEVIK CENTRE ABROAD

The relevant portion of the indictment (*Trial*, p. 39) begins thus:

The conspiracy against the people was conducted by the counter-revolutionary Menshevik organisation on the basis of direct guidance from the Menshevik Centre abroad. It has been shown above that the very establishment of the United Bureau was the result of the organisational influence of the same centre abroad. It has been established that direct instructions from the Centre abroad played a decisive role in the adoption of decisions and directives by the United Bureau with reference to sabotage, as well as decisions on forming a bloc with the Industrial Party and the TKP. This, however, was not all. From February 1928, when the United Bureau began its activities, to 1930, a number of its individual members held conferences with leading members of the Central Committee of Mensheviks abroad: written correspondence was carried on all the time, and finally two members of the Central Committee of the Mensheviks – the leader of the Mensheviks abroad, Abramovich, and the member of the Menshevik Central Committee Brounstein – came secretly to the USSR.

As far as the material in *Trial* shows, not a single Menshevik made a trip from the USSR to any foreign country in order to renew or maintain contacts with the Menshevik organisation abroad, let alone receive any directives from it. Apparently five of

[1] *Trial*, p. 323.

the accused were abroad at different times, and some of them saw one or more leading Mensheviks there; but they went on other business, and all their trips apparently occurred not later than the end of 1927, i.e. before the alleged organisation of the 'United Bureau' and before the alleged conferences.

Groman was in Germany in 1923, 1925 and 1927, stopping in Berlin on the way out and back. All these trips were made for health reasons. Each time he took the cure at Bad Nauheim, and at least twice he visited a famous physician in Berlin. In 1925 he visited the Menshevik leader Dan, and at his house he met Abramovich and Dallin. Groman mentioned that he spent three years in exile together with Dan, and that the meeting with the latter was for mutual information and as 'between old acquaintances' (*Trial*, p. 68). This meeting with Dan, Abramovich and Dallin was the only occasion on which Groman met Mensheviks abroad who had official positions in the Menshevik organisation as members of either the Central Committee or the Foreign Delegation. The disagreements which arose in subsequent years were so great that in 1927 Groman preferred not to see official representatives of the Delegation. About his stay in Berlin in 1927 he said specifically (*Trial*, pp. 69–70): 'I did not undertake the establishment of organisational connections with the Menshevik *émigré* organisation.'

In his testimony Groman also mentioned meetings in Berlin with Brounstein in 1923 and 1927 and with Denike in 1927. According to the recollection of this writer, Groman saw Denike also in 1923 and most probably in 1925. A main reason for the meetings was that Denike was on close terms with the German Social-Democratic Party, in which Groman was much interested. The meetings with Brounstein may have been due to Groman's desire to get more detailed information about the position of the various groups of Mensheviks abroad. But neither Brounstein nor, for that matter, Denike were members either of the Central Committee or the Foreign Delegation of the Social-Democratic Party. Groman's testimony makes it evident that the meetings with Brounstein and Denike were not regarded as 'organisational connections'.

Ginzburg (*Trial*, pp. 76–7) visited the United States in 1927. Stopping in Berlin on the outward journey according to *Trial*, he twice saw the *émigré* leaders Theodor Dan, Peter Garvy and Dan's wife, L. O. Kanzel-Cederbaum. On the way back he merely spoke to Dan by telephone.

According to Groman's testimony, it was only in 1925 that he saw Mensheviks abroad who held official positions in their organisation, but the indictment (*Trial*, p. 40) says: 'Until 1929 personal contacts with foreign countries were maintained by Groman and Ginzburg.' The statement is not true of Ginzburg either. In the period here discussed, he was abroad only once, in 1927. Finn-Enotaevsky was made to testify (*Trial*, p. 105) that Groman 'maintained relations with Dan of the (Menshevik) Foreign Delegation'.

The earliest trip abroad of a Menshevik described in detail in *Trial* is that of Berlatsky in 1925. He travelled to the United States at the end of that year, with stops at Berlin in both directions. His activities in Berlin were undertaken on the initiative of Sher, he said in his testimony. On that occasion, according to the indictment (*Trial*, p. 62), he saw in Berlin Boris Nikolaevsky, who was allegedly assigned to conduct official talks with him (p. 62). Nikolaevsky is supposed to have said that the operation of the NEP must be greatly intensified in rural areas, and that the Social-Democratic Party should take measures to strengthen it in industry. The Soviet Union would not succeed in restoring its industry without foreign capital. Emphasis was laid on the expansion of Social-Democratic work in government offices – a harmless directive inside Russia, if ever there was one (pp. 62–3).

According to *Trial*, p. 40, Shtern had the most extensive contacts with the Menshevik organisation during his trips abroad. Yakubovich testified (p. 40):

On each trip he [Shtern] stopped in Berlin and met all members of the Central Committee Abroad and attended its meetings. In addition, he visited the most prominent leaders of the German Social-Democratic Party. I know about his visits to K. Kautsky, E. Bernstein and R. Hilferding. On the instructions of the Russian Central Committee, A. B. Shtern reported in detail to the Centre Abroad and received from it directives and information. Sher was indeed allegedly appointed to represent the Menshevik Centre in Moscow and, if necessary, in the USSR as well.

77

There is, however, a contradiction with reference to dates. Yakubovich said that Shtern's trips 'started, I believe, in 1925'. But the indictment stated that 'the trips of Shtern belonged to the period after 1928'.[1]

The last trip of a Soviet Menshevik abroad reported in *Trial* was that of Petunin late in 1927. Petunin operated on the instructions of Sher, he testified. In accordance with these, he obtained directives from Dan, one of the Menshevik leaders abroad. There were three directives, of which the third was not specific. The first two, according to the interpretation of Krylenko, the prosecutor, were: (1) to support the Trotskyist opposition with the aim of wrecking the VKP, and (2) to support and carry out disorganisational work, in order to disrupt the economic machinery (*Trial*, p. 86). The third directive concerned the inevitability of foreign intervention. At first this question was left open (*ibid*. p. 87), but it was allegedly answered in the affirmative with the arrival of Abramovich in 1928. Since the whole trip of Abramovich to the USSR has been proved to have been a myth, the charge that the Mensheviks accepted the idea of foreign intervention collapses also. The material in *Trial* itself indicates that they did not do so until some time after the alleged visit by Abramovich.

The prosecution badly needed to prove that there had been contact between the Mensheviks in the USSR and 'the Foreign Delegation' in Berlin. Abramovich would be highly suitable as an emissary from 'the Foreign Delegation', and accordingly a trip by him to the USSR in 1928 was fabricated. Brounstein actually came to Russia in the spring of 1929, but he did so not as an emissary of 'the Foreign Delegation' but because of the sickness of his son, who was in Moscow with Brounstein's estranged wife. Brounstein was a man of modest abilities. He was neither a member of the Menshevik Central Committee nor of 'the Foreign Delegation'. Nevertheless an emissary was fabricated out of him. In *Trial*, p. 229, Krylenko called him a representative of the Foreign Delegation, and at another stage he was called a member of the Central Committee.

The principal testimony on Brounstein's stay in Moscow was

1 *Trial*, p. 40.

that of the defendant Sher (*Trial*, pp. 229–31). It may therefore be of some significance that he gave Brounstein's patronymic as Abramovich (*Trial*, p. 229) instead of Adamovich (I knew Mikhail Adamovich Brounstein personally for many years). Sher may have known Brounstein only fleetingly, if at all.

The Soviet potentates would have been happy to have among the defendants a self-confessed emissary from abroad, but were obviously unsuccessful in getting a 'confession' from Brounstein. The latter was arrested a few months after his arrival in Moscow, so that he was condemned by the Cheka even before the Menshevik trial (*Trial*, p. 46). Incidentally, he probably would not have come to Moscow if he had realised the meaning of the abolition of the NEP and had foreseen subsequent developments in the USSR.

Although much space is devoted in *Trial* to the imaginary visit of Abramovich to Moscow and to that of Brounstein, allegedly a member of the Foreign Delegation, and although the prosecution would have liked to make capital out of correspondence between Moscow and the Foreign Delegation, such correspondence is touched on only very briefly in *Trial*. The few letters which fell into the hands of the prosecution were from or to Ikov, the only defendant who had organisational contacts with the Menshevik political organisations in and outside the USSR. On the other hand Ikov did not have any connections with the 'United Bureau', if this body existed at all. The letters to him from abroad which figured in *Trial* were dated 25 August and 4 and 23 October, when Groman, Sukhanov and some other defendants were already in jail. Ikov's only letter to Berlin was dated 9 January 1931, when practically all the defendants were in jail. The letters did not contain anything criminal, and served no purpose except to bear out the existence of direct connections between the accused and the Foreign Centre (*Trial*, p. 45). There actually was only one accused involved in the correspondence. And there is really nothing exciting in the fact that Vladimir Ikov, a member of RSDWP(m) from 1901, wrote or received an occasional letter to or from a member of the Menshevik organisation abroad.

FINANCIAL HELP

It sounds like a joke, and was indeed nothing but a bad joke, when Petunin and Sher testified that, in about one and a half years, the 'United Bureau' received, for expenses connected with its counter-revolutionary activities, subsidies to the extent of 480,000 roubles (*Trial*, pp. 37 and 185). Of this amount 280,000 roubles were supposed to have come from the German Social-Democratic Party via the *émigré* Menshevik organisation abroad (the so-called 'Foreign Delegation'). This is the same organisation which had published *Sotsialistichesky vestnik* for forty years. From my personal experience I know that so far as finances were concerned, it was a pauper organisation and a pauper journal. From about 1925 to about 1960 I contributed to the journal from time to time, totalling a substantial number of contributions in all those years. I did not receive a cent by way of a fee or anything else. From 1933 onwards I lived in Washington, D.C. If I could arrange for the typing there, I paid for it myself. In a few cases I was compelled to mail my work to the editor in the form of a long-hand MS. The journal did not charge me for the typing. The balance of the above subsidies, also an absurdly large figure, is supposed to have come from organisations of Russian *émigrés*.

Two things are not clear to me with reference to Finn-Enotaevsky. The first is, why did they include him among the defendants at all? They had thirteen defendants and six witnesses, who 'confessed' fully and without reservation,[1] and there was no apparent reason to introduce a discordant note by including a man who confessed only partially. Was Finn-Enotaevsky so prominent as a scholar that it would have been a loss not to have him in the trial, even with only a partial confession? Or were the charges to which he 'confessed' believed so important that his failure to confess others was found acceptable? The second question involves the extent of the confession. Was there in fact a partial confession, or was there no confession at all?

[1] The testimony of Zheludkov, the sixth witness, is not definite enough to be classified one way or another.

Finn-Enotaevsky (*Trial*, pp. 104–7 and elsewhere), a former Bolshevik of long standing and a great expert on world economics, was professor at the Polytechnical Institute in Leningrad. In 1928–30 he visited Moscow perhaps three or four times, including one stay of less than fifteen minutes between trains. Apparently on each of his longer visits to Moscow he was asked to dinner, mostly by Groman, but once, I believe, by Kondrat'ev. One or two people would drop in (Bazarov and Kondrat'ev have been named) and a professional conversation would take place. Finn-Enotaevsky energetically insisted that the discussions were strictly theoretical and that problems of practical policies and action were not touched on (his testimony on p. 106 of *Trial*). It was said that 'it was necessary to influence the Soviet power in a certain direction' (*ibid.*), 'but there was absolutely no talk to the effect that it was necessary to overthrow the Soviet power' (*ibid.*).

Finn-Enotaevsky confessed that he had become a member of 'The United Bureau' in April 1929, but he insisted (*Trial*, p. 188) that he was not a member either of the programme committee or any other. His testimony does not include any statements concerning a proposed foreign intervention. His harmful activities were, according to his testimony, limited to twice passing 50,000 roubles from the Menshevik Foreign Delegation to the Mensheviks in Moscow.

Since the transfer of money from abroad to the Mensheviks in Moscow was his principal 'crime', and for other reasons also, it is worthwhile discussing the matter here. So far as the testimonies other than that of Finn-Enotaevsky are concerned, they, having been dictated by the GPU, agree as regards the financial help received by the Menshevik 'United Bureau'. Petunin, for example, testified (*Trial*, p. 37) that the total of such subsidies was about 500,000 roubles and that the calculations of the finance committee yielded 480,000 roubles. Sher (*Trial*, pp. 185 and 186) testified that 200,000 roubles were received from the Industrial Party and 280,000 roubles from the Menshevik organisation abroad, the money having originated in the Second Socialist International, and that the total from all sources was 480,000 roubles, but, still according to his testimony, it might have been as much as 500,000 roubles.

Larichev, who had been found guilty at the trial of the Industrial Party, gave evidence at the Menshevik trial (p. 185) that he had passed to Groman from the Industrial Party about 200,000 roubles in three instalments: two in the autumn of 1929 and the last early in 1930. A detail in Larichev's statement is very illuminating. With reference to the first two sums of money, he said that they were passed to Groman after the latter's return from vacation. Since the third payment occurred early in the following year, it follows that the huge sum of 200,000 roubles was paid out within six months or less. 200,000 roubles of subsidy from only one of the two sources, in at most half a year, for an organisation, one of whose chief members, Sukhanov, used on Sundays to entertain a couple of dozen guests, making do with three chairs and tea without sugar! And with reference to such testimony Groman is supposed to have said, 'I confirm the figures [given by Larichev], and the dates on which I received the money.' (*Trial*, p. 186).

Finn-Enotaevsky, however, also testified that in 1928 Groman asked his help in transmitting money from the Menshevik Central Committee abroad. 'At the end of October' (evidently still in 1928) he received 50,000 roubles for transmission to Groman. It is stated elsewhere that he transferred to Groman 50,000 roubles 'at the end of October': the year is not stated, but these 50,000 roubles must have been the same as those mentioned above as having been received by Finn-Enotaevsky. Continuing, he is supposed to have said: 'The second time, in April 1930...I received 50,000 roubles [for transmission to the Mensheviks]'. (*Trial*, p. 186.) Groman, cross-examined after Finn-Enotaevsky's testimony, said (p. 188): 'Then he [obviously Finn-Enotaevsky] stated that in February 1930 he received 300,000 roubles.' Groman went on to say that it must have been not 300,000 roubles, but 200,000 roubles. The statements of Finn-Enotaevsky indicated, however, that only 100,000 roubles had passed through his hands. If anything to do with the money were true, there would not have been such discrepancies.

THE VERDICT

The verdict was ten years' imprisonment for seven men – Groman, Sher, Sukhanov, Ginzburg, Finn-Enotaevsky, Yakubovich and Petunin; eight years for four – Sokolovsky, Salkind, Berlatsky, and Ikov; and five years for Teitelbaum, Rubin and Volkov. Ten years of jail is a pretty high price for the few dinners or suppers that Finn-Enotaevsky enjoyed at the houses of Groman and Kondrat'ev. Of course the reservations which he made in his confession must have gone a good way to earn his ten-year sentence.

Ten years of jail, though an inhuman sentence for guiltless people early in 1931, seems almost a trifle compared with the death penalty meted out by Stalin to innumerable members of his own Party in 1936–8. But, after all, some of those sentenced to jail in 1930 and 1931 were executed after secret trials in 1936–8, and the same fate was in store for others, like Bazarov, who were not openly 'tried' in 1930 or 1931. The only advantage that the Bolsheviks who perished in 1936–8 enjoyed was that they were free during part of the intermediate period (Stalin's brand of freedom, of course).

AN UNDESIRABLE WITNESS

Anton Ciliga, a fairly senior Yugoslav Communist, spent over nine years (from October 1926 to December 1935) in the USSR. He went there because: 'The Bolshevist revolution which... boldly tried to build a society founded on the brotherhood of nations and the enfranchisement of the workers had, from its very inception, gained my wholehearted sympathy'.[1] While in the USSR Ciliga became a Trotskyist. As a result, he spent three years in jail (from May 1930 to the summer of 1933) and two and a half years in exile (from the summer of 1933 to the end of 1935). Ultimately his insistence on being allowed, as a citizen of a foreign country, to leave the Soviet Union was crowned with success (to a certain extent with the help of a hunger strike).

Ciliga writes: 'Experience has proved, I am sure, that all means are *not* [Ciliga's italics] permissible in the service of revolution.

[1] Ciliga, *The Russian Enigma*, p. 1.

Shameful means end by compromising the best of causes.'[1] He goes on to say: 'My only aim is the truth – a valuable thing in these days when so many conscious and obvious lies are told about that country [the USSR]. I am fully convinced of the necessity of writing about the USSR and the Russian revolution in a spirit of absolute sincerity, putting aside the Bolshevist principle of deforming facts in the interests of the revolution.' Ciliga reverts to the same topic on p. 210, where he says: 'I consider it my duty to give a faithful and objective picture of this Soviet opposition...be it communist, socialist or anarchist.'

Despite his bitter experience in the USSR, Ciliga did not become a pronounced rightist. On p. 197, for example, one finds an enthusiastic description of the giant metallurgical construction at Magnitogorsk. There seems to be no reason not to accept him as a sincere, faithful witness, though errors may be found in his book, as in others of this type. From November 1930 almost to the end of his time in jail (1933) he was held in the political 'isolator' at Verkhne-Uralsk. Soon after the Menshevik trial in March 1931, all those condemned in it were imprisoned in the same isolator and held there for years. This makes Ciliga an interesting witness for the present study.

Ciliga declares the testimony of the defendants in the Menshevik trial to be a 'flagrant lie'.[2] He writes also: 'In contrast with what had happened in our prison during the trial of the "industrial section" [the trial of the Industrial Party at the end of 1930], the prison's verdict on the Menshevik trial was unanimous: we all thought it a manoeuvre of the GPU.'[3] Even of the Industrial Party trial he says merely: 'The only truth in the affair was the discontent of the specialists and their secret desire to see the communists come to grief in a failure of the Five-Year Plan... All the rest of the accusations were lies and moonshine on the part of the GPU.'[4]

Uncertainty remains only about how the defendants in the Menshevik trial were made to 'confess'. Ciliga makes a few general observations on the trials from 1928 to 1938. He writes: 'The

[1] *Ibid.* p. xi.   [2] *Ibid.* p. 225.
[3] *Ibid.* p. 222.   [4] *Ibid.* p. 223.

staging and the successful carrying out of the trials were the characteristic traits of the Stalin era...Such trials are only possible if the rule of an immoral government coincides with a phase of profound apathy in society, tired of disinterested motives...'[1] And furthermore: 'The GPU knew the art of shattering the nervous system of their victims,' (p. 228). Ciliga has evidence specifically on the use of all kinds of tortures (pp. 149, 153, 158–9, and 184). With reference to the Menshevik trial, he tells us: 'One day I asked one of them [those condemned in the Menshevik trial] how they had been able to make those monstrous statements. His answer was eloquent: "We ourselves don't understand it, it was all like a horrible nightmare".'[2]

The most interesting item of Ciliga's evidence on this score is this: 'A few years later Sukhanov...had a copy of his appeal to the government circulated throughout the prison, in which he demanded that they should fulfil their promises of releasing those willing to make untrue confessions. As a result of this incident the GPU had Sukhanov removed, but he was not released.'[3]

This last statement becomes more plausible if it is linked with Ciliga's evidence on Ramzin (p. 222). As stated, Ramzin was the leading defendant in the Industrial Trial in November–December 1930. The engineers:

...were accused of having organised a vast network of sabotage and espionage for the benefit of the French High Command, which was preparing for the military intervention of France against the USSR. The accused admitted everything down to the smallest detail...The accused were condemned to death. But the Government, 'taking the candour of their statements and admissions into consideration', commuted the death sentences to various terms of imprisonment. Thousands of people throughout Russia were being shot for infinitely lesser crimes; this unexpected clemency did, for that reason, strike a very suspicious note.[4]

Further:

Members of the Moscow Opposition who had been arrested after the Ramzin trial gave us further particulars. Ramzin had not even been sent

---

[1] *Ibid.* p. 226.
[3] *Ibid.* p. 227.
[2] *Ibid.* pp. 226–7.
[4] *Ibid.* p. 222.

back to prison after the trial. Immediately upon the termination of the trial, that is, after an interval of only six months, Ramzin resumed his lectures at the Institute of Thermodynamics, pronouncing the professors' ritual phrase, 'We had left off at...'[1]

Also: 'After a very few years he [Ramzin] was fully re-established in all his rights and was decorated with the Order of Lenin...(p. 224). Ciliga says of Ramzin (p. 224): 'According to the general opinion in Russia, Ramzin had consciously played the part of *provocateur*.'

Finally an interesting detail to round off the picture of the Menshevik trial. In describing the political isolator at Suzdal, Ciliga writes: 'That [political isolator] at Suzdal is the ancient and famous former convent of that name near Moscow. There the Menshevik trials were rehearsed before their final staging in Moscow.'[1] Trials are not rehearsed, but performances based on lies need rehearsing.

[1] *Ibid.* p. 223.　　　　[2] *Ibid.* p. 252.

PART III THE ECONOMISTS

6

VLADIMIR GUSTAVOVICH GROMAN

There are people, including some of my friends, who believe that I am biased in favour of Groman. I doubt this. At least, as always, I do my best to tell the truth, the whole truth and nothing but the truth. Actually I consider that Groman was a giant of a man with great abilities and a great heart, and I have accumulated and presented a good deal of material in support of this view. That my appraisal is not unreservedly favourable, the reader will see from my remarks on Groman's actions in 1917.

To understand Groman, a non-Russian has to do the impossible: to understand Russia and the Russians; even many or most Russians are incapable of doing this properly. The Russian nation produced a number of geniuses who displayed a deplorable tendency to die in early years. Goethe lived to be 83; Pushkin was killed in a duel at 37. There were many other able Russians, but much of their ability was wasted owing to the amount of time they spent in idle conversation, excessive drink, etc. This is still true to some extent. The President of the United States makes half-hour speeches, whereas Khrushchev's used to last up to eight hours, the audience being warned to bring their lunch. Again, able people have no time to study thoroughly in their field. It has happened quite often that important discoveries were honestly claimed by Russians which, upon examination, turned out to have been made in a foreign country years before.

All these traits were exemplified above all by the Russian intelligentsia, especially the left wing. And Groman, although half-German by blood, was one of its truest representatives. He was certainly an exceptional man in everything. Immense drive, great intuition, and honesty in the highest sense of the word were probably his main features. When I first met him he was a huge, heavy man, slightly over 40. He did not walk, he almost ran. Fat people often take small, delicate steps. Groman sauntered with long, heavy steps; you could hear him approaching from afar. He did not open the door, he tore it open. He did not eat, but devoured, and his drinking was on a par with this.

Groman was very careful about figures, but immensely negligent about words written on the basis of the figures – words were a mere form and he had no understanding for form. Preparing for a trip to Moscow (I am thinking of St Petersburg days), he would hastily dictate an important document to a typist, push the typescript into his pocket, drive off to the railway station, order a borshch, glance over the typing while gulping down the borshch, and send the thing off to the printer. The only times when he was cross with me were when I delayed for a few hours' revision some document which he wanted sent off immediately, insisting that it was perfect as it stood. Groman's style was certainly not the best imaginable, and did not improve as time went on. Omissions of words occurred even in his published material.

Groman was not a widely cultured man: he spent too much time working and drinking, nor was he systematic in the use of his time. In the United States, of course, it is quite usual for scholars to know only one language – American English. Things are different in Europe, and especially in Russia, but Groman did not know a single foreign language. Amazing as it may be, he had difficulty in ordering a meal in German. His father was a German who taught that language somewhere in the heart of Russia, but he never imparted it to his own son. In later years, when Groman became a man of importance, he had to have somebody read foreign material for him. However, his relative lack of knowledge was more than compensated for by his immense ability to grasp the essence of a problem, and by a corresponding gift of intuition.

Honesty played a great part in making him the man he was. His frank recognition of errors, which occurred in spite of his intuition, greatly reduced their harmful effect. His open, generous appreciation of his collaborators and assistants, together with his burning enthusiasm for work, won him the exceptional devotion of his staff.

EARLY YEARS

Groman was born in 1873, a son of a teacher of German nationality and a Russian mother. His untiring energy and fighting spirit probably came from his father's side. His Slav blood was responsible for a deficient sense of reality, cured only after bitter experience and then perhaps not fully.

His adult life until 1906 consisted of political activity, a spell in jail, and exile combined with statistical work. From his youth he was a Social-Democrat, and when the Social-Democratic Party split into Bolsheviks and Mensheviks, he beame a Menshevik. Like most Mensheviks, he remained an unwavering Marxist until 1931, the last year when anything is known of him.

The editorial in *Vestnik statistiki*, No. 2, 1927, when the thirtieth anniversary of Groman's statistical and scientific work was celebrated, naturally concentrated on his work in statistics. It traced his biography from 1897, when he was 24 years old. In that year he was arrested while a student at Moscow University and exiled to Orlov, Vyatka guberniya (in the north-east of European Russia). Here, and later at Vyatka itself, he became extremely active as a zemstvo statistician,[1] and was the effective head of the statistical bureau of the Vyatka guberniya zemstvo. It was at this time that he developed his own method, which he called 'typology', of analysing the material obtained by the surveys conducted by the bureau. After completing his sentence at Vyatka in 1901, he moved to Simferopol in the Crimea, where he was assistant chief of the guberniya zemstvo statistical bureau, but soon he was arrested again and after half a year in jail was deported to Ekaterinoslav, where he worked on a newspaper. Yet another arrest followed in 1902, and after a further half-year in jail he was exiled to eastern Siberia. He was not released until February 1905.

After a short stay in Tver, whence he was expelled, he returned to Moscow, where he published several works under the pen name Vladimir Gorn, the most important being probably 'The peasant movement [i.e. unrest] during the past 150 years'. Still in 1905, he

---

[1] The zemstvo was an agency of local self-government within each *guberniya* (province); an *uyezd* was one of the districts into which the provinces were subdivided.

represented the Union of Statisticians at the Congress known as the 'Union of Unions' in Finland, a central body of professional and other organisations concerned with public issues. Here he rightly predicted that the Bulygin Duma was doomed to be swept away by the revolutionary movement. Groman of course participated in the 1905 rising. In 1908, after he had graduated from the University (without attending any lectures), the eminent Professor N. A. Kablukov offered to have him trained for a university career. But Groman's thoughts were elsewhere. In 1909, on the recommendation of the same Kablukov, he accepted a job as chief of the statistical bureau of the Penza guberniya zemstvo, south-east of Moscow. This opened up a period of work important both to the guberniya itself, and for the credit of Russian zemstvo statistics in general. In Penza, he developed a method of surveying all branches of economic life statistically by a combination of samples of different size. His plan led to a conflict with the governor; the zemstvo being disinclined to support its chief statistician, Groman conducted the fight single-handed and, surprisingly, won.

The above account is taken from the editorial in *Vestnik statistiki*, which concludes as follows: 'During this difficult period of intensive work and fight for the right to work, Groman managed to arouse among his collaborators in the Penza bureau an exceptional ardour and exceptional enthusiasm. All who worked with him at this period or subsequently well remember his ability to inspire his staff with that zest for work which is typical of all units organised by him.'[1] An article by V. I. Zeilinger and D. V. Shub on the same occasion[2] concludes in exactly the same vein as the editorial, with the difference that they spoke as actual members of Groman's staff.

His statistical work in Penza did not preclude Groman engaging in literary activities of a broader nature.

WORLD WAR I

Food prices began to rise very soon after the outbreak of war in 1914. The Constitutional-Democratic (Kadet) Party was not

---

[1] No. 2, 1927, p. viii.   [2] *Ibid.* No. 6, 1927, p. viii.

alarmed,[1] but Groman took a different view. He was deeply concerned with the interests of the working class, whose wages were unlikely to keep pace with the rapidly rising prices. He may also have foreseen that the Tsarist government would be unable to prevent a runaway inflation, a situation exceptionally dangerous during a war. At all events, he at once made for Moscow, where, through the Chuprov Society (Chuprov was an economist of distinction), a 'Committee to Study the Current High Prices' was organised. With fiery enthusiasm Groman raised funds from some twenty sources and three volumes of *Trudy komissii po izucheniyu sovremennoi dorogovizny*, were published, covering economic developments during the first year of the war.[2] One of these contained a substantial upward revision of the official estimates (by A. N. Ivantsov)[3] of pre-war grain production, acreages and yields: each of these, in Groman's estimate, was raised by 9 per cent, and output consequently by 19 per cent. These estimates played a great role after the Revolution; they were accepted by Gosplan and served as the basis for official statistics for many years until Stalin took over.

The disorganisation of the economy from the very start of the war forced the Tsarist government, as early as 1915, to set up four Special Committees, for defence, fuel, transport and food. The Special Committees comprised representatives of numerous government agencies with a sprinkling of what were called 'civil elements'. The Special Committee on Food was to include a representative each from the Union of Zemstvos and the Union of Cities. The former of these was the well known economist, P. B. Struve, who played a rather inactive role; but the Union of Cities happened to choose Groman, or *vice versa*. To assist him in his work on the Committee he built up a huge statistical apparatus with bureaux in Moscow and Leningrad – given a free hand, he would have spent the whole State budget on statistics. But the money he did spend

[1] Its spokesman on this question was A. I. Shingarev, a medical doctor who was a brilliant speaker and a good politician, but not an economist.
[2] *Trudy komissii po izucheniyu sovremennoi dorogovizny* (Studies of the Committee to study the Current High Prices), Moscow, 3 vols. 1915.
[3] Unfortunately, in the environment of Tsarist émigrés in Prague, Ivantsov in later years went back on his estimates, although their correctness, by and large, was and is beyond doubt.

was not wasted: he influenced greatly the work of the Committee and thereby the organisation of food supplies throughout the country.

The armed forces were vast, and their need for food was correspondingly large. In spite of a fair crop in 1914 and a good one in 1915, plus the cessation of the huge pre-war exports, the government found it hard to procure all that it needed through free-market channels, and limited the use of railways for the transport of private supplies for the non-agricultural population. Shortages in urban centres, especially the provincial capitals, aggravated the effects of inflation. It was natural for the representative of the Union of Cities in the Special Committee on Food to demand that the needs of at least the largest cities be added to those of the armed forces in the government's procurement plans. Groman attained considerable results in this important endeavour.

There is no doubt that the clumsiness of the Ministry of Agriculture,[1] which was in charge of food procurements, was one of the strongest inflationary factors. Before the start of the 1916–17 procurement campaign, the Committee called a special meeting of the local representatives of the Ministry in charge of procurement; at this meeting attempts were made to establish prices which Groman believed to be too high, but he fought like a lion and succeeded in keeping them down. In a crumpled suit, with dishevelled hair, he thundered away at the big landlords, most of them nobles, who attended the special meeting, and made himself heard to good purpose.

It is outside the scope of this study to describe all Groman's activities in the Special Committee on Food. His fight against inflation of the price of grain has been mentioned. On his initiative the grinding of more than one grade of flour was eventually prohibited, so as to facilitate control and increase the capacity of the mills. This was violently opposed by the millers, who called the spokesman of the Union of Cities – the present writer – a traitor. The credit for my having the chance to make suggestions belongs wholly to Groman; but the detailed history of those fights will never be told.[2]

---

[1] The Special Committee on Food was subordinate to this Ministry.

[2] There is a whole volume almost entirely devoted to the work of the Special Committee on Food: viz. K. I. Zaitsev, N. V. Dolinsky and S. S. Demosthenov, *Food*

Vladimir Gustavovich Groman

In about June 1916, on Groman's insistence, I was transferred from a minor position in the Union of Cities to his organisation in the same Union; he placed me in his St Petersburg bureau. Before this I never met Groman and had scarcely heard of him, except that N. I. Astrov (the head of the Union of Cities, who was Groman's and my immediate chief), as well as the other staff in my room, spoke of him with esteem but also with considerable reserve: 'He is not a good man to cross.' The only person on Groman's staff who I happened to know personally – namely Vera, the wife of Vladimir Osipovich Levitsky, who was Yu. O. Martov's youngest brother – spoke of him with admiration and reverence, as of someone quite apart.

My transfer to Groman's office gave me an inside view of him as a chief who inspired general adoration. Even Lenin's sister Maria and the other Communists in our bureau were of the same opinion. In my long years of work I served under different chiefs, some really good and some less agreeable; but none of them even remotely reminded me of Groman. Groman would not pass on the most

Supply in Russia during the World War, New Haven, 1930. I am glad of the opportunity to point out the mis-statements and suppressions of fact in this production of the Prague-Sofia *émigrés*. Written by former employees of the Special Committee on Food (it had a large special staff), the work in question is no less mendacious than similar products of the Stalin era in the USSR itself. The authors of the volume disliked Groman and all his works because after the October Revolution he remained in the USSR and worked 'for the Soviets': *ergo*, he was a traitor, an enemy and an un-person as far as Russian history is concerned. While the *émigré* work mentions (on p. 358) the three important volumes (see footnote 2, p. 93), it suppresses the fact of Groman's editorship and his decisive hand in them. Similarly, although he played a great role in the work of the Special Committee, his name is mentioned only once in this connection (p. 46). On pp. 128–9 much is made of the flour-mill census carried through by the Special Committee, but it is not stated that the initiative was Groman's. There is a special section on standardisation of flour milling, which again does not mention that the initiative was entirely that of the representative of the Union of Cities. On pp. 85–6, for example, it is stated that standardisation of flour production based on a three-grade extraction rate was introduced; but we do not learn that the initiative was that of the representative of the Union of Cities, that from the start he suggested a one-grade extraction rate, and that such an extraction rate was actually prescribed only shortly after the establishment of the three-grade extraction – in this case on the initiative of the government itself.

At a later stage, Groman instructed me to collect for publication the numerous papers submitted to the Special Committee on Food and the Central Bureau for Milling attached to it, the reason he gave being that he wanted to make it perfectly clear which of the papers signed by him were written by him and which by me. The reason did not impress me at the time; I did not understand that history was being made, and carried out the assignment inadequately.

insignificant thought of mine without emphasising that it came from me. He was unhappy that he had to sign his name to papers prepared by me for the Special Committee on Food (he did so of course in his official capacity as representative). He told everybody who would listen that the papers were by me and not him. He took me to Moscow, which he need not have done, and introduced me to the Chief Council of the Union as the man who was successfully defending the interests of the urban population in regard to the distribution of State supplies. When, soon after my transfer to Groman's office, the Special Committee for Food transferred a large part of its functions to a specially organised Central Bureau of Milling, Groman, without forewarning me, told our Central Council that he declined to represent the Union of Cities in the Central Bureau of Milling, and suggested that I, no more than a provincial miller, be appointed to the post. In short, in those eight months, he made me capable of standing on my own feet when our ways subsequently parted.

My own impressions of Groman are fully supported by the statements made on the occasion of his thirtieth anniversary as cited above. Other published evidence provides similar testimony.

Articles by Groman, A. Petrov, and S. Strumilin on the balance of the national economy were published in *Vestnik statistiki*, No. 1, 1927. All three authors naturally had help in the work involved, but only Groman's theses were marked 'with the participation of R. Ya. Broitman and D. V. Shub'. In Groman's paper in *Planovoe khozyaistvo*, No. 1, 1925, all credit for the work on the 1922–3 balance of national economy is given to A. B. Gukhman, although the basic idea was his own. Gukhman was Groman's man and certainly consulted him extensively on the various phases of the analysis. S. G. Strumilin, who now enjoys the reputation of the doyen of Soviet economists, worked in close co-operation with Groman in those years, but did not imitate him in this respect, and acted quite differently even in his attitude to the same men.[1]

Kontrol'nye tsifry na 1925/26g. is largely Groman's work, Strumilin having played a minor role. Yet Groman mentioned Strumilin's co-operation, while Strumilin did not mention Gro-

[1] Personal information from Valentinov.

man's name in either of his two articles on these same *Kontrol'nye tsifry*[1] (incidentally in striking contrast to Bazarov).[2] Naturally a good many people were trained by Groman, and all or most of them are mentioned in various works of his.

THE REVOLUTION

In the first hours of the February Revolution of 1917, a Food Commission of the Soviet of Workers' Deputies and the State Duma was organised in Petrograd. Groman naturally became its chairman. The first item on its agenda was grain supplies, which were running dangerously low. In many areas, supplies to feed the immense armed forces were sufficient only for a few days. Later some absurd things were said about the grain monopoly: most frequently the responsibility for its introduction was put on Groman,[3] but this measure was adopted by the state commission, so far as I remember, unanimously. Y. A. Bukhshpan, an employee of the Special Committee on Food and a friend of the authors of the Prague–Sofia product discussed above, wrote eloquently in *Rech'*, the organ of the Kadet Party, on 21 March 1917, a few days before the grain monopoly was enacted: 'A long-standing national problem, brooking no delay, must be tackled immediately by the new government. The measure that has long been needed is a grain monopoly.' Certainly Groman was not powerful enough to enforce a nation-wide grain monopoly single-handed. Whether he was from the start in favour of such a monopoly, I cannot tell. It may be that a grain monopoly was essential for a rational procurement policy (the experience of World War II tends to confirm this), but in any case it seems beyond doubt that the clumsy handling of procurement by the Tsarist government in World War I speeded up this

---

[1] See *Planovoe Khozyaistvo*, No. 10, 1925, and No. 1, 1926.

[2] V. A. Bazarov (*Planovoe khozyaistvo*, No. 6, 1926, p. 54) mentions Groman's work on the Control Figures.

[3] The very fact that the credit or blame for the grain monopoly is attributed to Groman testifies that already at the time he had great influence. This was largely based on his work in the Special Committee on Food prior to the Revolution. The almost complete absence of any mention of Groman from the history of this Committee, as presented in the Prague–Sofia *émigré* product mentioned above, indicates the latter's bias still further.

process. The present writer argued in this sense in a pamphlet, *The Regulation of the Grain Market*, Petrograd, 1917, published by the Union of Cities, and written just before the February Revolution and the formal introduction of the grain monopoly. Unfortunately I could not find a copy of this work in Washington D.C.

While the need to introduce the grain monopoly was not disputed, an unexpected complication occurred, causing unfortunate delay. It was clear that the fixed purchase prices for grain, established in the preceding autumn, had been overtaken by the pace of inflation. Everybody in the Food Commission agreed that they ought to be raised; but by how much? At this point Groman insisted that owing to the disturbed economic conditions fair prices could not be established at once. Believing that the February Revolution had opened up immense new possibilities on the economic front, he proposed that the old prices be maintained for the time being; in addition, producers were to be given a kind of certificate. A commission was to be set up immediately and instructed to work out in the next few weeks a 'Unified Plan' to regulate the national economy and labour. This plan would fix prices to be paid for the grain to the producers, who would then get the balances due to them as indicated by the certificates. The argument in the Food Commission was in fact for or against the issue of certificates.

Politically, it was very unwise to suggest that the newly-formed government demand grain from the peasants in return for pieces of paper (the certificates). It was rightly objected that the general backwardness of the country, the bad state of the economy with daily worsening inflation, the lack of statistics and general disorganisation would preclude the elaboration of any sort of plan, let alone one to be devised in a matter of weeks and for immediate operation. This was a glaring demonstration of Groman's lack of practical sense; but he was unfortunately not the only person of his type at this period.

I fought bitterly against Groman's proposal, and was the only 'Gromanite' to do so. I insisted that the Revolution had not created any great new possibilities on the economic front, that there was no-one competent to work out the 'Unified Plan'. (Groman had said – it sounded like a joke to me – that I and 'others' would do the job.) When I told him 'You have no sense of reality', he shouted 'How dare you! I have spent twenty years in statistical offices studying peasant life.' I was rude enough to retort 'Yes, you saw the figures, but you did not see the life behind the figures.' And so on. In any case our ways parted.

Groman's idea of postponing payment of the full price for grain until the projected commission had worked out the Plan was defeated in the Food Commission by a small majority. The idea of working out a single Plan was ignored, whereupon Groman submitted it to the Soviet of Workers' and Soldiers' Deputies. Finally the Government organised a Supreme Economic Board, but the incompetent S. N. Prokopovich was appointed its president. In this Board not only Groman's idea, but the idea of any plan, or even any action, disappeared without trace.

A good illustration of Groman's obsession with the unrealistic idea of a Unified Economic Plan in 1917 is an anecdote recounted by Kondrat'ev during the Gosplan discussion of the Five-Year Plan for agriculture in 1925. When Groman was in charge of distribution of consumer goods in Petrograd, he allegedly declared: 'I shall not distribute a single pair of shoes until the national economy as a whole has been regulated.'[1]

I am not seeking to exculpate Groman; at that time I even used the word 'crazy' about him in a conversation with Cherevanin.[2] In fact, his mentality at that time is still incomprehensible to me. So far as the Unified Plan is concerned, it may be some excuse that his enchantment with central planning sprang mainly from descriptions of the central regulation of the German economy during World War I by Yu. Lur (alias Larin), whom even Lenin (chastened by the experience of War Communism) believed to have been crazy.

Kondrat'ev's story shows that Groman's obsession with central planning was quite widely known. It supports my opinion that, while Groman deserved the greatest blame for the way in which he wanted the central plan to be realised, he must also be given credit for having been the first to ventilate the idea of such a plan.

---

[1] *Puti sel'skogo khozyaistva* (*The Ways of Agriculture*), No. 3, 1925, p. 137.

[2] Cherevanin was Groman's deputy in the office in which I worked and officially my superior.

Grinevetsky, who must be recognised as the father of long-range planning, is unlikely not to have known of Groman's views and may well have been inspired by them to write his book.

It may be of interest here to quote a passage from Sukhanov's statement in *Trial*, which shows that people could be crazy not only in 1917 but also fourteen years later. In Sukhanov's testimony we read:

Groman was the author of War Communism. When did he proclaim it? He proclaimed it soon after the February Revolution, in his capacity as the head of the Menshevik-Socialist-Revolutionary Committee [presumably of the Soviet of Workers' and Soldiers' Deputies]. He took the Kadet Shingarev by the throat and squeezed out of him the basic element of War Communism, namely the grain monopoly. But matters did not stop with the grain monopoly. The Menshevik-Socialist-Revolutionary Committee accepted at the same time, on 16 March, a programme which in effect presupposed the system of War Communism in its entirety.[1]

However, Sukhanov also said that the programme was approved by Lenin.

The fact that Groman's position could be misinterpreted in this way by Sukhanov testifies to its absurdity.[2] Still the grain monopoly had little or nothing to do with War Communism, nor would it have had even if Groman's Economic Plan had been realised.

I have dwelt in some detail on events during World War I, including the early days after the February Revolution, because otherwise the immense and highly commendable change which occurred

---

[1] *Trial*, pp. 386–7.
[2] Before the Revolution Groman's position was to the right of mine. I believed that our policy toward the government agency with which we had to deal must be such as to make it clear that we were not responsible for its actions, even if this or that measure was taken at our suggestion, since there was no knowing how persons in the employ of the Tsarist government would execute the measure in question. Groman regarded this view of mine as irresponsible. Like me, he used the organ of the right-wing Mensheviks whenever he had something to say to the public – but the choice of this paper was due to personal reasons and does not mean that either of us was definitely a right-wing Menshevik. In any case, everything changed for Groman with the Revolution. It was a frequently repeated joke that after the Revolution 'Groman ran round Jasny and turned up on his left'. In the same way, he switched from the right-wing Menshevik paper to Gorky's *Novaya zhizn'*, considered a second-grade Bolshevik publication by the ruling Mensheviks and socialist-revolutionaries, according to the same Sukhanov (*Trial*, p. 386).

in Groman in the course of barely five years would hardly be appreciated. After March 1917, I did not meet him until early summer 1923, when almost his first words were 'You were right in those days.' Thirty-seven years later I found out from Valentinov's memoirs that I was not the only one to whom Groman acknowledged his error: in fact, he admitted it and even joked about it.

Groman's ability to face the facts, his readiness to acknowledge an error frankly, without looking for excuses, was a vital asset in the great job he was already doing in Gosplan at the time of our conversation in 1923 and was to do for five or six more years. Without this he never would have gone so far in getting rid of beliefs in fantasies, in pieces of paper drafted by a handful of more or less intelligent people (his Economic Plan of 1917 would have been just such a piece of paper!).

The great change in Groman's attitude towards Soviet policies had probably already occurred when the NEP was introduced early in 1921. When the NEP was proclaimed, he was indeed among its most ardent adherents, believing with Lenin that it was destined to endure for a long time. He may even have thought of taking the process further. Groman was a member of 'the League of Observers' as described by Valentinov (see Chapter 2) from the very inception of that organisation late in 1922.

Groman's position in those years is well characterised by his statement in 1931, reported by R. Vaisberg who regarded it as criminal:[1] 'A change in the socialist form of the economy [I would have said, "a change to the socialist form of economy"] is possible [he meant desirable] only under the following conditions: (1) an expansion of productive capacity; (2) improvement of the well-being of the labouring masses in town and village, and (3) avoidance of non-economic coercion.'

Groman's great error in 1917, and the salutory effect that his frank recognition of it had on his subsequent career, are hardly known. A similar case is more or less common knowledge, however: namely the introduction and abolition of Communism by Lenin in 1919–20. From this angle there is indeed a great similarity between Groman and Lenin.

[1] *Planovoe khozyaistvo*, No. 2–3, 1931, p. 12.

(i) *The error*

Lenin wanted to introduce Communism almost overnight, with grain forcibly obtained from the peasants practically without payment as the foundation of the system. Groman wanted a Unified Plan to regulate the national economy and labour for Russia as a whole, to be worked out in several weeks immediately after the February Revolution.

(ii) *Background*

Lenin knew a great deal about the economic life of Russia (this is evident from his publications), and should have realised the impossibility of his enterprise. It is some excuse, however, that much of his adult life before the Revolution was spent in emigration. Groman also knew the Russian economy well, and should have realised that the immensely primitive nature of the country and the disturbed conditions of the time completely excluded the elaboration of a Unified Economic Plan or anything even remotely similar to this in a period of weeks, months or even years. Moreover, he had spent much of his working life in provincial statistical offices investigating day-to-day life. Neither he nor Lenin displayed any ability to visualise what the possibilities of such a country as Russia were at the time.

(iii) *Redemption*

Lenin recognised his error after his experiment made a shambles of the Soviet economy. Groman recognised his error with no damage done, except that the country might have benefited if he had directed his genius to more realistic problems; the failure of the Provisional Government, led by the moderate revolutionary wing, to solve these problems resulted in the October Revolution.

THE GLORIOUS PERIOD

Groman testified in the Menshevik Trial (*Trial*, p. 377):

Five days after the October Revolution, on 1 November [O.S.] I published in *Novaya zhizn'* an article stating that it was time to realise that this was not an adventure but a popular action, that the Bolsheviks were at the head of this popular action, and that policies of coalition belonged to the past. Already in September I had taken up a position in the Social-Democratic faction in favour of a people's socialist government, and received 5 votes among Dan's faction. I did not take part in any sabotage [of the Soviet government] and continued to work in food organisations [after the October Revolution].

This and other work for the Bolshevik Government went on until some time in 1922. In 1922 Groman was appointed by Krasin, People's Commissar for Trade and Industry, to the important post of chairman of the Committee for Estimating the Losses Suffered by the USSR from the Intervention and Blockade (*Trial*, p. 378). However, the *Great Soviet Encyclopedia* (XIX, pp. 437–8) gives *Glavtop* (Chief Fuel Office) as the place of Groman's activity in 1919–20.

Groman at this time continued to stress, wherever and whenever he could, the idea of a central plan (e.g. in at least one conversation with Lenin, of which I know from Groman himself). He also started in 1920 – still under War Communism – to publish his reviews of economic conditions ('conjuncture reviews', as they were and still are called in Russia) in *Ekonomicheskaya zhizn'* and professional journals. The reviews, of which there soon were yearly, quarterly and monthly issues, became famous in a very short time. At first Groman had to publish them anonymously owing to the political situation. But the yearbook *Narodnoe khozyaistvo v 1921–2 godu*, published by *Ekonomicheskaya zhizn'*, already listed Groman as editor (Krumin, ostensibly the chief editor, was merely a supervisor).

While Groman apparently did not take up a hostile position toward the Soviet Government immediately after the October Revolution, the proclamation of the drive for full Communist organisation in 1919 must have had a decidedly sobering effect on him. He may not have been invited to participate in the preparation of GOELRO, because Lenin in his ignorance thought this was a job for engineers. When Gosplan was organised, early in 1921, S. G. Strumilin, a former Menshevik who had recently changed allegiance, was the only economist invited to participate. Groman was not invited to join Gosplan till 1922, and then at first only as a consultant in Strumilin's section. Bazarov was probably brought in somewhat earlier (he had an important paper circulated in Gosplan in May 1922). Any Gromanites whom Groman was able to recruit became staff members in Strumilin's section.

No sooner was Groman in Gosplan than he began to advocate the enormously ambitious idea, for that time, of preparing a balance-sheet of the national economy. In theory, the idea of such a balance was by no means new. It dated indeed as far back as Quesnay's *Tableau économique* in the eighteenth century, and was discussed by later scholars including Marx. But it is one thing to develop the idea of a macro-economic balance sheet in one's study in a purely theoretical way, with no specific country or period involved, and another to prepare one for a particular country and for a given year or years. Groman's was the first example of a scientific enterprise of this type. His first report on the subject was made to the Statistical Section of Gosplan very early in 1923.[1] A more detailed report, illustrated by a rough attempt at a balance for 1922–3, was presented by him to the Presidium of Gosplan on 21 November 1923;[2] but Gosplan did not then have sufficient man-power for its elaboration. On the insistence of Groman and his friends, the Council for Labour and Defence (STO), a commission of the Sovnarkom enjoying great power, ordered the Central Statistical Office to prepare such a balance for 1923–4; the CSO completed the job in 1925. Many years later, the idea of a macro-economic balance sheet was imported into the United States in the modified form of 'input–output analysis'.

Developments on the economic scene in the USSR in 1922–3 were by no means encouraging. While Krzhizhanovsky dreamed of a revised GOELRO and a general plan for ten to fifteen years, an immense disproportion between the prices of farm and non-farm products, aptly called 'price-scissors' by Trotsky, developed in that year. With the peasants' purchasing power declining sharply, great amounts of unsold industrial goods piled up, although indus-trial output was only about one-third that of 1913. The recovery of the economy was certainly jeopardised, and the authorities were

[1] *Byulleteni Gosplana*, January 1923, p. 31.
[2] *Ibid.* Nov.–Dec. 1923, pp. 119–22.

impelled to give power to Groman, who had shown a real ability to deal with current economic developments. In December 1923 Gosplan organised a Conjuncture Council with a Bureau attached to it. While Communist controllers numerically dominated the Council, it was Groman's organisation and the Bureau that became his working machinery. Almost immediately Groman began preparations with a view to planning the economy as a whole for the immediate future, but not for ten to fifteen years.

Groman's study 'On Certain Regularities Empirically Discovered in Our National Economy' (in *Planovoe khozyaistvo*, No. 1, 1925, pp. 89–100, and No. 2, pp. 125–141), was a milestone in the development of Soviet planning. It is significant that Groman was assigned to work only on what was to become the annual plan, while long-range planning went to Osadchy, a GOELRO engineer, who in 1927 was replaced by N. A. Kovalevsky. Perspective planning, i.e. the eventual Five-Year Plan, was put under Strumilin. It is possible, though not certain, that this arrangement was a result of Groman's wishes. Work on annual plans fitted in well with his work on conjuncture, which he started in earnest in 1920 and continued through 1928.

Even the preparation of a good annual plan turned out to be a matter of the relatively distant future. All that Groman could produce in 1925 on the basis of 'On Certain Regularities' and other findings were *Kontrol'nye tsifry* at first for 1925–6, but even the work on these by no means went altogether smoothly. They were prepared in the course of four months and published in July 1925. The harvest prospects, which were the deciding factor for the whole economy in those years, were good, and the projection was compiled accordingly. But, owing to heavy rain, the harvest turned out worse than expected, and the *Kontrol'nye tsifry na 1925/26g.* had to be revised. They were issued in revised form in October, but this was not the end of their misadventures.

Both in their original and in their revised form, the *Kontrol'nye tsifry* consisted of a booklet of less than 100 pages, not very closely printed. I often wonder whether Groman felt a sense of bitterness when he looked at this booklet, the result of so much labour and preparation, marred as it was by serious shortcomings – did he remember the Unified Plan which had had to be drawn up in the space of a few weeks? But it is more probable that he had shelved the thought of the Unified Plan and was simply glad to have at last accomplished the difficult first step towards the fulfilment of his beloved dream. In any case the complications which had attended the birth of his brain-child can hardly have left room or time for any other feelings.

In Gosplan's memorandum to the Council of Labour and Defence on the revision of *Kontrol'nye tsifry na 1925/26g.*, we read:

The fate of *Kontrol'nye tsifry* has been an extremely sad one. In the discussions, the most varied and contradictory views were advanced. The VSNKh drew attention to the insufficiently rapid tempo envisaged for the development of industry and the over-estimate of the production of agricultural goods. Narkomfin and Narkomzem complained that the interests of agriculture had not been sufficiently taken into account. Other comrades strongly criticised some aspects of the arrangement of the work and conclusions...The Council of Labour and Defence made no use of Gosplan's work.[1]

The attitude specifically of the neo-narodniks to planning was rather cool. Albert Weinstein began his paper 'On the Control Figures of the National Economy of the USSR for 1925–6'[2] by saying that he was not an adversary of control figures on principle, and indeed believed them necessary and useful, but 'with a restricted scope and in the sphere assigned to them'. Weinstein wrote further: 'Last year, the appearance of the Control Figures made a great impression, created much debate and attracted many attacks, sometimes fully deserved.' But then he went on to say that 'the idea that the control figures must provide a model for the situation a year hence is frankly a chimera, a guessing from tea-leaves, and cannot be anything else at the moment...It is a pointless task to draw up all those endless columns for next year.' Weinstein's appraisal of the Control Figures, it is true, was probably the most unappreciative of all. It should probably also be added that the development of Control Figures and after them of the annual plans did not proceed in the direction suggested by him.

[1] *Planovoe khozyaistvo*, No. 2, 1926, p. 44.
[2] *Sotsialisticheskoe khozyaistvo*, No. 6, 1926, pp. 6–18.

Milyutin, attacking Kondrat'ev for his criticism of Control Figures for 1925–6, said: 'You know that on the whole the forecast of 1925–6 was realised',[1] neglecting to mention that the forecast was that of Groman. The fact that the modest book of control figures, this first attempt, made 'a great impression', that 'it led to great debates', shows clearly how important it was to produce at least some semblance of a plan, and that for a first attempt the *Figures* were not bad.

M. Birlrauer,[2] while finding in the *Control Figures* for the first two years sufficient material for criticism, nevertheless wrote:

The group of economists who worked on the control figures for 1925–6 and 1926–7 fully realised the need of scientific methodology for their work. To comrade V. G. Groman belongs the undoubted merit of putting in the foreground the laws of 'the recovery period' and generally of regularity in the national economy. His works were used as the basis for the drafting of the 'control figures'. We believe that the method suggested by comrade Groman will prove very useful in the future.

It is hard to describe all the obstacles that confronted the authors of *Kontrol'nye tsifry*. In the first place, there were the purely methodological difficulties of making forecasts when each year differed sharply from the previous one (approaching the end of the period of restoration, achieving its end and then beginning the reconstruction period). Meanwhile there was a many-sided struggle between different authorities, political groups and factions. Perhaps the greatest difficulty of all was caused by the fact that two types of demand were made on the economy – viz. high growth rates and the rapid expansion of socialism – and these demands contradicted each other, since the running of State enterprises – industry, trade and especially building – was fantastically expensive. But despite all these huge difficulties the work not only continued but rapidly increased in scope. *Kontrol'nye tsifry na 1927/28g.* was a large, 600-page volume, extremely rich in content.

Groman's influence was rising rapidly. Soon he was appointed a member of the Presidium of Gosplan. In 1926, after the dismissal of

---

[1] *Kondrat'evshchina*, p. 13.
[2] 'On the Problem of the Methodology of the "Perspective Plans"', *Ekonomicheskoe obozrenie*, No. 6, 1927, p. 87.

P. I. Popov as head of the Central Statistical Office, perhaps at least partly owing to criticism by Groman and his followers, Groman also became a member of the Council of the CSO (for liaison with Gosplan) and thus attained great influence on the work of the CSO, its publications and selection of personnel. In 1927, on the occasion of the thirtieth anniversary of Groman's activities as a statistician, he was named, on the suggestion of the CSO, 'a distinguished scholar' by the RSFSR government.

It would be quite impossible here to give even the main features of the first three sets of Control Figures or even those for 1927–8. In my *Soviet Industrialisation*, I put forward the view that if there was a single sentence which cost Groman his position, it was the following from Control Figures for 1927–8, p. 28: 'It must, however, be stressed with all decisiveness that for the coming year the very difficult problem of improving the quality of work throughout the socialist sector is far more important than changing the quantitative relationship of one social sector to the other.'

In actual fact Groman probably lost his post because Stalin wanted to go over to the 'all-out' policy with its completely unrealistic plans (cf. what has been said about the Five-Year Plan), and in all this there was, of course, no place for Groman. For the time being Strumilin was tolerated, but two years later he too was removed from all responsible planning work.

After the 1928–9 edition, the compilation of annual control figures passed to other hands. At first sight the new edition resembled the old, but in fact it represented a long step in the direction of transforming a more or less realistic plan into one of fantasy: e.g. the demand for a 7 per cent increase in sown areas and a 3 per cent one in crop yields, a 7 per cent reduction in industrial prime costs within a single year.[1]

Kontrol'nye tsifry na 1929/30g. represented a further descent of the slippery slope. In those for October–December 1930 and the plans for 1931 and 1932, planning turned into a phantasmagoria. However, annual plans as opposed to five-year ones revived. Except for the years of the 'Great Purge' (1937–40), these plans, although

---

[1] Cf. G. M. Krzhizhanovsky, 'On Control Figures for 1928–9' in *Planovoe khozyaistvo*, No. 2, 1929, p. 17.

they showed great defects, especially in the field of agriculture, nevertheless broadly approximated to reality. This, of course, was not in itself good enough. From 1955 onwards attempts were made to improve planning and especially to modify the five-year plans so that they should not only have propaganda value but also play a part in running the economy.

On 15 December 1929, Vaisberg, one of the most prominent Communists in Gosplan and a former member of the editorial board of *Planovoe khozyaistvo*, opened an attack on a broad front against the Mensheviks and narodniks, in particular Groman, Kondrat'ev and Bazarov. Shortly before, on 20 September 1929, he had published an article in *Pravda* entitled 'The first five sets of *Control Figures*, 1925-6 – 1929-30', which was a kind of precursor of the great campaign. There were savage attacks on Groman and his associates in that article, but in *Kontrol'nye tsifry* he wrote:

In their time, the *Control Figures* were a great step forward in the process of summing up results as regards the methodology of planning.

These attempts to provide a statistico–economic conspectus of the national economy as a whole, to define the trends of the most recent past and the coming year, constitute a great historical merit of the first *Control Figures*, which it is hardly possible to overrate.

The *Control Figures* have undoubtedly played a revolutionary role in planning. They have become a reliable guide in the process of broadly developed socialist construction.

We must not forget that if it was possible for a five-year plan to be drawn up in 1929, this was due to the accumulation of a long experience of planning work and the compilation of *Control Figures* over many years.[1]

THE MENSHEVIK PROGRAMME

The programme of Groman and the Gosplan Mensheviks in general had been formulated repeatedly by him and Bazarov since 1923 at the latest. The following is taken from a paper presented by Groman to a conference on the Control Figures for 1927-8, held on 29 June 1927:

[1] The importance of the statistical and dynamic coefficients used by Groman as a basis for Control Figures may be judged from the fact that vicious attacks on them continue to appear in the Soviet press even now, more than thirty-five years after their publication.

There are criteria which will enable us to arrive at an objective appraisal of the situation, as well as to establish the role of each branch...These criteria were formulated by comrade Bazarov thus: the optimum combination of the development of productive forces, growth of well-being of the working masses, and the development of socialist forms of the economy. [Note that socialisation comes last.] I used always to add: concern for the maintenance of a dynamic equilibrium in the national economy, which requires a balanced development of its components.[1]

The idea of equilibrium was formulated by Groman with great clarity in 'On Certain Regularities etc.' (*op. cit.* p. 91): 'Equilibrium, be it a dynamic one, of the economic body of a country is the highest requirement, each violation of which at once leads to a crisis, and compels conjections of the permitted departures from its requirement.'[2] In 1926 Groman wrote on the Control Figures for 1925–6:[3]

The Control Figures are a co-ordinated system of figures, reflecting a certain system of real relationships [p. 8 of *Kontrol'nye tsifry na 1925/26g.*] When they were submitted to S.T.O. by the author of these lines, it was emphasised that, if one of the elements in the system of Control Figures is changed, all others are changed also, for the system of Control Figures reflect a definite system of dynamic equilibrium of the national economy.

The first formulation of the concept of equilibrium by Groman which this writer has found goes back to 1923, though there may well have been earlier ones. He wrote: 'The planning feature must be strengthened by the adequate co-ordination in Gosplan of all measures of economic, financial (especially credit) and social policies (wages, anti-unemployment measures), from the point of view of national-economic unity...Objective contradictions and antagonisms must be modified on the basis of the principle of equilibrium of the social organism.'[4]

In fact, the idea of equilibrium was already implicit in Groman's Unified Economic Plan of 1917 and in his 'statistics of the national economy as a whole', also advocated in or after 1917.[5]

[1] See V. G. Groman, 'On the Appraisal of the Economic Situation of the USSR', *Planovoe khozyaistvo*, No. 7, 1927, p. 137.
[2] *Planovoe khozyaistvo*, No. 1, 1925, p. 91.　　　　[3] *Ibid.* No. 2, 1926, p. 85.
[4] 'The Economic Condition of the USSR', *Byulleteni Gosplana*, No. 10, 1923, p. 40.
[5] But his encounters with the brilliant Bogdanov, an advocate of the idea of equilibrium, dated back to his Penza days.

An important feature of dynamic equilibrium as advocated by Groman and Bazarov was the growth of agriculture, not as rapid as that of industry, but still quite substantial. However, the implications of the idea of equilibrium were much greater than this, having actually been the cornerstone of the planning method developed by Groman.

The idea of economic equilibrium may seem quite elementary, even from the viewpoint of almost forty years ago. But influential Bolsheviks at that time were galloping like unharnessed but blinkered horses. What they wanted was industrialisation at all costs. In the early 1920s it was only the left wing of the Party who failed to show any understanding of equilibrium. In the second half, disregard of it had become Stalin's credo and the cornerstone of the so-called General Line. Accordingly Groman's insistence on the need for equilibrium had become ever more urgent as time passed.

By 1930 the cards were put on the table. M. Rogal'sky, one of Groman's accusers, wrote: 'It is necessary to keep in mind that the theory of equilibrium was deliberately put forward by Groman in order to prove the impossibility of abrupt shifts in our economy and the devastating effect they would have on it.'[1] Rogal'sky's assertion was incorrect. Groman's enthusiasm for equilibrium dated back to the time before the Bolsheviks attained power. But his ever-growing emphasis on this idea may well have been caused by his realisation of the Party's inclination to disregard it and the immense danger that this involved.

All Groman's accusers felt like Rogal'sky. In his paper read at a meeting of Gosplan specialists on 15 December 1929, R. Vaisberg, having quoted Groman's statement that 'Equilibrium of the economic organism, although dynamic, is the highest requirement', etc., continued:[2] 'That is untrue, Mr Groman. Not mechanical... equilibrium is wanted, but...unity of contrasts and skilful utilisation of reality for the purpose of a revolutionary aim. The good of the Revolution is the supreme law, and, when this law demands, we must accept the violation and disregard of equilibrium.'

[1] 'On the Damaging Theory of Planning of Groman and Bazarov', *Planovoe khozyaistvo*, No. 10–11, 1930, p. 63.
[2] *Ibid.*

While the idea of equilibrium was violently attacked, hostility and distortion were also the fate of Groman's view concerning the relationship between marketed farm products and those of industrial goods – which is one aspect of the idea of equilibrium. In 'On Certain Regularities...'[1] Groman tells that Gukhman in working out the balance of the national economy for 1922–3 noticed that the ratio of farm to industrial output *at current prices* in 1922–3 was close to that obtaining before the war. After having his attention drawn to the phenomenon, Groman, together with Gukhman, investigated the situation in 1921–2, 1922–3, and 1923–4. On the basis of the data obtained, an attempt to forecast 1924–5 was made. The percentage distribution of total sales between farm and industrial products, calculated at current prices, proved to be as follows:[2]

Year	Farm	Industrial
1913	37	63
1921–2	52	48
1922–3	41	59
1923–4	38	62
1924–5 (forecast)	37	63

It is easy to make Groman's idea (which became famous) of the ratio of 37 to 63 look absurd by ascribing to him the claim that the 'stated ratio' would exist forever. This was done by Groman's enemies and sometimes also by others. But there is no trace of such a claim in his writings. The essay 'On Certain Regularities, etc.' in which the idea of the proportion of marketed industrial and farm products to total marketings was developed fully, is restricted to the recovery period, and in 1924, when Groman wrote his study, he expected that period to end by about 1926 or 1927. He said: 'The great probability is that in future years we will come still closer to the pre-war pattern.'[3] But by 'future years' he meant only the next year or two. As is obvious from the table above, he actually attempted a forecast of the distribution of marketings only for one

[1] 'On Certain Regularities Empirically Established in Our Economy', *Planovoe khozyaistvo*, No. 1, 1925.
[2] *Ibid*. p. 96.
[3] *Ibid*. p. 99.

year (1924–5). Groman even discussed what happened to this relationship in the first two months of 1924–5, prior to the time he was writing his paper. Six to seven years was, so to speak, an eternity at the time in question. Rogal'sky wrote of Groman's theory in 1931:[1] 'The hidden purpose of the theory was to prove that a rise in the prices of farm produce was an inevitable result of the unavoidable and unrestricted growth of industry relative to agriculture. Such inflation was in the interests of the *kulaks* [read: peasants] and to the disadvantage of industrialisation.' Rogal'sky did not even take the trouble to show that Groman's calculations were wrong.

Vaisberg did not, of course, miss the opportunity to attack Groman's coefficients for the relationships between marketed products.[2] He alleged that Groman had persistently cited his proportion of 37 to 63. He instanced as a particular crime that Groman 'managed for some time to include his proportions in the Control Figures'. No statistical data on the phenomenon can be found in Vaisberg either.

Unfortunately criticism not much different from that of Vaisberg and Rogal'sky can be found also in Western literature. This seems to make it advisable to dwell on the problem a little longer. The Control Figures for 1927–8, pp. 474–5, give the following proportions of the values of the marketed farm and industrial products at current prices in 1924–5 and 1926–7 and the plan for 1927–8 (per cent):

Item	1924–5	1925–6	1926–7	Plan 1927–8
Farm products	42.7	37.9	36.8	35.8
Industrial products	57.3	62.4	63.2	64.2

Groman was entitled to be satisfied with his calculations. In 1926–7, when the recovery period as then interpreted ended, the pre-war proportion of 37 to 63 was reached precisely.

The industrial drive was intensified in 1927–8 and especially in

---

[1] M. Rogal'sky, 'On the Damaging Theory of Planning of Groman and Bazarov', *ibid.* No. 10–11, 1930, p. 65.
[2] 'The Objective Science of the Gosplan Saboteurs', *ibid.* No. 10–11, 1930, p. 39.

1928–9, and it would hence be expected that extrapolations of the relationships in marketed products made in 1924 would no longer hold good. But the deviation was small, indeed almost negligible. According to *Kontrol'nye tsifry na 1929/30g.*, pp. 422–3, the ratio of the values of marketed farm and non-farm products to the total values of marketed products at current prices was as follows (in per cent):

Item	1926–7	1927–8	1928–9 (estimates)
Farm products	33.1	31.9	32.0
Industrial products	66.9	68.1	68.0

In the two important years 1927–8 and 1928–9, the share of the value of farm products in total marketing went down by 1.1 per cent. These data show a degree of accuracy which is rare in statistics.[1]

In spite of Groman's insistence on equilibrium, growth of productive powers may still have been the basic item in his programme. In any case, it played a major role in it. In *Kontrol'nye tsifry na 1926/27g.*, p. 5, he wrote: 'In preparing the Control Figures for 1926–7, we set ourselves the question: *Does growth of productive forces occur? What rate of growth in 1926–7 is implied as compared with the preceding years, and what are the prospects for 1927–8?*' 'Growth of productive forces...' This is of course strictly Marx. But the question implies an unwelcome (for the Bolsheviks) implication that further socialisation of the economy should proceed only in so far as it would not affect unfavourably the growth of productive powers, i.e. general economic development.

Groman was not satisfied to have this restriction present only as an implication. As early as March 1924, i.e. five and a half years before the start of Stalin's 'all-out drive', Groman is supposed to

[1] The data in the three tabulations above show some discrepancies between themselves. Thus for 1926–7 the proportions were 36.8:63.2 according to Control Figures for 1927–8, and 33.1:66.9 according to Control Figures for 1929–30. The difference is not large, but, more important, only the statistics from the same source are compared in the above tables. Finally no one more than Groman untiringly stressed the defects of statistical material. (In *Planovoe khozyaistvo*, No. 1, 1925, p. 93, he wrote: 'The statistical data are very imperfect; the method of working them up is very approximate.')

have made the declaration to the Presidium of Gosplan, quoted above (p. 21), that changes should occur only if growth both of production and personal consumption could be assured without coercion.[1]

The future rate of socialisation visualised by Groman and Bazarov certainly was not such as could have kept them in favour with the Party leadership. Control Figures for 1926–7, p. 27, stated: 'The structure of the social sectors...is the legacy of decades and centuries'; 'prolonged and gigantic efforts would be needed to change this structure radically.'

Bazarov's statement quoted below dealt with the relation between growth of productive forces and socialisation in a Five-Year Plan.

Circumstances may occur which would make it necessary to retard the quantitative rise of wages in the socialised sector and, so to speak, to consolidate the position already reached, in order to clear the way for a further intensive expansion of productive forces. But it is impossible to visualise the reverse, i.e. the necessity of temporarily retarding the rise of productive forces with the aim of rapidly raising the well-being of the population or the processes of socialisation. The development of productive forces is the chief link. In an optimum plan this indicator must show a smooth rise. Any kind of fluctuation, interruption or lag would testify to a defective plan.[2]

This restriction on the extent of further socialisation (the Mensheviks, and specifically Groman, did not suggest the re-privatisation of activities already socialised) was important, because the socialised economy operated at higher costs than the private economy had done before the war. Production costs in industry and trade margins were higher, the only exception perhaps being in rail transport, which had been largely State-owned prior to the Revolution.

The Communists could not be satisfied with this attitude toward the socialised sector. The rates of growth of the socialised sector provided in the Control Figures from 1925–6 to 1927–8 – for it was impossible not to plan for some amount of socialisation – seemed

---

[1] The citation is taken from an attack on Groman by R. Vaisberg in *Planovoe khozyaistvo* No. 2–3, 1931, p. 12; Vaisberg, of course, had access to material not accessible to us.

[2] 'Principles for the Construction of Perspective Plans', *Planovoe khozyaistvo*, No. 2, 1928, pp. 42–3.

to them grossly inadequate. A statement in the summarising part of Control Figures for 1927–8, p. 28, on this point has already been quoted above. It is worth repeating, with added emphasis: 'It must, however, be stressed with all decisiveness that for the coming year the *very difficult task of improving the quality of work throughout the socialist sector* is far more important than changing the quantitative relationship of one social sector to the other' [i.e. more socialisation.]

It required a lot of courage at that time to put such a statement in the Control Figures; and, as already mentioned, this may have played a great role in depriving Groman, immediately after the publication of Control Figures for 1927–8, of control over the work on the Control Figures.

The issue was settled by Stalin's blunt declaration in April 1929:[1]

Is it true that the central idea of the five-year plan in the Soviet state is represented by the growth of productivity of people's work? No, it is not. It is not just any growth of labour productivity that we need, but a definite type of labour productivity, namely that which ensures a systematic preponderance of the socialist economy over the capitalist sector.

And further:[2]

Every society, capitalist and pre-capitalist, is interested in the growth of productivity of labour. The difference of the Soviet society from all other forms of society consists in the fact that it is interested not in every growth of labour productivity, but in such growth as ensures the predominance of the socialist form of the economy over all other forms, especially capitalist forms of economy, and thus ensures the overcoming and elimination of the capitalist forms of economy.

Actually Stalin was willing to sacrifice growth in labour productivity, and even to accept its temporary decline, for the sake of what he called 'socialism'. Stalin certainly achieved a large measure of 'socialism', but productive forces grew only moderately, in spite of immense sacrifices. In 1931 and 1932 the national income even declined.

[1] Stalin, *Voprosy leninizma*, 11th edn., Moscow, 1947, p. 253. The tirade was directed against the Right-Wing Opposition, specifically Rykov, but this is immaterial.
[2] *Ibid.* pp. 253–4.

Vladimir Gustavovich Groman

THE END

Nineteen-twenty-seven, the year when the Control Figures for 1927–8 were produced, must probably be considered the peak of Groman's activities. It so happened that it was also the anniversary of thirty years of his scientific work. Some of the statements published on this occasion are worth quoting.

In an unsigned leading article in *Vestnik statistiki* for May 1927 we read: 'Groman is incapable of thinking in a fragmentary, disconnected manner, by fits and starts: his thought always takes the form of a synthesis, his analyses always embrace a whole range of separate factors...'

In Bazarov's article, this approach of Groman's to problems of the national economy is already expressed in the title: 'Economic planning and the Groman conception of the national economy as a whole'.[1] In the article itself we read:

I should like to say just a few words about the quite exceptional and, I would say, intimate link between planned economy and the scientific activity of V. G. Groman. The research he has carried out over the past thirteen years is inspired by a single guiding idea of 'the national economy as a whole'... In this respect he is to some extent a pioneer.

But that is not all Bazarov had to say about Groman. I will quote the most significant passage: 'Groman, as an eminent artist in the economic sphere, possesses a spark of mysterious vision which, by its very nature, cannot be translated into the ordinary language of our discursive, scientific and methodological knowledge.'

The editorial in *Vestnik statistiki*, quoted above, concludes with a wish that 'Groman may turn a new brilliant page in the history of his activities and help towards the full clarification of what he calls statistics of the national economy as a whole.' But fate ruled otherwise. The anniversary was in April 1927. The New Economic Policy was already very much on the decline; in a few months it would be dead. Stalin's 'General Line' proved victorious. Groman could not accept even a fraction of it.

Groman did not lay down his arms. On the contrary, he fought

[1] *Planovoe khozyaistvo*, No. 6, 1927, pp. 162–5.

furiously, but Stalin's 'General Line' was moving like an avalanche. In the discussion of Kovalevsky's paper 'Methodology of the Plan of Reconstruction' prepared for Gosplan and discussed also in the Club of Planning Staffs early in 1928, Groman thundered:

> We must completely abandon this inclination toward fantastic constructions. Look at the facts, do not invent but study the environment. The first thing that must be done is to grasp fully that, in addition to the forces which are making our plan one of minimum growth, there are also those which drag us back. We must not close our eyes to these forces.
>
> The moment you cease to operate with *real forces* or *real development*, you embark on fantasies. The great danger is that fantasies will suddenly enter into our construction.[1]

One of the last statements in print clearly in opposition to the 'General Line' is to be found in Sukhanov's paper 'Economic Conditions for a Rise in Farm Output', read to the Agrarian Institute of the Communist Academy on 4 December 1928.[2] His speech in the discussion of Kritsman's paper 'Analysis of the Peasant Household' in the Conference of Marxist–Leninist Scientific-Research Organisations in April 1929 was the penultimate public utterance by the opposition.[3] The very last was Groman's open letter to Rykov, the chairman of the Council of People's Commissars and of the Council of Labour and Defence (Gosplan, the centre of Groman's activities, was a committee of the latter body), published in a Moscow paper on 10 October 1929, in which he had the courage to refer to himself as a 'socialist who does not share the point of view of the Communist Party'. Gorlunov, secretary to Rykov, answered Groman on Rykov's orders. He correctly interpreted Groman's position as that of an adherent to the Second International.[4]

Groman's open letter to Rykov preceded by just under a month the famous Stalin article on 'The Year of the Great Turning-point',[5] proclaiming the collectivisation of peasant farming on the whole front. Stalin's article gave the signal for violent attacks in the specialist press against the Mensheviks, neo-narodniks and others. So far as Groman and his followers are concerned, the cannonade

[1] *Planovoe khozyaistvo*, No. 4, 1928 (italics in the original).
[2] See *Kondrat'evshchina*, p. 111.   [3] *Na agrarnom fronte*, No. 7, 1929, pp. 101–2.
[4] See also the present writer's *Soviet Industrialisation*, p. 439.
[5] *Pravda*, 7 November 1929.

began with R. Vaisberg's paper, read at a meeting of Gosplan and published in *Planovoe khozyaistvo*, No. 1, 1930, under the title 'Bourgeois Distortion in the Field of Planning'. We may further note Rogal'sky, 'On the Damaging Theory of Planning of Groman and Bazarov', *ibid.* No. 10–11, 1930, pp. 60–97, and Vaisberg, 'The Objective Science of the Gosplan Saboteurs', *ibid.* pp. 27–59.[1] Vaisberg's last shot in *Planovoe khozyaistvo*, No. 2–3, 1931, has already been noted.

Reports presented to the Society of Statisticians are also mentioned in *Planovoe khozyaistvo*, No. 10–11. The lady who presided at the reading of these reports was M. N. Smit, who in the winter of 1916–17 shared an office with me in the Statistical Bureau (headed by Groman) of the Petersburg Department of the All-Russian Union of Cities. Papers were read by Professor Yastremsky – who, till shortly before, had no doubt considered himself a friend of Groman's – by Starovsky, the present head of the Central Statistical Office, and others.[2] The object of attack was in all cases Groman, and in Starovsky's case Vishnevsky as well.

Towards the end of this campaign a review appeared sharply criticising Groman's small book *Introduction to the Planning of National Economy*, published by the Communist Academy, Moscow. Writing in *Planovoe khozyaistvo*, No. 2, 1931 (pp. 82–91), the reviewer said:

As was already pointed out by *Pravda* [No. 347, 1930], this book represents a sly attempt, disguised as a purely formal critique of some particular aspects of the Groman–Bazarov wrecking 'theories' of planning, to smuggle in all the remaining features of that Menshevik 'ideology' and of a capitalist restoration. The book is permeated by the Groman spirit, it is absolutely of a piece with the Groman–Bazarov theoretical endeavours...

The review spoke throughout of Groman, Groman and Bazarov, Groman–Bazarov etc. Anyone who takes the trouble to study *Planovoe khozyaistvo* for 1930 and Groman's work of 1931 – all other journals connected with planning had ceased publication

---

[1] As a crude yardstick of how those in power gauged their enemies' relative importance, we may note that the name of Groman was mentioned in these three articles some 110 times, or twice as often as Bazarov's, while those of Kondrat'ev and Osadchy each appeared a dozen times. [2] See p. 123.

earlier – cannot fail to conclude that Groman was the founder of Soviet planning, with Bazarov in a major auxiliary role.

When most of those attacks were published, the victims were already in jail; the culmination came in the trial of Groman and thirteen other Mensheviks in March 1931. By that time Groman had long been on a sick-bed and was more or less a wreck. He had suffered from incurable *angina pectoris* as early as 1923. By 1927 he had weakened considerably, although he had been lucky in the years since his symptoms appeared. When in 1927 he visited me in Hamburg after treatment at Nauheim he was 52 years old, and although he was in the best state of health possible for him, people spoke of him as of an old man. I did not see him again after 1927, but I can well imagine how greatly he must have deteriorated by 1928–30, when conditions were very grave for him and when he could no longer travel abroad for cures.

It was in 1927 that he was deprived of responsibility for his beloved Control Figures. He was retained in Gosplan for two more years, but only on unimportant tasks. On 22 May 1929, he read in the collegium of CSO (and previously in Gosplan) a paper on a new method of forecasting grain crops. The collegium buried his proposals in these words:[1] 'Noting the great interest aroused by this work of V. G. Groman, it [the collegium] believes, however, that the supposed law of a ten-year period during which harvests offset one another is not proven.' When Groman was arrested in mid-1930, he was already in the employ of the Central Sugar Office (Tsentrosakhar), which for him meant exile from real work. He testified in *Trial*, p. 120:

I must mention that recently I was ill every year and about twice a year I had attacks, each of which threatened disastrous results. As a result of my arrest I have, for the first time in all these years, spent eight months without an attack. I was kept under careful medical observation and received an exceptional diet, devised by a specially convened committee of professors.

Krylenko and the others apparently did not mind including in the minutes of *Trial* a confession of the painstaking efforts made by

[1] *Vestnik statistiki*, No. 2, 1929, pp. 99–118.

them not to lose their star performer. Without Groman among the accused, the whole *Trial* would hardly have been worth a candle.

While, by the time of the trial, Groman was merely a shadow of the strong man he had once been, the great reputation acquired by him in the preceding years made him by far the most prominent among the accused. This has been shown already in the chapter devoted to the *Trial*. There are some additional points which can be made.

When Krylenko, the prosecutor, came in his introductory speech to the part played by individual defendants, he spoke first of Groman in this way (*Trial*, p. 354): 'Groman – the old man, the leader, the authority, the organiser. The man who enjoyed great trust, who with his authority systematically covered up the wrecking activity' ...etc. Krylenko perhaps meant the words 'leader, authority, organiser' to sound ironical. But there is no irony when one reads this statement – it was perfectly accurate.

When, in the trial, several names were given including Groman's, his usually came first. This was true not only in lists of the defendants, as in Ramzin's statement: 'I pointed out the principal workers of the centre with whom I had to do. There were five persons: Groman, Sukhanov, Ginzburg, Sokolovsky and Shtern' (*Trial*, p. 176). The same Ramzin, after stating that all memoranda of the bloc of the three organisations involving economic analysis were prepared under Groman's direction, said 'A special memorandum (or note) presented to the Torgprom was prepared jointly by Groman, Ginzburg and Kondrat'ev.' Groman testified (as reported in *Trial*) that he was appointed financial 'dictator' of the 'United Bureau'.

Anyone who takes the trouble of reading the Soviet press regularly is familiar with its habit of calling the current leader by his first name, patronymic and surname, while all others, even those immediately below him, are called simply by their surnames. In the Menshevik trial, the prosecutor and the court called the defendants by their surnames only. The defendants and witnesses also mostly did the same, probably for convenience. But exceptions were made fairly often for Groman, Sukhanov and Finn-Enotaevsky. Ramzin said for example: 'This contact was made by the following persons: in the Gosplan – by Vladimir Gustavovich Groman; in the VSNKh by Ginzburg, Sokolovsky, and Shtern.' (*Trial*, p. 172.) Kondrat'ev testified (*Trial*, p. 195): 'I used to meet, firstly with Vladimir Gustavovich Groman, secondly with Nikolai Nikolaevich Sukhanov, and thirdly with A. L. Sokolovsky.' The major role of Groman in *Trial* was merely a reflection of the major role that he played in planning at the time when serious planning was still being done. The trial took place at the time when 'Bacchanalian planning' had replaced sensible planning.[1]

For the subsequent period, all that this writer knows for certain is that (according to Ciliga) shortly after the trial, together with other defendants, Groman was brought to the Nizhny-Uralsky political 'isolator'. According to some rumours he was later transferred to a jail in a big city, where he worked as a statistician, earning a good salary by day and returning to jail for the night.

It would be a mistake to infer that I have a low opinion of Ginzburg and the other VSNKh Mensheviks. Ginzburg was undoubtedly an able and energetic man. I always maintained that the Mensheviks ought to be proud that one of their number was responsible for what became known as the 'Ginzburg' Five-Year Plan. But one must add that in the post-NEP period Ginzburg, unlike Groman, did not have to struggle with anyone. The Plan that bears his name was drawn up with the full blessing of Dzerzhinsky, the head of VSNKh. When he was taken off this work he devoted himself to the economics of industry, of which he was also a professor, in such a way as not to offend those in authority – though he did not capitulate either, up to the time of his arrest. I had no personal knowledge of the other Mensheviks in VSNKh, as opposed to knowledge of their writings. But Groman told me that he had a high opinion of Shtern.

The main point is, however, that though there was not a profusion of able and energetic men, there was at any rate more than a handful of them. Groman, despite his ignorance of foreign languages, was in a class by himself by reason of the originality and boldness of his thoughts and actions and his ability to attract devoted advisers. As Krylenko rightly said, he was the leader.

---

[1] As regards 'Bacchanalian planning', see the present writer's *Essays on the Soviet Economy*, pp. 231–5.

Vladimir Gustavovich Groman

It was a lucky stroke of fate that made Bazarov Groman's adviser. They complemented each other in important respects. Bazarov was a far more cultivated man than Groman: for one thing, he was a man of letters, which Groman certainly was not. On the other hand, Groman had more originality, and above all he was a leader. When he moved from one organisation to another he took a whole band of advisers with him. There were something like a dozen people, perhaps even more, of real ability who could truthfully be called Gromanites. I cannot, of course, give a full list, but one may mention D. V. Shub, Zeilinger, Gukhman, Broitman, Vishnevsky, Pistrak and E. P. Groman. In addition, Cherevanin was a Gromanite for many years. In *Planovoe khozyaistvo*, No. 10–11, 1930, p. 28, Vaisberg wrote spitefully that Groman was 'surrounded in Gosplan and the Central Statistical Office by a clique of his own statisticians, occupying the most varied positions in the Soviet hierarchy and in that of sabotage'. He added (*ibid.* p. 34): '[Groman] at one period monopolised work on conjuncture problems, being in complete control of statistical work both in the CSO and in the USSR Gosplan.' Nobody could have done this single-handed: it required a small, but devoted, band of supporters.

None of the workers in this field became known as a 'Bazarovite'. One may go further and say that Bazarov himself was to some extent a Gromanite. The two men parted company soon after the XV Party Congress (December 1927), when Groman stuck to his guns while Bazarov began to seek for a compromise. But the latter acquired no following after he had separated from Groman. The separation itself was perhaps one reason, though of course not the chief one, why Bazarov became practically a cipher.

7

VLADIMIR ALEXANDROVICH BAZAROV[1]

Bazarov, the party name and pen-name of Rudnev – a philosopher, economist, and journalist – was born at Tula in 1874. He entered Moscow University in 1892 and in 1896 began to engage in revolutionary activities. In 1897 he was expelled from Moscow and settled at Tula, where he was active in social-democratic work. Together with A. Bogdanov and Skvortsov-Stepanov, he organised a kind of secret university for Tula workers. The triumvirate thus formed was a prestigious one: for a considerable time Bogdanov ranked next to Lenin in the Bolshevik Party. After the revolution Skvortzov-Stepanov played an important role and from 1925 on he was chief editor of *Izvestiya*. He died in 1928.

Bazarov was expelled from Tula in 1899. After spending some time abroad, he returned to Russia and became a member of the Moscow Social Democratic Committee. In the fall of 1901 he was again arrested and exiled for three years to eastern Siberia. In 1904 he joined the Bolshevik faction of the Social Democratic Party after its split. In 1905, and also in 1906–7, he wrote for both legal and underground Bolshevik publications. He was a member of the editorial board of the Party's chief publication, and also a member of the so-called Bolshevik Centre. In subsequent years he dissociated himself from the Bolsheviks, without however becoming a Menshevik. He was arrested in 1911 and deported for three years to Astrakhan. During World War I and the February Revolution he was on

[1] For the period prior to 1922, extensive use was made of the article on Bazarov in the *Great Soviet Encyclopedia*, Moscow, 1926, Vol. 4, pp. 333–6, by E. A. Preobrazhensky. It was written before falsification had become standard in Soviet publications; nevertheless, it strongly reflects sharp political disagreements between Preobrazhensky and Bazarov, who was a much bigger figure than the article indicates. Alexander Erlich, *The Soviet Industrialization Debate, 1924–1928*, Cambridge, Mass., 1960 devotes considerably more space to Bazarov than this writer (pp. 60–75, 135–40 etc.), and differs somewhat in his appraisal of the relative importance of Bazarov and Groman. Erlich writes: 'V. A. Bazarov, one of the intellectual lights of the Bolshevik movement during its first decade, and later the leading, though non-party, economist of Gosplan.'

the staff of various leftist publications, lastly *Novaya zhizn'*, Gorky's daily, which was to the left of everyone except the Bolsheviks.

Bazarov's philosophic interests date from the earliest days of his literary activities. The first more or less comprehensive exposition of his views ('Authoritarian Metaphysics and Autonomous Personality') was published in 1904. Already at that time he had ceased to accept Marx's dialectical materialism. Together with Bogdanov and Skvortsov-Stepanov he was an adept of the Mach-Avenarius school, which advocated a form of positivism and made many adherents among the Bolsheviks. Bogdanov was the unofficial leader of this school in Russia (where it was frequently referred to as 'Bogdanovism'), but Bazarov also played a considerable role in it.

Under the editorship of Bazarov and Skvortsov-Stepanov, with Bogdanov as general editor, the three volumes of Marx's *Das Kapital* were retranslated and published in 1907-9. This translation is still used in the Soviet Union, but the fact of Bazarov's and Bogdanov's editorship is suppressed.

IN THE PLANNING OFFICE

After the October Revolution, with which he was not in great sympathy, he moved to Kharkov, where he wrote for Menshevik publications, some of which were considerably to the right. In 1922 he joined the USSR Gosplan. It was in Gosplan that the Groman-Bazarov team was formed, which lasted for over five years. The two men complemented each other admirably. Whether the characterisation by R. Vaisberg in *Planovoe khozyaistvo*, No. 2-3, 1931, of Bazarov as Groman's 'theoretical henchman' is an understatement of his role depends on how we interpret this phrase; but it was broadly accurate. Groman, however, never treated Bazarov merely as a 'henchman' of any kind.

On 21 November 1923, Bazarov read to the Presidium of Gosplan a paper entitled 'Problems of Planning the National Economy as a Whole'. The emphasis was on 'as a whole'. Groman's paper on the balance of the national economy, read at the same meeting,[1] likewise

[1] *Byulleteni Gosplana*, 1923, section 'In the Presidium of Gosplan', Nov.-Dec. pp. 119-20.

emphasised that the balance must be that of the national economy as a single unit.

Bazarov in his paper argued that 'the importance of the principles of planning and of planning activities in the national economy is not only not lessened by the transition to the NEP, but, on the contrary, has become stronger'. The restoration of commodity markets and the transition of the state enterprises to *khozrazchet* (cost accounting) had created for the first time the material conditions for operative planning, i.e. the inducements which made it possible to put forward plan proposals. Bazarov further held that 'an automatic control of performance success has been created'. He emphasised *inter alia* that: 'The past year was characterised by big successes of planning within individual groups and branches of industry and big strides forward in the rationalisation of the technical division of labour. This meant an end of the period of crises of under-production, the period of catastrophes which paralysed first one and then another branch of the national economy.' However, extremely little had been done 'as regards rationalisation of the social division of labour, i.e. in planning the economy as a whole, as a result of which we have a general crisis of sales (relative over-production), i.e. the first post-war and post-revolutionary crisis of a purely capitalistic nature'.

In 1924 Bazarov published a pamphlet *On the Methodology of Drafting Perspective Plans*, dealing with such important problems as the transition from the restoration to the reconstruction period, the relation between agriculture and industry in different stages of development etc.[1]

As soon as Gosplan turned its attention to planning for the national economy as a whole, the problem arose whether, and for how long, the very high rates of recovery experienced after the proclamation of the NEP could be maintained. The inevitable decline of these rates was baptised 'the diminishing curve'.[2] The problem arose first with reference to money in circulation. According to Groman this was discussed in a commission of Gosplan in

---

[1] *K metodologii perspektivnogo planirovaniya*, Moscow, 1924.
[2] V. G. Groman, 'On Certain Regularities...', *Planovoe khozyaistvo*, No. 1, 1925, pp. 137–8.

1923, and on Bazarov's proposal specific rates of decline in the velocity of money circulation were assumed by the commission.

It seems probable that Groman was the first to distinguish the declining growth rate as a phenomenon of an economy in the process of recovery, but Bazarov played a great role in the development of the idea and its later history. In his article in *Ekonomicheskoe obozrenie*, 1925, published about the same time as Groman's 'On Certain Regularities etc.', Bazarov formulated the 'extinguishing curve' concept more broadly than just in application to paper money in circulation; but he gave Groman credit for the formula of the 'recovery period' as a special period with its own laws.

It was, I believe, Bazarov who introduced in the literature on planning the term 'teleological' in the sense of a directive. In an article published in 1926 he wrote:

In appraising perspective plans originally only one criterion is considered, viz. agreement with reality. This criterion could be recognised as exhaustive for adaptation to a scientific forecast of economic development, constructed strictly genetically, i.e. exclusively on the basis of consideration of the objective regularities and tendencies of an elementary economic process. But a 'perspective plan' is not only a forecast but a directive – not only a genetical study, but also a teleological construction – not only a consideration of objective possibilities, but a system of measures necessary for an optimum utilisation of these possibilities.[1]

And also:

The basic task of perspective planning leads to the necessity to combine genetic and teleological methods of determining optimum ways of development. The field of teleological constructions broadens at the expense of the geneticist forecast, in proportion as a given branch of the economy is embraced by the direct operative influence of the State.[2]

Agriculture, split into more than 20 million small individual units and, as regards its marketable output, oriented to a considerable extent towards export, is the branch where genetical analysis plays a dominant role. The State sector of the national economy is the area of predominantly teleological constructions.[3]

[1] V. A. Bazarov, 'On the Methodology of Drafting Perspective Plans', *Planovoe khozyaistvo*, No. 7, 1926, p. 9.   [2] *Ibid.* pp. 9–10.   [3] *Ibid.* p. 10.

Considering the tendency toward unbridled enthusiasm in the USSR, the statement on the role of the teleological factor in State enterprises might with advantage have been a little more cautious. It was also perhaps premature, to say the least, when Bazarov in 1926 spoke of 'our hope to overtake and surpass in our development the advanced countries of the capitalist world'. 'This hope', he added, 'is based on the fact that we expect to find a shorter and more economical way of reconstruction than if our economic policy were oriented exclusively by consideration of the elementally (*stikhiino*) changing situation.'[1]

Of considerable interest are Bazarov's remarks on the application of mathematics to planning:[2]

We are unable to draw the optimum lines of perspective development with full exactness and rigidity...The calculation of even a very short optimum line...presents one of the most difficult problems of accounting technique. Modern mathematics shows how to solve such problems in only a few of the simplest cases...In the meantime we are compelled, in looking for the optimum, to take refuge in crude approximations.

Only now, after over thirty years, is Soviet planning coming to use mathematics in the way Bazarov recommended.[3]

A LONG-TERM PLAN

Bazarov probably spoke for Gosplan when he described the form of plans needed at that time: 'The general plan as the foundation; the perspective plan as the first specification; the control figures as the fully concrete yearly portion of the general perspective plan.'[4] In stating this formula, he declared that it represented the logical and rational sequence which Gosplan hoped to realise some time in the future. At present, he said, the sequence was the reverse. The Control Figures were being prepared already for the second year. In six weeks or two months, work on the Five-Year Plan would be completed (so it was, but it became only another rough draft),

---

[1] *Ibid.* p. 21.   [2] *Ibid.* p. 13.
[3] Rudolf Schlesinger drew attention to this contribution by Bazarov in *Soviet Studies*, July 1964, p. 25.
[4] 'On the Methodology of Drafting Perspective Plans', *Planovoe khozyaistvo*, No. 7, 1926, p. 9.

while the preparation of the general plan was only in its beginnings. Explaining this reversal, Bazarov said: 'Considering the acute need [for a five-year plan], Gosplan proposes to give a sketch of the five-year perspective plan in the near future, although the figures therein, especially at the present stage when the outlines of the general plan are not indicated with sufficient exactness, can have only very general and provisional validity.'[1]

The role of the general plan in planning as a whole, envisaged in Bazarov's article and by some other prominent planners, was rather unrealistic. Even if the schemes in the Party Programme for 1980, approved by the XXII Party Congress in 1961, are accepted as a general plan (which they scarcely are), the delay in working out the general plan as compared with expectations in the mid-twenties amounted to more than thirty years. Bazarov's contention of 1925 would suggest that all planning until 1961 was of a preliminary nature. Actually even most of the Five-Year Plans adopted from 1926 to the present time lacked adequate material to serve as a guide for the drafting of the annual plans, and, as Soviet experts now recognise, more or less successful planning was in the past practically limited to annual plans. The approach of the neo-narodniks on this point turned out more realistic than that of the Mensheviks. While the former in general went too far in their criticism of planning and the plans, scepticism as regards long-range planning seems largely justified.[2]

Bazarov's next article devoted to planning seems to have been that published in *Ekonomicheskoe obozrenie*, No. 5, 1927.[3] This is the article containing his well-known statement that he was 'an honest non-Party man, standing on the Soviet platform'. Although this article was published early in 1927, it already indicated the new thoughts that were brewing. It was preceded by the following editorial note:

[1] *Ibid.* p. 8.
[2] On doubts regarding the possibility of preparing the general (long-range) plan before the shorter plans and using it as a guide in drafting the latter, see, for example, A. N. Chelintsev, 'The Problem of Methods and Principles of Constructing Perspective Plans for Agriculture', in *Puti sel'skogo khozyaistva*, No. 2, 1927, p. 53.
[3] 'On Our Economic Perspectives and Perspective Plans', *Ekonomicheskoe obozrenie*, No. 5, 1927, pp. 31–53.

The author of this article attempts to find abstract theoretical principles of the consistent rationalisation of our industry. While believing this topic to be very urgent, the editors nevertheless cannot agree with him that the obstacles to the realisation of his theoretical scheme are only due to our organisational shortcomings and wrong traditions; in our view he goes too far in criticising the latter.

In early 1927 it was still possible to write, without being ferociously attacked: 'Only by amply supplying the village with good industrial products at very low prices can we create a real impulse toward the development of our backward agriculture, which represents the basic foundation, and in its present condition also the principal obstacle to the economic development of the country.'[1]

Not long afterwards (in *Kondrat'evshchina*, p. 111), Sukhanov was 'excoriated' for expressing the same opinions in a paper read to the Agrarian Institute on 4 December 1928.

Bazarov's article contains many good ideas, but also some doubtful statements, showing *inter alia* the lack of a fully realistic approach and some lack of discrimination in making suggestions. The most interesting suggestion was perhaps the following: 'On every rouble passed by the State to industry, the State should charge a certain, not too large, yet measurable rate of interest.' As is well known, suggestions according to which the use of capital by State enterprises would have to be paid for by them in one way or another have become popular recently, e.g. those put forward by Liberman more than thirty years after Bazarov.

In his article Bazarov assigned particular significance to increasing the effectiveness of capital. He said for example that to be effective the prices of industrial goods sold to the peasants must be reduced by two to three times.[2] Even then, this was not a fully realistic approach: such a reduction was simply impossible.

Surprisingly careless statements were made by Bazarov on the relation between cotton and flax as well as on sugar beet. He first quotes some absurd statements by a commission of Gosplan on the relative significance of cotton and flax (*op. cit.* p. 42) – possibly these were suggested by him personally – and then goes far beyond

---

[1] *Ibid.* p. 33. [2] *Ibid.* p. 46.

them. On p. 43 he writes 'In the USSR, where all conditions exist for developing a flourishing flax industry, conditions are unsuitable for cotton growing'. He envisaged a fifty-fold increase in the utilisation of flax by industry. To make this possible the output of flax must exceed tenfold what he called the 'pre-war norm'.[1] As regards sugar beet, 'Assuming a real rationalisation [of the sugar industry] and a corresponding reduction of prices, not only would our domestic consumption of sugar increase several times, but simultaneously a most valuable export product would come into existence' (*op. cit.* p. 43). The Soviet Union imports huge amounts of sugar, and yet Khrushchev discovered that sugar is a most valuable fodder. Bazarov's wrong statements on sugar beet were made thirty years earlier and are contrary to the views of Khrushchev, who claimed to be an expert on agriculture. Elsewhere in the article (p. 42), Bazarov admitted that he was 'an ignoramus as regards technology'.

In No. 2 of *Planovoe khozyaistvo* for 1928 he published an article 'Principles for the Construction of Perspective Plans', in which he continued to emphasise the importance of increased efficiency. He was still on the previous track when he argued that: 'First we must reconstruct the industries producing consumer goods, particularly those for which something like large-scale demand already exists.'[2] He suggested that as regards all other industries, until they had acquired a broad enough base within the USSR, it would be preferable to purchase essential products abroad or grant concessions to foreign capitalists.

As is apparent from the chapter devoted to the economy after the NEP and also from Chapter 4, an error was made in forecasting the rate of growth in the first years after 1925–6. Contrary to expectations the 'diminishing curve' not only failed to operate but there was actually an increase in the rate of industrial growth. While Stalin's policies would hardly have been affected whatever turn developments in the Soviet economy had taken, the error which led to underestimating the rate of industrial growth at the end of the

---

[1] The output of flax fibre in 1962 was only equal to that in 1913. See *SSSR v tsifrakh v 1962g.*, Moscow, 1963, pp. 142–3.
[2] Here cited from Nicolas Spulber (ed.), *Foundations of Soviet Strategy for Economic Growth*, Bloomington, Indiana, 1964, p. 222.

NEP and the beginning of the post-NEP period greatly facilitated the first stages of Stalin's all-out drive.

Bazarov, and no other, seems to have been the first to offer a sensible explanation of the fact that industrial growth developed more favourably in the late NEP and early post-NEP years than it had been expected to. He did this in the discussion of the general plan in the Krzizhanovsky Club of Planning Staffs after only half of the 1927–8 fiscal year had passed:[1]

When I consider these two years [1926–7 and 1927–8], I must ask: Why did this optimum increase develop instead of a decline in the rate of growth of industrial production? You have said that in 1926–7 the recovery period was exhausted. But then 1927–8 showed an even greater growth. Of course cyclical factors were at work, but the fact is that the growth of output of this type without new investment, by means of enlarged output from old investment, did not cease. In a capitalist economy there can never be full utilisation [of capital] up to the technical limit. In such a society, the economic limit of utilisation is below the technical limit. But full utilisation does happen in our specific conditions. I think that this 20 per cent rate of expansion [in one year], in the face of admittedly rather mediocre attainments in new capital formation, occurred because an over-recovery utilisation of the same enterprises took place, and we can give perhaps 30 per cent for this.[2]

In other words, the recovery period must be considered as ended and the 'diminishing curve' may be expected to start operating when not the pre-war output, but the pre-war productive capacity is reached. The fact that the 'diminishing curve' failed to materialise when expected came as a complete surprise to Bazarov and everyone else, planners as well as the government and Party.

In May 1928 Gosplan issued special directions and methodological instructions for the drafting of the first Five-Year Plan. When Groman and Bazarov raised violent objections to these, Gladkov attacked them as follows ('On the History of the First Five-Year Plan', *Planovoe khozyaistvo*, No. 4, 1935, pp. 128–9):

[1] *Planovoe khozyaistvo*, No. 6, 1928, p. 153.
[2] Bazarov is unclear with regard to the additional 30 per cent growth. It seems that he meant that the full level of pre-war production may be exceeded by 30 per cent to reach the post-revolution limit of possible expansion based on full utilisation of old equipment.

Vladimir Alexandrovich Bazarov

The wreckers Groman and Bazarov in their monstrous theses, reports and speeches on perspective planning tried to prove that we need not a directive plan but an orientation based on the dynamics of the past. Bazarov insisted that 'the type and style of our national economy is determined in advance by the existing condition of our productive capabilities, their geographic distribution and the relationship of social forces which determine the road of our future economic development'. He therefore argued that to attempt to force socialisation was equivalent to discrediting socialism, because the old social forms were as yet unripe for this, and hence the new form would be artificial and would fetter productive forces. According to Groman, the supreme criterion of the plan was the growth of productive forces; and hence the perspective plan should not be subordinated to the task of development of the socialist economy, because this might lead to a standstill of production and goods turnover, to the paralysis of productive forces.[1]

It seems that the great expansionist drive then in progress prevented Bazarov from stressing the teleological method, as he may have been inclined to do somewhat earlier. Groman had never shown any such inclination.

In *Ekonomicheskoe obozrenie*, No. 6, 1928 may be found Bazarov's article 'On the Prospects of Economic and Cultural Development'. The article seems to have been closely linked with the discussions on the preparation of the Five-Year Plan in the Presidium and sections of Gosplan in May 1928. In this article, Bazarov discussed the latest available draft of the Five-Year Plan by the VSNKh, which scheduled for State industry a growth of 135 per cent in the five years from 1927–8 to 1932–3 (*op. cit.* p. 56). Bazarov calculated the total increase in ten and fifteen years at this 'dynamic' rate, and exclaimed: 'What a fascinating, enchanting perspective' (p. 58). He added that he did not altogether deny its possibility, but wanted only 'to underscore the need of gigantic organisational strides for maintaining such a dynamic tempo' (*op. cit.* p. 62). The editorial note stated that the article was published at length for discussion purposes only, and then proceeded to criticise Bazarov at length (p. 54). *Inter alia* the editors wrote:

[1] Gladkov apparently took his material from the Archives of the Presidium of Gosplan, probably about May 1928.

'It appears to us that comrade Bazarov under-estimates the advantages inherent in the Soviet system.'

The growth of State industry by 135 per cent in the five years from 1927–8 to 1932–3 was not the last and not the highest target: in the approved version of the first Five-Year Plan it was raised to 179 per cent. The unfriendly attitude of the editors toward Bazarov's article makes it understandable that the article proved to be his last publication not only in *Ekonomicheskoe obozrenie*, but in any professional journal.

THE END

At the VSNKh Valentinov, before leaving Moscow for Paris in December 1928, saw Shtern, whom death was to save from being an actor in the Trial. Shtern told him that the Mensheviks in VSNKh were in a panic because of the aggressive behaviour of Kuibyshev: 'Even Bazarov panicked, and this is reflected in the papers he wrote for Gosplan', Shtern is supposed to have said.

In the chapter devoted to Groman we have cited his speeches against Kovalevsky in the Krzhizhanovsky Club of Planning Staffs in the spring of 1928. Compared with these, Bazarov's speech at the same conference[1] was modesty itself. But the two men were very different anyway. Shtern hardly would have made his remarks on Bazarov's papers for the Gosplan on the strength of his speech in the Club of Planning Staffs. The position taken up by Bazarov in the debates in Gosplan on the Five-Year Plan in May 1928 and his article in *Ekonomicheskoe obozrenie*, published shortly after, also do not indicate a retreat. If Shtern was right that Bazarov was panicky, this attitude is likely to have developed only in the second half of 1928.[2]

---

[1] *Planovoe khozyaistvo*, No. 6, 1928, pp. 149–56.

[2] Gladkov (*Planovoe khozyaistvo*, No. 4, 1935, p. 136) writes as follows on the basis of the materials in the Gosplan archives about the discussion of the final drafts of the first Five-Year Plan in the Presidium of Gosplan on 12 February 1929. 'Osadchy declared: "I must on my conscience say that if I were told: subscribe to this variant as the basic one [i.e., the lower variant of the final draft of the first Five-Year Plan], I would say no." He [Osadchy] was seconded by Bazarov, who regarded the basic variant as unrealistic because of the shortage of skilled personnel capable of preparing a draft of a construction and fulfilling it. "If you", he declared, "undertake simultaneously a number of measures on such a gigantic scale and do not know the organisation in advance, do not have the needed cadres and do not know what to teach

Vladimir Alexandrovich Bazarov

The All-Out Drive period, which ended disastrously with the great famine of 1932–3, began in this writer's view with Stalin's article 'The year of the Great Turning Point', in *Pravda*, 7 November 1929. This date was not long after the time when the period of 'Bacchanalian planning' started. (Actually, Bacchanalian activities began about a year earlier.)[1]

The discussion on the general plan which took place in the spring of 1928 in the Club of Planning Staffs was repeated in February 1930, i.e. less than two years later.[2] What an immense difference between the two conferences as regards who spoke and what was spoken! While in 1928 some Communists, for example Vaisberg and Trakhtenberg, participated in the discussion, Groman still could take the floor twice and the Mensheviks Gukhman and Maslov, the neo-narodnik Weinstein, and A. S. Gordon, who was certainly not a Communist, could take part in the discussion.

N. A. Kovalevsky, who read the papers in the two great discussions of 1928 and 1930, was also a 'driver', although a more moderate one than those named above. Still, according to him, a rouble invested in the national economy would produce fourteen roubles after twelve years.[3] The discussion of Kovalevsky's paper in the All-Union Conference of Planning Staffs in 1930 was actually a meeting of extremists. All non-Bolsheviks disappeared from the list of speakers. In addition to Vaisberg, Rogal'sky, another sworn adversary of Groman and Bazarov, participated in the discussion,

them, you will get into utter confusion. Not only would the fulfilment of the programme be delayed and, at best, be fulfilled in seven, if not ten years, but there would be even worse results, namely such a clearly irrational waste of resources as would discredit the whole idea of industrialisation".'

The information of Valentinov obtained from Shtern would be entirely omitted in view of this quotation from Gladkov, if the printed evidence about Bazarov's behaviour in the discussion of the general plan in the spring of 1930 were not available.

[1] The first relevant articles were published by Feldman in the November and December issues of *Planovoe khozyaistvo* for 1928 and by Sabsovich in the January 1929 issue. Feldman and Sabsovich were the best-known 'drivers' or exponents of 'Bacchanalian planning', but Zolotarev may be given the doubtful honour of being included in this company. According to Feldman's maximum variant, national income was to rise in twelve years (from 1929 to 1941) by 45.9 times (implied in Feldman's table quoted on pp. 486–7 of Spulber (ed.), *op. cit.*).

[2] Paper read by N. A. Kovalevsky on 'On the Methodology of the Plan of Reconstruction'. The paper and related discussion were published in *Planovoe khozyaistvo*, No. 3, 1930, pp. 117–211.

[3] *Ibid.* p. 118.

as did Mendelson and Feldman (Sabsovich was in the audience).
To my great regret I have to state that Bazarov not only was present,
but participated in the discussion with a brief speech (*Planovoe
khozyaistvo*, No. 3, 1930, pp. 153-4). To avoid being involved, he
said: 'At the present moment I will not try to give a systematic
critique of the whole structure [of Genplan], because I am not
prepared for this.' In general, Bazarov spoke so vaguely that
Kovalevsky in his concluding remarks was able to include him
among the 9 out of 16 speakers who 'were in general agreement with
my exposition of the problem but criticised various parts of the
work' (*ibid*. p. 183). These nine included Rogal'sky and Feldman,
the arch-planner. Among the seven other speakers at the conference
were some for whom Kovalevsky did not go far enough.[1]

Bazarov, while not one of the defendants in the Menshevik trial
of 1931, is repeatedly mentioned in *Trial* as having been engaged in
the same activities as those who were tried. Among the testimony
involving Bazarov was the following: Groman 'testified' that the
counter-revolutionary group in Gosplan (it was supposed to have
existed since 1923) was headed by him and Bazarov (*Trial*, p. 36),
and that he formed from among his immediate staff as well as those
close to him in their work ('I have in mind Vladimir Alexandrovich
Bazarov', he said) a group which tried to incorporate in economic
surveys 'that very line...of influencing the economic policy of the
Soviet authorities so as to hold to the position of 1923-5.' (*Trial*,
p. 69). Groman also testified that he and Bazarov in 1926 and 1927
pursued a line sharply opposed to the policy of the Soviet authorities (*Trial*, p. 71).

According to the indictment (*Trial*, p. 17) Bazarov was one of
those who, while not a member of the 'United Bureau' (alleged
Menshevik wrecking organisation) were informed of the latter's
work and assisted in it. According to the same source, he was chairman of the programme committee of the 'United Bureau'. Accord-

[1] In addition to the open session or sessions reported in *Planovoe khozyaistvo*, No. 3,
1930, there was a closed session in which Strumilin said that by the method employed
by Kovalevsky the production of steel could be increased to four times the size of the
earth (discussion speech of A. Kon, pp. 155-6). Clearly it was forbidden to talk sense
at the open session in February 1930, while the retention of Strumilin's statement in
Kon's speech was probably an oversight.

ing to still further testimony by Groman (*Trial*, p. 26), Bazarov was a member of the committee which produced the 'Circular letters' put out in limited numbers by the 'United Bureau'. Finally Finn-Enotaevsky (*Trial*, p. 189), testified that in 1930 he was invited for dinner at Kondrat'ev's and the next day at Groman's by Bazarov. Finn-Enotaevsky believed it necessary to mention or to emphasise that Bazarov was not present at Kondrat'ev's home.

Rumour has it that a major role was intended for Bazarov in the Menshevik trial. A great Bolshevik for many years in the past, he should have repented his 'crimes' publicly. If the evidence in the cited parts of *Trial* were at all truthful, one would have to assume that he participated in the anti-Soviet activities of the 'United Bureau' but possibly not in those of the bloc of the three organisations. His activities in the 'United Bureau' also were apparently more limited than those of some others, particularly Groman and Sukhanov. However, this would hardly have played a role in the fact that he was not among the defendants in the trial. The most likely reason is that, although Bazarov seems to have shown an inclination toward compromising with Stalin's policies, the GPU did not succeed in breaking him completely enough to make him a desirable member of the trial.

Since *Trial* makes Bazarov out to be a Menshevik and the same is frequently done by Soviet and non-Soviet writers, it is useful to mention that in numerous statements in which Bazarov is mentioned by Groman, the latter avoided calling him a Menshevik. The reason is probably that adherence to Marxist dialectical materialism was probably regarded by Groman and many other Mensheviks as part of the Menshevik *credo*, and therefore Bazarov did not qualify in their eyes.

In any case, Bazarov disappeared from view around the time of the Menshevik Trial. An article in *Pravda*, 24 December 1938, 'What is Machism?', included the statement that Bazarov was sentenced in 1931 for wrecking activities. This evidently took place *in camera*, which goes to confirm that he could not be broken sufficiently to be an actor in the open trial of the Mensheviks.

A letter from the USSR in *Sotsialistichesky vestnik*, (the Menshevik journal then published in Berlin), 12 December 1931, p. 15, reported that Bazarov was in the 'isolator' at Yaroslavl. According to the *Great Soviet Encyclopedia* he died in 1937, a year in which Stalin murdered thousands, of whom Bazarov may have been one. Valentinov informed me that he had heard from some recent *émigrés* that Bazarov had been shot.

8

ABRAM MOISEEVICH
GINZBURG

Abram Moiseevich Ginzburg was another veteran revolutionary of Tsarist times. According to his own account (*Trial*, p. 396), he started his political activities in 1895 when he was 17. He spent two years in jail from 1902 to 1904, followed by exile to the Yakutsk Province. He escaped in 1905, took part in the 1905 revolution and was active politically for several years after 1905, living various times under false names (a nerve-racking existence when one's passport was a 'second soul'). From 1909 to 1921 he belonged to different legal and semi-legal organisations. During the period of the 3rd Duma (1907–12) he was again arrested, and, after spending some time in jail, was expelled from St Petersburg for life. From 1912 he lived in Kiev and for a few years wrote for *Kievskaya mysl'* (*Kiev Thought*), a democratic daily of high standing, under the pseudonym of Naumov.

He was always a Social-Democrat, and was a Menshevik after the split of the Social-Democratic Party. After the October Revolution he was deputy mayor of Kiev for about one and a half years and subsequently worked for sometime in consumer co-operatives. After the proclamation of the NEP he became deputy head of the Kiev *guberniya* planning commission.

In 1922 he joined the VSNKh, and was at once given the responsible post of deputy head of the economic division. His short periods of work as deputy mayor and in consumer co-operatives may have given him some administrative experience, but his career prior to entering VSNKh does not suggest the degree of familiarity with the economics of industry which was necessary for his new position. Reading Marx and even the more modern Hilferding, which was common among Russian Social Democrats in those days, was not quite adequate for this, yet Ginzburg soon developed into the greatest expert on industry the country then had. Such an expert on planning as V. A. Bazarov referred to him as 'one of the greatest inspirers and leaders in the work of drawing up the perspective plan of the VSNKh'.[1]

Dzerzhinsky, the former head of the GPU, who was head of the VSNKh for a short period till his death in 1926, on one occasion expressed his pride in having Abram Ginzburg on his staff, along with three other Mensheviks.[2] In spite of the condemnation of his Five-Year Plan by Kuibyshev (Dzerzhinsky's successor) in 1927, Ginzburg retained considerable prestige. On 25–28 April 1929, i.e. a considerable time after the abolition of the NEP, when the storm-clouds were already heavy, an all-Russian Conference on the economics of industry took place. Ginzburg was a member of the presidium representing the Plekhanov Institute and presented the principal paper to the Conference.[3] Even later, in 1930, the *Great Soviet Encyclopedia* (Vol. 17, p. 44) declared his two-volume work on the economics of industry to be 'the only fundamental text on the economics of industry in the Russian language'.

On 18 March 1924, Ginzburg read a report to a conference of senior economic workers on 'The Problem of Labour Productivity and Wages'. The main section of the report was published in *Sotsialsticheskoe khozyaistvo*, No. 2, 1924, pp. 62–106. The topic was a crucial one. The output per head in industry was amazingly small in those years. According to Gosplan it was 38 per cent below the pre-war level, small as that was, in 1922–3, and 31.3 per cent below pre-war in the first half of 1923–4 (presumably in State industry) (*op. cit.* p. 69). As major reasons for this were cited (*op. cit.* p. 78): (*a*) Deterioration of equipment, (*b*) Deterioration of the quality of raw materials, (*c*) Decrease in utilisation of enterprises, (*d*) Profusion of unprofitable subsidiary enterprises, (*e*) Inflation of the number of subsidiary workers.

While wages were low, they were still higher than pre-war relative to output, with considerable variation from industry to industry (*op. cit.* p. 74). The situation in two important branches of industry in 1923–4 was approximately as follows (in per cent of 1913):

[1] Bazarov, 'On Our Economic Perspectives and Perspective Plans', *Planovoe khozyaistvo*, No. 3, 1927, p. 31.
[2] Valentinov, *op. cit.* p. 224. The other three Mensheviks were A. L. Sokolovsky, L. B. Kafengaus and Valentinov himself.
[3] *Sotsialisticheskoe khozyaistvo*, No. 4, 1929, pp. 233 ff.

	Metallurgy	Engineering
Labour productivity	45	37
Wage earnings	67	75

The task ahead was thus formidable.

In 1926–7 Ginzburg was deputy head of the industrial planning division (*Promplan*) of the VSNKh and chairman of a special commission for the preparation of its Five-Year Plan for industry. After the completion of the Five-Year Plan in the summer of 1927, Ginzburg made a prolonged trip to the USA. From March 1928 he continued as deputy chairman of the economic planning division of the VSNKh (but without administrative functions) and was also head of the Conjuncture Bureau of the same organisation.

In April 1929 he was deputy chairman of the Institute of Industrial Economic Research at the VSNKh (*Trial*, p. 295) – obviously an even less active role. At the time of the trial he was 52 years old, and considering the long years in prison and exile, cannot have been in his prime. He seems indeed to have lost a great deal of his courage long before the trial.[1] A spell of almost six months in jail prior to the trial (he was arrested on 16 September 1930 – *Trial*, p. 323), under conditions which will probably remain unknown for ever, was quite sufficient to break his spirit and turn him into a good performer at the trial. I am happy to say, however, that a search in literature of that time did not disclose any compromising statements in print by Ginzburg prior to the trial.

As already stated, the VSNKh Five-Year Plan for industry was completed in the early summer of 1927, i.e. almost four years before the trial. The Five-Year Plan was already history at the time when the trial took place; yet the preparation of the Five-Year Plan for industry by Ginzburg was the only item in the indictment against him which made any sense at all. However, the only truth in the accusation was that a Five-Year Plan was prepared and that this was done under the direction of Abram Ginzburg. There is no trace of anything criminal in the Five-Year Plan. Whatever errors

---

[1] I have heard on good authority that in his youth he transported the whole equipment of the printing office for the *Yuzhny rabochii* (*Southern Worker*) (illegal of course), tied to his body, from one city to another.

were in it, they were a trifle as compared with those in official plans. The same is, of course, true of similar charges against the other defendants.

For reasons stated, the Ginzburg Five-Year Plan is the only item discussed below in this chapter.

THE GINZBURG DRAFT FOR THE FIVE-YEAR PLAN

The Five-Year Plan in question was the Five-Year Plan for industry, to operate in the years 1927–8 to 1931–2, and published in VSNKh, *Materialy*. The commission for the preparation of the Five-Year Plan was set up in September 1926, and its final decisions were taken in May and the first half of June 1927 (*Materialy*, p. 9). In addition to Ginzburg, more than twenty persons are named in the volume as members of the commission, chief participants in the work or both. The three most prominent were probably A. L. Sokolovsky, V. V. Sher and A. B. Shtern. The first two of these later figured as defendants in the trial: Shtern was saved from this by his death. Among the other participants were a few more Mensheviks who were not in the trial.

The work on the Five-Year Plan was facilitated by that of the OSVOK (Special Conference on the Restoration of Fixed Capital) at the VSNKh, which operated in 1925 and produced many volumes on individual industries. On the basis of this work, a committee headed by Ginzburg worked out a very rough draft of the five-year plan for industry in the period 1 October 1925 to 1 October 1930. This draft soon became obsolete.

The new commission working on the Five-Year Plan did not have the final data for 1926–7, which turned out somewhat more favourable than expected as regards the volume of industrial production, but much less favourable with regard to labour productivity, production costs and prices. But the Bolsheviks saw only the data for the volume of output, and this brought about a soaring of their hopes for future industrial growth. V. V. Kuibyshev, who acquired a bad reputation as head of VSNKh, especially during the 'all-out drive' period which was soon to come, declared in the preface to the Five-Year Plan (*Materialy*, pp. 3–4):

Abram Moiseevich Ginzburg

The experience of 1926–7...shows with absolute clarity the need to make important corrections in the basic features of the five-year plan....

Everything compels us not to consider the present work as final but to subject it to a revision on the basis of the experience which the proletarian state made during this year [1926–7].

Hence we consider it necessary, in publishing this work as *Materialy*, to draw the widest possible attention to the task of preparing a five-year plan of development of industry, and simultaneously undertake the work of revision of the *Materialy*, which are of immense value for the clarification of the methods of preparing a plan and the dynamics of development of its individual components in their mutual interdependence.

In other words, a first-class funeral! A full-scale draft was titled simply *Materialy*, and this word was even included in the title of the Five-Year Plan. Although Ginzburg's work was thus killed before it was fully born, the Five-Year Plan, as already stated, brought him a great deal of recognition, and the draft was frequently referred to not as *Materialy*, but as the 'Ginzburg Five-Year Plan'.[1]

The Ginzburg draft of the Five-Year Plan is a product of which one might be proud. It consisted of 740 large, closely printed pages. Of this total, 340 pages were taken up by the table section. The past was covered by preliminary estimates for 1926–7, but in some cases there were also data for 1925–6 and 1913. The future in general was dealt with by annual estimates from 1927–8 to 1931–2. Considering the wretched state of statistics at the outbreak of the Revolution, the mass of material presented is astounding. The basic indicators of the Five-Year Plan for large-scale industry planned by the VSNKh alone occupy 10 pages. Particular stress was laid on furnishing, along with data on production, those on distribution and consumption, the latter being divided into productive and personal. Thirteen large groups of industries were distinguished, the last of which (group 13, food) comprised twelve industries. *Per capita* consumption of industrial goods was given for more than 20 of them.[2]

---

[1] See for example the important article by L. M. Sabsovich in *Planovoe khozyaistvo*, No. 1, 1929, Tables 2 and 6.

[2] Considerable credit for the data on the performance of industry in and before the base year goes to L. B. Kafengauz, another Menshevik, who was in charge of statistics in the VSNKh and whom I had the honour of knowing also.

The section devoted to agricultural statistics gave detailed balances for about twenty raw materials of agricultural origin, showing acreage, yield per hectare, gross production, utilisation by producers, marketable output, reserves held by industry at the beginning and the end of the Five-Year Plan period, imports and exports and utilisation (total, state, co-operative and private).

As will be seen, the balancing method, so forcefully advocated by Groman, was extensively used. Ginzburg made it perfectly clear that the use of the balancing method would have been general but for circumstances beyond the commission's control. He wrote:[1]

Unfortunately the state of statistical and accounting data on the economy is such as to exclude all possibility of preparing reliable balances. For many components of the national economy we do not have exact data, for example on small-scale [mostly cottage] industry; on the numbers and earnings of transient workers; on the size of private procurements etc., and even on the real harvest of grain. Under such conditions it is impossible to prepare balances of demand and supplies. We do not even have unimpeachable data on the output of industry and its value. Estimates differ even as regards the output of the State sector, not to speak of the private and co-operative sectors. The arbitrariness of statistical calculations with computation of absolutely abstract averages for an immense number of very different enterprises, with a multitude of extrapolations and assumptions, makes it necessary to distinguish between statistical balances and economic interconnections in the true sense of the word. Nevertheless, failing better means of checking the results obtained, it is necessary to make use of the balances based on statistical data.

Space prevents our describing in greater detail the valuable material in the Ginzburg Five-Year Plan, to which even Kuibyshev assigned immense significance for the preparation of the future Five-Year Plan. So let us turn to the features on account of which the Five-Year Plan was condemned in 1927, and which made Ginzburg and two of his colleagues actors in the show trial of March 1931.

[1] *Materialy*, p. 12. It is natural to assume that the general report, called 'explanatory note' (pp. 9–72), was written by the chairman of the commission. In any case, Ginzburg's publications in journals leave no doubt on this score.

Abram Moiseevich Ginzburg

Targets for output

As regards the targets of the Ginzburg Five-Year Plan and its other components, it cannot be over-emphasised that any defects in the draft plan cannot be treated as certain, and whatever errors may be found in it were trifles compared with the enormous errors in setting the targets in the drafts of the Five-Year Plans produced later, especially the targets of the last draft of the Five-Year Plan and the subsequent boosting of these by decisions of the Party and Government down to as late as March 1931.

The Ginzburg draft envisaged for 1931–2 an output of the industry controlled by the VSNKh which was 82.1 per cent higher than the estimate for 1926–7.[1] According to this Five-Year Plan, total industry and large-scale industry were to grow, until 1931–2 inclusive, by 73 per cent and 78.7 per cent respectively.[2] The output of small-scale industry, without the value of customers' materials, milling and other non-planned branches, was to rise by 1931–2 by 29.2 per cent.[3]

The Ginzburg draft was down-graded to just *Materialy*, as explained above. The first revision of it was ready at the end of 1927. For industry controlled by the VSNKh the new target involved a rise by 108 per cent in 1931–2 over the base year 1926–7. But this was only a cautious start. The great madness, the feeling that the sky was the limit, was only just beginning: the orgy began in earnest in 1928. In August 1928 the VSNKh already believed that the State industry under its control could raise its output by 121.0 per cent in the five years from 1927–8 to 1932–3.[4] Then in the VSNKh Control Figures accepted at the end of 1928 the figure for the percentage rise in 5 years was boosted to 167.7 per cent – more than double the rise scheduled by the original Ginzburg Five-Year Plan. The target of the optimum variant for the state industry controlled by the VSNKh, which had been approved as the target of the Five-Year Plan, turned out even higher (179.2 per cent for the period

---

[1] *Materialy*, p. 696.   [2] *Ibid.* pp. 17 and 698.
[3] *Ibid.* p. 698. The source speaks of 'small-scale and *kustarny* out-put'.
[4] N.B. this period is one year later than that of the original draft. Thus the Party was setting a target for the growth of industrial output more than twice as high as the reasonable ones.

1927-8 to 1932-3, as against 167.7 per cent for the same period in the VSNKh Control Figures of the end of 1928).

As mentioned in Chapter 3, there were further increases of the target figures at the XVI Party Congress in June–July 1930, while the VI Congress of Soviets of March 1931 demanded that the Five-Year Plan targets for industry be fulfilled in four years and those for the 'basic and decisive industries' in three.

The continuation of the raising of the Five-Year Plan targets into 1930 and especially into 1931, when the disorganisation of the economy had already reached high proportions and targets even one-half as high as the new ones were very unlikely to be reached, testified to the extreme disorganisation of planning. Yet those setting these absurd targets were extolled while the cool-headed Ginzburg was prosecuted.

It seems to be of considerable significance that the Gosplan draft of the Five-Year Plan, announced in April 1927, i.e. very shortly before the Ginzburg draft, scheduled for large-scale industry an increase, in the 5 years from 1925–6 to 1930–1, of 79.5 per cent,[1] as against 82.1 per cent in the Ginzburg draft for a somewhat later period, 1926–7 to 1931–2, which *ceteris paribus* could be expected to show a smaller rate of growth than Ginzburg's plan for the period 1925–6 to 1930–1. Yet nobody accused S. G. Strumilin, the communist responsible for Gosplan's draft, of sabotage.

Ginzburg certainly would have revised his Five-Year Plan if given a chance. As already mentioned, his commission did not possess the final results on the output of industry in 1926–7, which turned out somewhat larger than expected. This unexpected development was due, possibly entirely, to the fact that the Ginzburg draft was fully based on the idea of the diminishing growth rate. Ginzburg would have arrived at higher targets if he had acted along the lines laid down, for example, in the corresponding portion of Bazarov's speech at the meeting of the Krzhizhanovsky Club of Planning Staffs on the general plan in the spring of 1928.

Bazarov certainly wanted to go as high as possible. But accept-

[1] *Perspektivy*, table section, p. 17. The draft was worked out under S. G. Strumilin and neither Groman nor Bazarov were allowed any hand in it. The chief participants are listed in the source.

ance of his suggestions would hardly have led to a boost of the Five-Year Plan target for industry controlled by the VSNKh, greater than the first raising of the target from 79.5 per cent (Strumilin) or 82.1 per cent (Ginzburg) to 108 per cent.

Ginzburg's text was completed at a time when the idea of the 'diminishing curve' was generally accepted. It was thus finally based on the idea of the 'diminishing curve', as was Strumilin's Five-Year Plan worked out at about the same time. Starting from 16.3 per cent in 1927–8, the annual rate of growth in the Ginzburg Five-Year Plan showed a decline to 10.0 per cent as the target for 1931–2. The Control Figures of the VSNKh released at the end of 1927, the first revision of the Ginzburg draft, were still fully based on the principle described: the rate of growth of industrial output was expected to decline from 18.1 per cent in 1927–8 to 12.8 per cent in 1931–2.

As was the case with the Gosplan draft, prepared under Strumilin and completed in the spring of 1927, nobody in the VSNKh was blamed because the targets for industrial output in the VSNKh Control Figures, completed at the end of 1927, were based on the idea of the 'diminishing curve'. Then, however, some miraculous powers of the planned socialist economy were discovered which exempted it from being subject to the 'diminishing curve'. This discovery was for the first time reflected in the VSNKh draft of the Five-Year Plan of August 1928, but only to the extent that the annual rates of growth in the Five-Year Plan, rather than declining as previously planned, remained unchanged for three years in succession, from 1929–30 to 1931–2. But the 'diminishing curve' was still strongly pronounced in the scheduled rate of growth of 14.4 per cent in 1932–3 as against 19.7 per cent in 1928–9.

In only a few months longer, by the end of 1928, this arrangement was fully eliminated. The wave of madness was swelling rapidly. The last two years of the Five-Year Plan in the Control Figures of the VSNKh at the end of 1928 and in the final draft of the Five-Year Plan already showed higher rates of growth than those of the initial year of the Five-Year Plan period. The rate of growth provided in the final draft of the Five-Year Plan for the last year of the period was no less than 2.5 times as large as that in the Ginzburg version, and the situation was the same if the Gosplan text accepted in the spring of 1927 were taken instead of Ginzburg's. Indeed, the annual rate of growth of large-scale industry, which, according to the Ginzburg project or the Gosplan Five-Year Plan in the version accepted in the spring of 1927, was to decline during the operation of the Five-Year Plan by one-third or somewhat more, had to more than double according to the final draft of the Five-Year Plan or the Control Figures of the VSNKh approved at the end of 1928.

Fulfilment of output targets

The rates by which output fell short of the ultimately accepted Five-Year Plan targets were discussed in Chapter 3 above, where it was shown that the targets in the final drafts of the VSNKh Control Figures and the final draft of the Five-Year Plan were missed by immense margins. How easy it would have been to accuse the authors of those drafts of deliberately setting targets which had not the slightest chance of fulfilment, and so undermining planning and in general sabotaging the national economy. We for our part do not go so far, seeing in those targets only absurdity or rather madness.

Another point to be made is this: for many years now over-fulfilment of targets has occurred quite regularly, and is always highly praised. At the end of 1964 the exceeding of targets was even declared inseparable from Soviet planning as A. N. Kosygin's report on the 1965 plan testifies. Echoing him, A. Korobov, Deputy President of the USSR Gosplan, wrote in *Planovoe khozyaistvo*, No. 1, 1965, p. 17: 'In our country we have a good tradition – to overfulfil our targets.' Regular over-fulfilment means of course that the targets tend to be underestimates – yet Ginzburg's action in 'deliberately' setting targets too low was branded as a crime.

The data in Chapter 3 show that the target of the Ginzburg Five-Year Plan for industrial output was approximately reached as regards the industry controlled by the VSNKh, but definitely not as regards total output. The difference is of course due to the catastrophic decline in the output of small-scale industry. Even if, given better all-round conditions than actually existed, the industry controlled by the VSNKh could have grown during the Ginzburg Plan draft period by more than 82.1 per cent, the excess could hardly have been large. Still more important, industrial output (total industry) actually increased by only about 45 per cent during the official plan period from 1927–8 to 1932, or of at most 55 per cent in the period from 1927–8 to 1933 (the year 1933 need not be included on the basis of official pronouncements). These fulfilment figures were obviously lower than Ginzburg's targets.

The exact rate of growth of industrial production during the whole period for which the Ginzburg draft of the Five-Year Plan was drafted is not the only thing to be considered. It is important that the Ginzburg Five-Year Plan, in its original form or with the needed adjustments for the final 1926–7 figures, as well as for the factor emphasised by Bazarov, was based on the expectation of a healthy growth of the economy, whereas in fact the development during the Five-Year Plan period was very unhealthy and ended in a catastrophe.

The 'diminishing curve', for the idea of which Ginzburg, together with Groman, Bazarov and others, was furiously attacked in post-NEP years, operated to a greater extent than he foresaw. The actual decline of the rate of growth was immensely stronger than according to the idea of the 'diminishing curve'. More specifically, rather than declining by about 40 per cent in five years as scheduled by the Ginzburg Five-Year Plan, the annual rate of industrial growth, as calculated from Hodgman's figures, went down almost fivefold in only four and a quarter years.[1] Actually the situation was even worse. The Five-Year Plan scheduled for the year 1932–3 a rate of growth for the industry controlled by the VSNKh of 25.2 per cent. Taking into account a serious deterioration in the quality of the goods produced, which is not adequately reflected in the official price statistics, the year 1932–3 probably did not witness any increase in industrial output at all, and there may even have been a decline.[2]

---

[1] Hodgman, *Soviet Industrial Production*, p. 73.
[2] According to Raymond Powell in Bergson and Kuznets (eds.), *Economic Trends*, p. 187, the value added in the whole of industry declined in 1933 by 2 per cent at 1928 prices and by 5 per cent at 1937 prices. Powell's calculation, like any other,

The rates of growth during parts of the period, its beginning, end, and the years in between, showed more or less significant departures from those foreseen in the various drafts of the Five-Year Plan. At the beginning of the period for which the Ginzburg Five-Year Plan was drafted, i.e. in the year 1927–8, the rate of growth of large-scale industry increased considerably as compared with 1926–7, while everybody, Ginzburg included, expected a slight decline in this rate.[1] The explanation offered by Bazarov in 1928 (see Chapter 7), viz. that the recovery of industrial output must be considered to have ended with the attainment of the pre-war level not of output but of production capacity, would in itself explain only the absence of a decline in the rate of growth, not an increase. The quotation from Bazarov in the chapter devoted to him also mentions, it is true, conjunctural factors which operated in the same direction as the factor referred to above; but unfortunately he did not specify which these were. According to him, the fact that the rise in the rate of growth in output of the State industry was larger in 1927–8 than 1926–7 (instead of remaining unchanged) was presumably due to the efforts toward expansion of output made in disregard of the so-called qualitative factors (labour productivity, production costs etc.). Those intensive efforts could have been successful because the economy was still in a fairly healthy condition.

The statistical material for the years after 1927–8 is doubtful. The growth of output of the industry controlled by the VSNKh is likely to have exceeded, perhaps substantially, Ginzburg's targets in 1928–9 and 1929–30. To a smaller extent the same may have been true for industry as a whole. In 1931 even the industry controlled by the VSNKh may have grown less than Ginzburg's target. With much greater certainty the same can be assumed for industry as a whole. The disastrous situation in the last year of the Five-Year Plan has already been discussed. Ginzburg's target for this year of course turned out to be much too optimistic.

could not possibly have considered in full the immense deterioration in the quality of industrial production in those years.

[1] The rate of growth of large-scale industrial output increased in 1927–8 by 23.5 per cent after it had grown by 18.1 per cent in 1926–7: see *Kontrol'nye tsifry na 1929/30g.* pp. 422–3.

Table 12. *Output per man in state industry as planned and
realised, yearly from 1926–7 to 1932–3*

| | Plan | | Fulfilment |
Year	Ginzburg's FYP[a]	1st FYP[b]	(Hodgman)[c]
1926–7	11.6 (expected fulfiment)	—	—
1927–8	10.9	—	—
1928–9	8.5	16.1	7
1929–30	8.7	14.9	−4
1930–1	7.7	15.0	−3
1931–2	7.0	16.1	−8
1932–3	—	17.3	12.6[d]

SOURCES: [a] See *Materialy*, pp. 542–3.
    [b] First Five-Year Plan, text, Vol. II, part 1, pp. 252–3, and II, part 2, pp. 206–7.
    [c] Hodgman, *Soviet Industrial Production*, p. 113. Hodgman's coverage is somewhat wider than State industry, but this hardly affects comparability in any significant way.
    [d] Calendar year 1933.

Other important factors

The targets for industrial output contained in the 740-page volume of the Ginzburg draft, which Soviet sources describe as much too low, were based on assumptions and conditions which fell considerably short even of those assumed by the Ginzburg targets.

The quality of the goods produced by industry fell considerably after the World War. In 1926–7 it was still inferior to pre-war, and all Five-Year Plans prepared at that time provided for a great improvement. In fact, the quality of the industrial goods produced deteriorated immensely during the period for which the Ginzburg Five-Year Plan was drawn up. In 1932 journals and even government documents were printed on wrapping paper. This deterioration was reflected, if at all, only very inadequately in prices used to calculate output, and consequently also in output statistics.

There was also the crucial problem of labour productivity. Ginzburg was abused in the trial for having assumed too modest a rise in output per man – 'only' about 50 per cent in 5 years.[1] The Stalin régime could not think in such petty terms; the first Five-

[1] *Materialy*, pp. 408–9.

Year Plan, as approved, scheduled for State industry an increase in *per capita* output of no less than 135 per cent in 5 years. The actual outcome is shown, together with the targets, in Table 12.

Hodgman's calculations imply an 8 per cent decline in output per head from 1927–8 to 1932. The failure to reach the targets for labour productivity was obviously huge, both in itself and as compared with the inexactness, if any, in Ginzburg's estimates for industrial output.

It is significant that labour productivity had already begun to decline in 1929–30. The data in *Narodnoe khozyaistvo, 1932*, p. 16, on productivity per head in physical terms, enable us to follow developments in greater detail. These data, which are certainly too favourable, show that a certain increase in labour productivity took place as late as the first quarter of 1930, which apparently marked the culmination of many years' development. Labour productivity remained at that level in the second quarter of 1930 and then started its prolonged decline. Ginzburg's arrest took place very soon afterwards, on 16 September 1930.[1] The fact that an absolute decline occurred in output per man instead of a projected growth of over 20 per cent per year was a good reason indeed for holding a show trial of those who, years ahead, had warned of the likelihood of this very danger.

The immense errors of official planners with respect to the growth in labour productivity were necessarily accompanied by corresponding errors in estimates of numbers of workers employed. The labour force in the State industry from 1927–8 to 1932–3 was to increase by 1,000,000, or 32.8 per cent, according to the final draft of the Five-Year Plan (II, part 2, pp. 206–7). The miscalculation was terrific: in only four and a quarter years from 1927–8 to 1932, the labour force in large-scale industry grew by 3.3 million.[2] In one single year, 1931, the very year of the trial, labour in large-scale industry jumped by 1.2 million, more than was provided in the last draft of the Five-Year Plan for all five years of the plan period and nearly three times as much as was scheduled for five years by the Ginzburg draft of the Plan. The labour force rose to 0.9 million and 1 million respectively in 1930 and 1932. What in fact amounted to

[1] *Trial*, p. 323.   [2] *Sotsialisticheskoe stroitel'stvo*, Moscow, 1935, p. 476.

a near catastrophe was soon to be hailed as evidence of fulfilment of the targets of the first Five-Year Plan. Again, as compared with the error of these 'plan fulfilments', the inaccuracies in Ginzburg's targets for industrial production were negligible. Heavy mortality due to poor food and starvation, and greatly reduced birth rates due to the same causes, added to the immense failure of the targets for increase in labour productivity. Those were the means by which Stalin solved the problem, which had seemed insoluble in the mid-twenties – the problem of getting rid of the great surplus of the farm population. The Mensheviks engaged in planning work in the mid-twenties were certainly guilty of not having been in sympathy with such a solution.

It was generally recognised at the time when the Ginzburg plan was prepared that the high production costs of state industry were a great obstacle to economic progress. The 'wrecker' Ginzburg wanted a reduction in production costs of that part of industry planned by the VSNKh of 16.5 per cent in five years (*Materialy*, p. 648). The 'heroes' who produced the final Five-Year Plan, heroes in paper-work and hurrah-shouting, were of course not satisfied with so 'modest' a figure. According to them production costs in industry were to decline by 35 per cent (*Materialy*, p. 85).

Even Stalin did not dare to claim fulfilment of the target of the last draft of the Five-Year Plan as regards reduction in production costs. Yet he claimed that the gains were large. Then, on the occasion of the 40-year celebration of the Revolution, when it seemed not to matter much any more, the information was slipped in that the figures for production costs, officially trumpeted for twenty-five years, were actually 'improved' by neglecting the increase in nominal wages.[1] The belatedly revised figure indicated, instead of a drastic cut in production costs from 1928 to 1932, their increase by 2.3 per cent, and with this little or no consideration of the immense deterioration in the quality of output.[2]

---

[1] *Dostizheniya Sovetskoi vlasti za 40 let v tsifrakh, statistichesky sbornik* (The achievements of Soviet power during the last 40 years in figures; a statistical compendium), Moscow, 1957, p. 55, footnote. Nominal wages actually doubled from 1928 to 1932.
[2] According to Malafeev (p. 406) production costs of comparable marketable industrial production declined by 5.2 per cent and 6.9 per cent in 1928–9 and 1929–30 respectively, but then rose by 6.8 per cent and 8.1 per cent in 1931 and 1932.

The Ginzburg Five-Year Plan was based on the assumption that wholesale prices of the goods produced by the industry controlled by the VSNKh would decline by 17.4 per cent.[1] Not satisfied with this, the last draft of the Five-Year Plan (*Materialy*, I, p. 135) called for a cut of 24 per cent, also in five years but starting one year later in respect of wholesale prices of the State industry. According to Malafeev (*op. cit.* p. 400) these prices increased by 26.9 per cent from 1 August 1928 to 1 April 1932.

Finally, wages. Gosplan's Five-Year Plan, approved in April 1927 (*Perspektivy*, etc., p. 12), provided for an increase of 33 per cent in nominal industrial wages, or 50 per cent in real terms. Real incomes of a large proportion of the urban population were scheduled by the Five-Year Plan to rise by 37.5 per cent. To make this somewhat unrealistic target possible, it was believed necessary to have a substantial decline (at least 17 per cent) in prices of industrial goods, with the prices of farm products fully maintained (*ibid.* p. 13).

The Ginzburg Plan draft, more cautious with regard to wages than the Gosplan Five-Year Plan (*op. cit.* p. 68), scheduled an increase of nominal wages in the industry controlled by the VSNKh of 20 per cent from 1926–7 to 1931–2,[2] while real wages were to rise by 29 per cent. What a shame, what treason: a rise in real wages, for the victors of the Revolution, of only 29 per cent in five years! The final draft of the Five-Year Plan scheduled a rise of 109.2 per cent in real wages in large-scale industry during the period from 1927–8 to 1932–3.[3]

But what was the reality? A rough calculation indicates that there was a decline of about 50 per cent from 1928 to 1932.[4] The approved

[1] *Materialy*, p. 406.   [2] Ibid. pp. 406–7.
[3] Five-Year Plan text, Vol. II, part 2, p. 190.
[4] See this writer's *The Soviet 1956 Statistical Handbook : a Commentary*. East Lansing, 1957, p. 41. Data by Malafeev indicate the possibility of a somewhat smaller decline than this, but he avoids supplying data on real wages in the years analysed here, and whatever other evidence is supplied pertaining to incomes is frightening. The annual nominal wage of hired labour in 1928 was somewhat above 700 roubles (*Kontrol'nye tsifry na 1929–30g*. p. 489). For 1932 Malafeev (p. 407) gives the nominal wage of workers and employees at 1,427 roubles. The data are supplied in one figure. Whether all wage-earners considered for 1928 were included is uncertain. The index of prices in state and co-operative trade stood, according to Malafeev (p. 407), at 255 in 1932 (1928 = 100). The data imply a decline in real wages of almost 30 per cent. This percentage would be much higher if the exorbitant rise in the prices in private markets were considered.

target of the Five-Year Plan for real wages was not fulfilled even as to one-third.[1] The forecast of the Ginzburg Plan draft fared better, but only a little better. Nobody can of course accuse Ginzburg in his Five-Year Plan of unjustified optimism, for he was guilty only of very moderate optimism in this respect. But there would have been much more reason to condemn him for excessive optimism than for the pessimism of which he was in fact accused and for which he was condemned, viz. failure to realise 'the immense possibilities present in the planned socialist economy'.

CONCLUSION

The Ginzburg draft had been prepared in the expectation of a healthy development (so far as such a thing was possible under Soviet conditions). Any adjustments in the Ginzburg draft of the Plan required to take account of modified assumptions or later data could easily have been made. Not all such changes would necessarily have led to raising the targets. In fact, in the first years of the five-year period there were moderately high rates of growth in the volume of industrial production, accompanied however by immense failures in the other indicators for industry (labour productivity, quality of output, size of labour force, production costs, wages, etc.).

Before the five-year period was over, even the volume of industrial output completely stopped growing, and in 1932–3 it was probably even declining. The other indicators of industrial production showed failures of near-catastrophic proportions.

The relevant part of the trial can be dealt with briefly. Of the principal indicators for industry in the Ginzburg Plan draft, only the targets for growth in gross output were featured (*Trial*, p. 296). The fact that targets for labour productivity and production costs, on which Ginzburg's targets for the industrial output had been based, were missed by immense margins was passed over in silence.

What then was Ginzburg's crime? He 'confessed' to having committed for wrecking purposes actions which he actually took in the country's best interests as he understood them. The authorities

[1] One should not in fact speak of fulfilment at all, since immense failures are involved.

needed a scapegoat because they could not attain what they promised and, even more likely, foresaw that they were heading towards disaster. Indeed, starvation rather than a doubling of real wages was in store for industrial workers. Actually, of course, Ginzburg did a very good job for that early time. It was not his fault that even his targets, allegedly set deliberately too low, were missed by immense margins, except for industrial output, which was missed only moderately. (But even this moderateness was only possible because the other targets were missed greatly.)

It is sad to have to record that Ginzburg was forced to give the names of fifteen persons as alleged conspirators (*Trial*, p. 34), although most of them were guilty only of being his co-workers in preparing the Five-Year Plan. This is clear from the following tabulation:

Named by Ginzburg as conspirators	Collaborators in Ginzburg draft of FYP[a]
1. Abramovich, S. D.	xx
2. Arkus, Ya. S.	no
3. Belotsvetov, V. A.	no
4. Galperin, M. B.	no
5. Grinzer, M.	xx
6. Dubovikov, F. G.	xx
7. Kukol-Kraevsky, S. A.	xx
8. Lavrov, V. I.	xx
9. Rabinovich, A. I.	x
10. Rabinovich, K. I.	xx
11. Sokolovsky, A. L.	xx
12. Uritsky, M.	no
13. Chernobaev, N. G.	xx
14. Shein, S. D.	no
15. Shtern, A. B.	xx

SOURCES: [a] xx indicates a member of the special commission preparing the Five-Year Plan.

x indicates a person who was mentioned in *Materialy* as chief participant in the preparation of the Five-Year Plan without being a member of the special commission.

Of the fifteen persons mentioned by Ginzburg, nine were members of the commission preparing the Five-Year Plan and one was a chief participant in the preparation without having been a member of the commission. These mentioned by Ginzburg in *Trial* and not listed in *Materialy* as chief participants may have been participants in less prominent positions. There is in *Trial* some confusion with regard to the initials of two persons.

Of the persons named above, Ginzburg designated five (in addition to himself) as Mensheviks: Grinzer, K. I. Rabinovich, A. I. Rabinovich, Sokolovsky and Shtern.

9

NIKOLAI DMITRIEVICH KONDRAT'EV[1]

The brilliant career of Nikolai Dmitrievich Kondrat'ev was very brief. He was born in 1892. Our paths crossed in 1916 and 1917. In 1916 he was working in the economic section of the Union of Zemstvos (headed by Chayanov). After the February Revolution, when only 25 years old, he was already Deputy Minister of Food responsible for providing the peasants with industrial consumer goods. In 1919 he began his famous work on long cycles (he himself spoke of waves rather than cycles), which has become an important part of the world's economic literature. He was jailed in 1930 and was not heard of again after the Menshevik trial of March 1931, in which he appeared as a key witness. He was then only 39 years old.

Although, outside the USSR, Kondrat'ev is known mainly for his work on long cycles, this played only a minor role, if any, in establishing the important position which he occupied in the eyes not only of his friends and well-wishers, but probably even more in the eyes of his deadly enemies in the USSR. This was established by his contribution to problems of domestic economy, especially agriculture, and, possibly most important, his great ability in organising research and defending its findings before such institutions as Gosplan and Narkomzem. It seems beyond doubt that just as Groman was the leader of the Mensheviks (Bazarov did not rank very far below him), Kondrat'ev was the leader of the neo-narodniks.

KONDRAT'EV AS A PUPIL OF TUGAN-BARANOVSKY[2]

Kondrat'ev's meteoric rise was probably due in considerable measure to the fact that he was privileged to be one of the 'closest' (his own expression) pupils of Professor M. I. Tugan-Baranovsky.

---

[1] In the scholarly connection for which he is best-known, that of the trade cycle, Kondrat'ev is usually written Kondratieff.

[2] This section was written with the assistance of Dr George Garvy. See also the latter's biographical article on Kondrat'ev in the *International Encyclopedia of the Social Sciences* (New York, 1968, Vol. VIII, pp. 443-4).

Nikolai Dmitrievich Kondrat'ev

In this writer's opinion, Tugan-Baranovsky was the greatest Russian economist of all time. Kondrat'ev recalled his connection with him in a pamphlet published in Petrograd in 1923 to commemorate the professor's death in 1919. Nineteen twenty-three was probably the latest date when, even with the greatest courage and restraint, anything good could have been published in the USSR on Tugan-Baranovsky, who had been a minister in Petlura's rightist Ukrainian government which fought the Bolshevik régime. (Tugan-Baranovsky was not the only genuine democrat whom the Bolsheviks pushed into the arms of reaction.)

Kondrat'ev's pamphlet was written with the greatest appreciation and love. He was, of course, unable to state his real attitude toward Tugan-Baranovsky's activities in the Ukraine, and he skirted this subject in his concluding words as follows:[1]

Everything short-lived will die and be covered with the ashes of oblivion. But ever more brilliantly will burn the sparks of real...inspiration, creativeness and talent of which Tugan-Baranovsky's life was so full. Ever more shall we be inspired by the scientific and ideological inheritance which he has left to future generations. He himself is dead, but his memory and spiritual influence will not die.

This pamphlet on Tugan-Baranovsky was dug up when the Bolsheviks made up their indictment of Kondrat'ev. He was viciously attacked for it *inter alia* in *Kondrat'evshchina*, the collection of reports and speeches delivered to the Agrarian Institute of the Communist Party on 1 October 1930. After quoting Kondrat'ev's statement cited above, a certain Uzhansky declared (p. 30): 'Short-lived – such indeed were the activities of Tugan-Baranovsky against the country of the Soviets. I tell you, Mr Kondrat'ev, the works of Tugan-Baranovsky and his faithful pupils, the Kondrat'evites, will soon be forgotten. But it will never be forgotten that Tugan-Baranovsky and Kondrat'ev were on the wrong side of the barricade in the class struggle.'

The above passage demonstrates the confused, indeed crazy conditions in the USSR in 1930, when the Bolsheviks were campaigning to create a socialist industrial state in two or three years. The views expressed in *Kondrat'evshchina* turned out in any case

[1] Here cited from *Kondrat'evshchina*, p. 36.

to be totally wrong. The works of both Tugan-Baranovsky and Kondrat'ev are part of world economic literature: Tugan-Baranovsky is known mainly for his analysis of business cycles,[1] Kondrat'ev for his 'long cycle'. Now, almost half a century after Tugan-Baranovsky's death, there is again considerable interest in him and specifically his monetary theory.[2]

THE THEORY OF LONG CYCLES

Kondrat'ev described as follows the history of this theory of long cycles:

I arrived at the hypothesis concerning the existence of long cycles in the years 1919–20. Without going into a special analysis, I formulated my

[1] See the article about him in *Encyclopedia of the Social Sciences*, Vol. xv, 1st edn., 1937, pp. 128–9, and Vol. xvi, 2nd edn., 1968, pp. 164–7. T. W. Hutchinson, in *A Review of Economic Doctrines, 1870–1929* (Oxford, 1953) calls Tugan-Baranovsky's *Industrial Crises in England* 'a book which may deservedly be taken as opening a new phase in the study of crises and cycles' (p. 377). A. Spiethoff called it 'the first scientific monograph on its subject which combines history, statistics, and analysis' (quoted by Hutchinson, *loc. cit.*). Alvin Hansen wrote 'He cut his way through the jungle to a new outlook. He began a new way of thinking about the problem' (*Business Cycles and National Income* (New York, 1951), p. 28).

[2] For an interesting attempt to assess the importance of Tugan-Baranovsky as an original thinker in the field of monetary theory, see V. E. Vlasenko, *Teorii deneg v Rossii : konets XIX v – dooktyabr'sky period XX v.*, (*Monetary Theory in Russia from the end of the 19th century to the October revolution*) (Kiev, 1963). Vlasenko says that 'There are reasons to believe that the views of Keynes on money and monetary circulation were formed to a certain degree under the influence of the monetary theory of Tugan-Baranovsky.' Vlasenko concludes that 'in any case one thing is certain: the basic monetary theories of Keynes expounded in *A Treatise on Money* were formulated almost a decade earlier by Tugan-Baranovsky in his *Bumazhnye den'gi i metally* (*Paper Money and Specie*), Moscow, 1917 (p. 215).' Already in 1925 S. A. Falkner in an introduction to the Russian translation of Keynes' *Treatise on Money*, Moscow, 1925, p. 4, remarked that 'similarly in a number of other places we find statements and thoughts undoubtedly borrowed from Russia' [implying from Tugan-Baranovsky].

By far the longest chapter in Vlasenko is entitled 'Tugan-Baranovsky's theory of the Monetary Business Cycle', section 5 of which is headed 'Tugan-Baranovsky – the founder of the nominalist-quantitative theory of money, the principal branch of bourgeois monetary theory in the period of general crises of capitalism'. If Vlasenko were not a Marxist, he would probably have agreed with my appraisal of Tugan-Baranovsky as the greatest Russian economist of all time.

In reviewing Vlasenko's book in the organ of the State Bank of the USSR, *Den'gi i kredit* (July 1964), Z. Atlas, the most eminent of Soviet monetary economists, remarked: 'It is a pity that we still do not have a study of the work of Tugan-Baranovsky that would bring out all that is valuable and useful for economics.'

general thesis for the first time shortly thereafter in my study *The World Economy and Economic Fluctuations in the War and Post-War Periods*.[1] During the winter and spring of 1925, I wrote a special study on 'Long Business Cycles' which appeared in Volume I of *Voprosy Kon'yunktury* (*Problems of Economic Fluctuations*), published in Moscow by the Institute of Conjuncture in 1925.[2]

On 6 February 1926, Kondrat'ev read a paper on long cycles at the Institute of Economics of the Russian Association of Research Institutes in Social Sciences (subsequently merged with the Academy of Sciences), which seems to have been his last contribution on this subject. The next week, at the same institution, Oparin presented a counter-report which was longer than Kondrat'ev's original one. Both reports, as well as the discussion (the latter obviously incomplete) were subsequently published as a book entitled *Long Cycles*.[3]

A detailed discussion of long cycles is beyond the scope of this book. Kondrat'ev distinguished three long cycles, the third as then unfinished, as follows:[4]

First Long Cycle   – Rise: From about 1790 to 1810–17;
                           Decline: From 1810–17 to 1844–51;
Second Long Cycle – Rise: From 1844–51 to 1870–5;
                           Decline: From 1871–5 to 1890–6;
Third Long Cycle – Rise: From 1890–6 to 1914–20;
                           Decline: Beginning in 1914–20.

The Bolsheviks took up arms against Kondrat'ev's long cycles, which they regarded as a deliberate distraction of attention from the imminent collapse of capitalism. In their conception, there was no room for an ascending capitalist cycle.

[1] *Mirovoe khozyaistvo i ego kon'yunktury vo vremya i posle voiny*, Vologda, 1922.
[2] N. D. Kondrat'ev and D. I. Oparin, *Bol'shie tsikly kon'yunktury* (Long Cycles), Moscow, 1928, p. 114.
[3] *Ibid.* The principal publication on the subject in English is 'The Long Cycles' in *The Review of Economic Statistics*, November, 1935. This is an abridged translation from the German version published in *Archiv für Sozialwissenschaften und Sozialpolitik* in 1926, and was reprinted in *Readings in Business Cycles Theory*, selected by a committee of the American Economic Association, Philadelphia, 1944. Editor's note: Oparin's publications appeared first in 1914, ceased in the early thirties and re-emerged in 1955; for a resumé of his career see M. Kaser, review of Oparin, *Multi-Sector Economic Accounts*, Oxford, 1963, in *Journal of the Royal Statistical Society* Series A, Part 3, 1964, pp. 460–1.   [4] Kondrat'ev and Oparin, p. 49.

Besides this, Kondrat'ev's theory of long cycles was not widely accepted in Russia, or accepted only with great reservations, by non-communist scholars. Numerous criticisms were published in various Russian journals.[1] A book was published against the long cycles theory in 1929[2] and M. Kraev attacked it in an article entitled 'The Theory and Practice of Wrecking Activities in Perspective Agricultural Planning', in *Planovoe khozyaistvo*, No. 1, 1931.

The attitude towards Kondrat'ev's theory of long cycles outside Russia was mixed, but it was universally recognised as a major contribution.[3] Joseph A. Schumpeter, a great economist in his own right, attached Kondrat'ev's name to long cycles, which are now commonly referred to in business cycle literature as Kondrat'ev's cycles. Schumpeter wrote that it was Kondrat'ev 'who brought the phenomenon [of long cycles] fully before the scientific community and who systematically analysed all the material available to him on the assumption of the presence of a long cycle, characteristic of the capitalist process'. Schumpeter also believed that the long cycles 'are associated (to say the least) with definite historical processes in industry which are of the same nature and produce the same symptoms as those which are responsible for and produce the symptoms of the generally recognised cycles'.[4]

Arthur F. Burns and Wesley C. Mitchell, who referred to Kondrat'ev's hypothesis as 'the most celebrated of the long-cycle theories',[5] devoted a section of their book to the examination of the evidence in its favour. The Burns and Mitchell study is only one among a whole literature on the theory of long cycles which

[1] See George Garvy, 'Kondratieff's Theory of Long Cycles', *The Review of Economics and Statistics*, Vol. xxv, 1943. This article contains a detailed examination of the empirical data used by Kondrat'ev in his several articles on Long Cycles and a summary of the discussion of his theory in contemporary Soviet publications. It was reprinted in *Readings in Business Cycles and National Income* (Alvin H. Hansen and Richard V. Clemence, editors, New York, 1953).

[2] A. G. Gertsenshtein, *Do Long Cycles Exist? A Critique of the Views of N. D. Kondrat'ev*, Moscow, 1929.

[3] Kondrat'ev was among the first Fellows elected by the [International] Econometric Society in the early thirties.

[4] See Joseph A. Schumpeter, *Business Cycles*, Vol. 1, New York and London, 1939, p. 164 and footnote.

[5] *Measuring Business Cycles*, New York, 1946, p. 431.

has come into existence since the publication of Kondrat'ev's article.[1]

Only a dedicated scholar could have turned to the historical problem of long cycles in the midst of civil war and the rapid approach of an economic catastrophe involving the starvation and death of millions as a result of Lenin's experiment with communism. There was, it is true, little that a scholar could contribute to current developments then. But Kondrat'ev found time for the subject also in the winters of 1924–5 and 1925–6, in spite of his hectic activities as director of the Conjuncture Institute.

THE CONJUNCTURE INSTITUTE

The October Revolution of course deprived Kondrat'ev of his job, but he was not a man to stop working. As early as 1919 he published a study, *Production and Marketings of Oilseeds in Relation to the Interests of the Peasant Economy*, and in 1922 his better-known book, *The Grain Market and its Regulation during the War and Revolution*,[2] appeared. Even before this, in 1920, he organised the Conjuncture Institute, which played a great role in the ensuing decade. He also began working on his index of retail prices, which soon acquired great significance.

In mid-1922 the publication of the *Ekonomichesky byulleten' Kon'yunkturnogo Instituta* (*Economic Bulletin of the Conjuncture Institute*) began. It was edited by Kondrat'ev, and after 1925 by 'N. D. Kondrat'ev with the close collaboration of Albert Weinstein'. This publication of course expanded after the first issue. Issue No. 10–11 for 1924 (80 pages) consisted of four parts, (1) domestic: overall economic indicators of the Conjuncture Institute; (2) domestic: indicators of the state of the national economy of the USSR; (3) foreign sections and (4) articles of general and theoretical nature. Part 1 had sections on various price indices, including the new retail-price index of the Conjuncture Institute; also short

---

[1] For a bibliography of studies on long cycles in six languages, see Gaston Imbert's book of more than 500 pages, *Des mouvements de longue durée Kondratieff* (Aix-en-Provence, 1959). See also Ulrich Weinstock, *Das Problem der Kondratieff-Zyklen* (Berlin, 1964).

[2] *Rynok khlebov i ego regulirovanie vo vremya voiny i revolyutsii*, Moscow, 1922.

sections on money circulation, credit, trade, transport, output of heavy and of light industry, and overall economic indicator (geometric average).

Part 2 of the next issue of the Bulletin contained domestic data in greater detail, specifically retail price indices. Separate indices were given for industrial and farm prices, with further subdivisions by groups. Most important was the calculation of the relation between the retail price index for industrial goods and that for farm products. The foreign section represented a compilation of various indices for the United States and Britain: this was the part which most irritated those in power, to whom it was anathema that Soviet citizens should be familiar with foreign conditions or foreigners with conditions in the Soviet Union. In a paper 'On Counter-revolutionary sabotage in Agriculture' read to the Agrarian Institute of the Communist Party on 1 October 1930, Milyutin commented:[1]

> The Conjuncture Institute of the Commisariat of Finance is basically the mouthpiece of the Kondrat'ev gang, which is directly connected with foreign bourgeois institutes to which it conveys detailed information on the situation in the USSR.

The information supplied to these institutes was 'deliberately falsified,' Milyutin insisted, although all that was wrong with it was that it did not slavishly reproduce the officially garbled data and interpretations on the same subjects. At the meeting, Uzhansky added in the same vein: 'Kondrat'ev with his staff of henchmen in the Conjuncture Institute was engaged in the study of the economy of foreign countries and described it in numerous bulletins and books' (*ibid.* p. 33). A great crime indeed!

After issue No. 4 of 1928, i.e. very early in the course of the industrialisation drive, the Conjuncture Institute was dissolved. The *Ekonomichesky Byulleten'* was transferred to the Central Statistical Office, where it soon quietly died.

[1] *Kondrat'evshchina*, p. 9.

Nikolai Dmitrievich Kondrat'ev

FARM INDICES

While the Conjuncture Institute's retail price index was not believed to cover the peasant economy adequately, the existing index of living costs was also found wanting in so far as the peasant economy was concerned. One reason, which alone would have been sufficient, was that the index of living costs did not include prices of producer's goods used in agriculture. There was in any case an urgent need for specifical 'peasant indices'. The Conjuncture Institute responded to this need adequately and promptly.[1]

In fact, 'peasant indices' consisted of twenty price indices for goods purchased and used by the peasants. These were classified as follows:

1. Industrial goods purchased for personal consumption;
2. Industrial goods purchased for use in farming;
3. Industrial goods purchased, total;
4. Farm products purchased for personal consumption;
5. Farm products purchased for use in farming;
6. Farm products purchased, total;
7. All goods purchased for personal consumption;
8. All goods purchased for use in farming;
9. All purchased goods.

There were furthermore nine indices for prices of products bought by the farm population, including prices of goods for use in farming, and finally there were indices for total farm products produced and total farm products sold. Additional indices were compiled for individual farm products sold by the peasants. The list included five different grains, potatoes, sugar beet, sunflower seed, flax-fibre, hay, beef, milk and eggs.

It is important that in addition to those for the USSR as a whole, indices were worked out for regions with different types of farming.

[1] N. D. Kondrat'ev (ed.), *Krest'yanskie indeksy; sbornik trudov* (Peasant Indices; a *Collection of Studies*), Moscow, 1927. Interesting material on this item is also found in Albert Weinstein, 'Peasant Indices as Indicators of the Conjuncture of Agriculture', *Sotsialisticheskoe khozyaistvo*, 1927, pp. 60–76. According to Weinstein (*op. cit.* p. 64), 'the initiative and the actual compilation of the system of peasant indices were due to I. N. Zhivkovich and I. N. Ozerov'.

Five such regional groups of subindices were calculated: potato region (Yaroslavl and Kostroma guberniyas); flax-fibre region (Smolensk and Tver guberniyas); sugar-beet region (Kursk guberniya); dairy region (North-east of the forest-steppe area; beyond the Urals); and the wheat region (North Caucasus). The index for the flax fibre region was calculated both as a whole and for two sub-areas.

Data were obtained for the first day of each month, mostly from 1 October 1925 on, but in some cases from 1 October 1926 only. The indices were calculated using 1913 as a base.[1] This was of course most important, because the decline after 1913 in the prices the peasants received for their produce relative to the prices of the goods they needed was a crucial factor in appraising the prospects of Soviet agriculture. The farm indices proved useful at once. They showed, for instance, that for the flax-fibre region the price index of products sold by the peasants declined from 1.90 on 1 October 1925, to 1.76 on 1 March 1927, while the price index of goods bought by them for personal consumption and production purposes rose from 1.96 to 2.20 over the same period.

Some of the last price indices, shown in *Krest'yanskie indeksy*, are reproduced in Table 13.

In the flax region on the same day (1 March 1927) the price indices were (*op. cit.* pp. 82–5):

Purchases, total	2.48
Sales, total	1.79
Flax-fibre	1.37
Flax seed	1.55

The 'peasant indices' strikingly illustrated the fact that the authorities expected great increases in farm output for the market under conditions of declining prices for farm products in relation to the cost of goods purchased by farmers.

The Conjuncture Institute was never given a chance to improve on its work in compiling the elaborate peasant indices. The Institute

---

[1] *Ibid.* pp. 82–3. According to *Krest'yanskie indeksy*, p. 30, 1913 prices were determined by consulting files and published sources, but also by means of estimates – the least reliable method.

Table 13. *Index of prices on 1 March 1927 (1913 = 100)*

	Potatoes	Sugar Beet	Dairy	Grain
Purchases of				
Industrial goods, total	243	229	214	236
Sales : Principal products, total	168	135	139	172
Potatoes	144	...	...	...
Sugar beet	...	117	...	...
Milk	...	...	164	...
Wheat	...	...	...	140

SOURCE: *Krest'yanskie indeksy*, 1 March 1927, pp. 78–9.

was taken away from Kondrat'ev and his collaborators within a year after the indices were published, and dislike of them may indeed have played a serious role in the demise of the Institute.

THE FIVE-YEAR PLAN FOR AGRICULTURE AND OTHER PLANS

The Five-Year Plan for agriculture prepared by Kondrat'ev in the Narkomzem in collaboration with N. P. Makarov as early as 1923 and 1924 was certainly a solid piece of work. The first draft of the plan was presented by him to Gosplan as early as 18 January 1924. The second draft was made available soon thereafter, on 8 July 1924: it was published as a small book entitled *The Bases of the Perspective Plan for the Development of Agriculture and Forestry*, as the fifth report of Zemplan (the planning organisation of the Commissariat of Agriculture of the RSFSR). Subsequent work on the plan continued for almost a full year, and the material published on the topic amounted to several thousand pages. Sixteen special plans were transmitted to Gosplan after the autumn of 1924. In July 1925, Kondrat'ev made a third report to Gosplan, with P. I. Popov, the Head of the Central Statistical Office and a member of the Agricultural Section of Gosplan, as seconding reporter; there were in addition five discussion speakers and the proceedings were summarised in *Puti sel'skogo khozyaistva*,[1] No. 2, 1927.

[1] *Osnovy perspektivnogo plana razvitiya sel'skogo i lesnogo khozyaistva*, Moscow, 1924.

Table 14. *Planned and Actual Agricultural Production in 1928.*
(percentage change over 1913)

	Planned	Actual
Gross Production	+ 3.5	+ 10.0
Cropped Ploughland	+ 0.8	− 3.2
Grain	− 5.6	− 8.3
Fibres	+ 11.6	+ 32.3
Sugar Beet	− 25.0	+ 18.7
Livestock		
Horses	− 21.7	− 6.4
Cattle	+ 3.8	+ 16.3
Cows	+ 6.7	+ 18.1
Hogs	+ 2.0	+ 24.9
Sheep and goats	− 10.7	+ 21.0

Note: See the notes to Table 17 in this writer's *Socialized Agriculture of the USSR*, Stanford, 1949, p. 219.

As Table 14 shows, the targets set for 1928 in accordance with Kondrat'ev's projection were overfulfilled for farming as a whole, though not by very much. However, the target for grain, an export commodity, was missed by a sizeable amount, probably in view of the less favourable prices abroad and at home than were assumed for 1928 relative to 1913. The subdivision of the larger land holdings may also have played a role here. The over-fulfilment of the targets for fibres was large, and even more so was that for sugar beet. This is understandable for such goods as flax, a product of medium-sized peasant farms. Sugar beet, however, was grown before World War I almost exclusively by large landowners, and it was not expected that the peasants would adapt themselves quickly to this crop after the subdivision of the land. In fact they did, although the yields per hectare which they achieved were less than those of the large landowners before the War.[1]

The overfulfilment of the targets of the Five-Year Plan for agriculture confirmed Groman's expectations. 'We were given a plan for agriculture which undoubtedly lagged far behind reality,' he said with typical bluntness in the July 1925 discussion. (*Puti*

[1] The average yield of sugar beet in the USSR as a whole was 150 quintals per hectare in 1909–13 and 135 quintals in 1927–8 (see this writer's *Socialized Agriculture of the USSR*, p. 507).

sel'skogo khozyaistva, No. 2, 1962, p. 186.) He explained the error as follows: 'Where are the basic reasons of errors of all plans, this and others? I think they are due to insufficient understanding of the recovery process by everybody, including me.'

Groman in the first place blamed Zemplan for not revising the targets upward between the second and third presentations of the drafts by Kondrat'ev. But he did not speak of 'gigantic errors' in the plan as Dubrovsky did (*op. cit.* p. 190). Dubrovsky, of whom I know nothing, and Kritsman, a well-known Communist concerned with farming, attacked the plan viciously. Dubrovsky (*op. cit.* p. 191) said that it was 'full of errors', that the Narkomzem had in fact no plan at all. According to Kritsman (*op. cit.* p. 184), the plan had a 'strange character' and was stillborn, being an attempt to combine the communist approach with something quite different. He suggested returning it to Narkomzem for revision. The co-rapporteur Popov, on the contrary, had 'no quarrel with the picture of the evolution of agriculture given by Narkomzem'; however, he believed that the problem of the surplus labour force did not receive due attention.

Professor Bushinsky declared in the name of the Agricultural section of Gosplan (*op. cit.* p. 170) that the theoretical portion (i.e. the principles) of the plan was not adequately linked with the 'factual realisation of the perspective plan'. So much importance was assigned to this item that it was included in the written appraisal of the draft of the Five-Year Plan by the agricultural section of Gosplan.

The Kondrat'ev Five-Year Plan for agriculture was actually a great achievement, considering that all planning was still in its infancy – as can be seen, for example, from the fact that in and after 1919 Lenin held to the absurd opinion that economic plans must be worked out by engineers. The engineers picked by Krzhizhanovsky, Lenin's deputy in this work, a Communist but also an engineer, made a farce of planning. The targets were in general much too low, and the actual course of events over the years bore no relation to the plans.[1] Really good forecasts were, it must be

[1] The greatest achievement of the engineers was the famous GOELRO (plan for electrification of Russia) which was worked out in 1920. In addition to electrification

12-2

admitted, impossible in the chaotic conditions of that time and with planning in its infancy.

While Kondrat'ev worked mainly for Narkomzem and in particular played a decisive role in drafting the early agricultural Five-Year Plan, he was by no means uninformed about planning as a whole.

On the release of the early draft of the five-year plan by Gosplan, prepared under Strumilin and discussed by him in *Planovoe khozyaistvo*, No. 4, 1926, the neo-narodnik group reacted with an extended analysis of the plan.[1] Although all contributions were mainly critical, the editors of the journal called them interesting and declared that the problems touched on in them deserved wide discussion (*op. cit.* p. 3). Of the three contributions, that of Kondrat'ev was confined to planning in general, with hardly any specific reference to agriculture. Makarov devoted his short article mainly to criticism of the Five-Year Plan for agriculture prepared by N. P. Oganovsky, A. E. Lositsky, and N. M. Vishnevsky. Chelintsev gave a broad analysis of problems involved in planning agriculture as such and as an important component of the national economy as a whole.

The first part of Kondrat'ev's contribution contained an exposition which was probably meant as a criticism of Bazarov (though he was not named) on the spheres of application of the genetic and teleological methods of planning. While Bazarov believed that the geneticist method was primarily applicable to the peasant economy and the teleological method to the socialised sector of the economy, Kondrat'ev wrote on p. 9: 'The drafting of perspectives in a plan of development of agriculture, as well as in a plan of development of industry, is based on teleological as well as on genetic methods.' And further: 'We cannot set the task and perspectives in the realm

targets this also included some other items, mainly for the output of major industrial products. The GOELRO can be praised, as is done in Soviet publications, only by neglecting to compare the actual developments with those forecast in it. Such a comparison was made briefly by the present writer in 'Perspective Planning', in *Essays on the Soviet Economy*. The effect of GOELRO on developments in the economy was actually zero or very close to zero.

[1] N. D. Kondrat'ev, 'Plan and Foresight (on the problem of Methods of Drafting Perspective Plans of Development of the National Economy and Specifically of Agriculture)', pp. 3–36; N. P. Makarov, 'Problems on Perspective Plans for Agriculture', pp. 37–44; and A. N. Chelintsev, 'On Methods and Principles of Preparing Perspective Plans for Agriculture', pp. 45–82; all in *Puti sel'skogo khozyaistva*, No. 2, 1927.

of development of industry arbitrarily, just because we so wish, without consideration of objective conditions, i.e., without resort to the genetic method.'

Kondrat'ev concluded that the difference in the use of the respective methods of drafting plans, if it existed, was quantitative rather than qualitative. He and other neo-narodniks strongly objected to the forms of plans that were then and still are common in the USSR. He argued first of all that the introduction into the plans of elements obtained arbitrarily should be completely given up (*op. cit.* p. 31):

It is possible and even certain that forecasts for the more distant future will become poorer and more modest. One of two things: either we want serious and realistic plans, and in that case we must base them exclusively on assured scientific foundations; or we shall continue to engage in all kinds of 'bold' calculations and computations for the future without sufficient foundations, and then we must accept from the start that the calculations are arbitrary, that such plans lack reality. But what is the purpose and value of such plans? At best they remain harmless, because they are dead from a practical point of view. At worst they will be harmful, because they may introduce serious errors into our practice.

Kondrat'ev objected furthermore (p. 34) that operative, i.e. annual, and perspective (i.e. five-year) plans scarcely differed from one another. Similarly, 'a plan for 10–15 years is basically nothing but a perspective plan', he stated in disapproval.

Kondrat'ev and the other neo-narodniks attacked with particular energy the huge tables in the draft plans ('bedspreads', as they sarcastically called them), with a mass of figures showing in detail a large quantity of data year by year. 'We must get rid of the fetishism of figures', he declared (*op. cit.* p. 31). In his opinion, only operative plans needed to contain such detailed data in tables (*op. cit.* p. 32). Albert Weinstein ('On Control Figures of the National Economy of the USSR for 1926–7', *Sotsialisticheskoe khozyaistvo*, 1927, p. 7), went still further in this respect. He applied to Control Figures, the early annual plans, the objections which Kondrat'ev made against medium and long-range plans. He wrote: 'It seems to me a useless game...to complete all these gigantic tables in the construction of Control Figures for the different branches of the economy.'

Chelintsev took the opposite attitude toward the Control Figures (he must have had in mind the same issue for 1926–7 to which Weinstein referred). He said:

We may say provisionally that the practice of working out control figures of the national economy, following the principle of mutual interdependence of all sectors of the national economy and all spheres of activity of all Commissariats by means of the balancing method...has acquired great importance. These calculations of interdependence can of course be worked out only in figures.[1]

Kondrat'ev demanded furthermore (p. 34) that: 'To avoid errors, forecasts of the future must be made not as exact single figures, but with indication of the probable error.'

The positions of Makarov and Chelintsev towards the plan cannot be discussed here. The most important problem of the relation of the plan for agriculture to the plan for the economy as a whole, as discussed by Chelintsev, is briefly touched upon in the next section.

One month after the publication of Kondrat'ev's 'Plan and Perspective' in *Puti sel'skogo khozyaistva*, No. 2, 1927, a number of reports prepared by Gosplan on the Five-Year Plan for 1926–7– 1930–1 were released in *Planovoe khozyaistvo*, No. 3, 1927. In the next issue of that journal Kondrat'ev reacted with 'Critical Remarks on the Plan for the Development of the National Economy'.[2] The remarks were certainly critical. They concluded: 'The basic error committed in the drafting of the plan is that those who drew it up sought to accomplish the series of tasks indicated above (i.e., maximum, crisis-free expansion of productive forces and maximum satisfaction of current needs) without taking sufficient account of the fact that where these partial tasks are expressed in extreme terms they come in collision one with another.'

KONDRAT'EV'S POLITICAL POSITION

In contrast to Groman, who accepted the NEP and merely wanted a few moderate revisions, Kondrat'ev desired a fundamental broadening of the NEP. He believed in favouring the more well-to-

---

[1] *Puti sel'skogo khozyaistva, loc. cit.* p. 47.
[2] Translated in Spulber (ed.) pp. 438–51.

do peasants because they were fostering the growth of production. Kondrat'ev also was not in favour of a State monopoly of foreign trade. With reference to the period before 1927, Kondrat'ev testified in *Trial* (p. 195): 'It is necessary to say that, although I was acquainted personally with Vladimir Gustavovich Groman, he and I held quite different positions. Not infrequently we used to fight the various organisations such as the Labour and Defence Council, Gosplan and others.'

Groman indicated in *Trial* that, while he himself espoused the cause of industrialisation, although based on a rate of investment lower than those proposed officially, Kondrat'ev favoured still lower rates and saw future developments from the point of view of agriculture.

The controversy between Kondrat'ev and Groman prior to the end of 1927 became, quite naturally, a controversy between their respective supporters and the influence of the Communist leadership of Narkomzem and Narkomfin. For a long time, the head of the planning organisation of the Commissariat of Agriculture of the RSFSR was I. Teodorovich. The Commissar of Finance was G. Ya. Sokolnikov and his mouth-piece was L. Shanin, the theoretical advisor of the Commissariat and a Bolshevik of the Bukharin persuasion. In 'The Economic Nature of Our Commodity Shortage',[1] Shanin insisted that investments in industry, and especially in heavy industry, were too large (he had in mind the years 1924–5). Shanin held that the development of consumers' goods production and of exports should be the central objective of the Plan: 'We must adopt a course of initially slower and more cautious development of heavy industry'.[2]

Both the Teodorovich and Shanin–Sokolnikov views were repeatedly attacked in *Kondrat'evshchina* for their pro-agrarian leanings, mainly by I. D. Laptev (p. 51) and Ya. P. Nikulikhin (pp. 66–7). Both these authors bracketed Bukharin, Teodorovich and Kondrat'ev together ideologically, Nikulikhin believing that the Shanin–Sokolnikov line favoured adopting extreme agrarian policies: 'The co-operation of the right-wing Communists with the

[1] *Ekonomicheskoe obozrenie*, No. 11, 1925, here cited from Spulber (ed.), pp. 205–9.
[2] Shanin, pp. 209–1c.

Kondrat'evites is most clearly reflected in a report of Zemplan over Teodorovich's signature, 'Materials on the Perspective Plan for the Development of Agriculture (1928)', wherein the commanding position in the development of the national economy was assigned to agriculture.

Contrary to the views of Kondrat'ev, of Teodorovich and of Shanin and Sokolnikov, Groman and Bazarov believed that all branches of industry should be developed at about equal rates. The point of view of Gosplan, including some mild criticism of Shanin, may be found *inter alia* in Bazarov, 'The Results of the Past Year and the Crucial Point of the Present Day'.[1]

With the passage of time, Kondrat'ev abandoned some of the more extreme views he held in the early NEP period, perhaps because he realised that developments had taken a turn contrary to his expectations. It was, for example, hopeless to expect that the foreign trade monopoly would be abolished. The shift in his position may have been sincere, or else he just preferred to keep silent.

Kondrat'ev was the leader of the neo-narodnik group which late in 1930 took the name Working-Peasant Party (TKP). Others prominent in this group were Makarov, Chayanov, Chelintsev and perhaps also Weinstein. It is possible that Kondrat'ev was more to the right than the others, although probably he was only more consistent than they. In any case the hostile press continuously bracketed him with Yurovsky and even with Litoshenko, and showed more hostility toward Kondrat'ev than toward the other neo-narodniks. Yurovsky at least was a member of the TKP in the late 1920s, according to Kondrat'ev's testimony at the trial of the Industrial Party; Litoshenko was definitely a Kadet, although not a left-wing one. Many more cases may be cited where Kondrat'ev was grouped with Litoshenko and Yurovsky and placed to the right of Chayanov, Makarov, and Chelintsev.[2] Whatever split existed

[1] *Ekonomicheskoe obozrenie*, No. 12, 1925.
[2] The resolution of the Conference of Marxist–Leninist Research Organisations on the Tasks of Marxist Science in the Field of Agriculture stated in April 1929:
    The conference notes the disintegration of the earlier united *petit bourgeois* ideological front of the neo-narodniks. As a result, part of this front is moving closer to the bourgeoisie (Kondrat'evites), while another part is yielding to Marxism (Chelintsev).
    The conference believes it necessary to conduct the most energetic fight against

within the neo-narodnik group was probably exaggerated in the official press.

The different positions of Kondrat'ev and Chelintsev indicated in the citation from the resolution of the Conference of April 1929 were at least partly due to the fact that Chelintsev was about a year ahead of Kondrat'ev in laying down his arms. Chelintsev did so, although reluctantly, in the second half of 1928; Kondrat'ev capitulated to a large extent by the end of 1929.

During the 'purge' of the People's Commissariat of Finance (December 1929), Kondrat'ev is quoted as follows:[1]

To the question whether large-scale organisation of the kolkhozes was possible without strong pressure on the kulaks, he replied: 'I believe it possible to organise kolkhozes on a large scale even without pressure on the kulaks, but the development would be more rapid if it were simultaneously accompanied by pressures on the kulaks.'

The above statement ascribed to Kondrat'ev is still somewhat vague,[2] but the following statement, allegedly made at the same time, amounted to a full capitulation: 'I did not object to the general line, anywhere or at any time' (*op. cit.* p. 107). Of course, the statement may not have been sincere. If it was actually made, it signified the end of Kondrat'ev's political career.

Krylenko, the prosecutor in the Menshevik trial, spoke of Kondrat'ev (*Trial*, p. 53) as one of the principal defendants belonging to what was called the S.R. counter-revolutionary kulak group headed by Kondrat'ev and Chayanov. It was evidently intended to

the bourgeois theoreticians Kondrat'ev, Litoshenko and others (*Na agrarnom fronte*, No. 8, 1929, p. 104).

O. P. Davidov, one of the discussion speakers, said (*Kondrat'evshchina*, p. 114): 'It was not by accident that we received confessions and condemnations of their former positions from a number of specialists [*spetsy*], as for example Chayanov, Chelintsev and lastly even such crazy counter-revolutionaries as Litoshenko and Kondrat'ev.'

[1] This and some other quotations are from the speech of V. S. Mullin in *Kondrat'evshchina*, Moscow, 1930, pp. 105-7. In this source there are references to a stenographic report of a discussion with Kondrat'ev during the 'purge' of the Commissariat of Finance in 1929. The same Mullin who twice spoke of a 'discussion' with Kondrat'ev (*op. cit.* pp. 105–6), finally (*op. cit.* p. 107) called it an 'interrogation'.

[2] In *Planovoe khozyaistvo*, No. 1, 1931, p. 299, M. Kraev interpreted Kondrat'ev's statement to mean that he favoured a socialist reorganisation of agriculture without attacking the kulaks; this was probably an arbitrary interpretation of Kondrat'ev's much less definite statement quoted in the text.

have three trials: that of the Industrial Party, which actually took place at the end of November and beginning of December, 1930; another for the Mensheviks discussed here, and, finally, one for the TKP (neo-narodniks) which, however, was never held, at least as an open trial. I have no evidence as to why it was not. One possibility is that Kondrat'ev was considered sufficiently broken in spirit to be a star witness at the Menshevik trial, but not sufficiently to be a star defendant in a trial against the Working Peasant Party. It may also have been felt that a trial of the neo-narodniks would be anticlimactic after the big Menshevik trial, with all the principal defendants having already confessed a year or two earlier. Indeed, the booklet *Kondrat'evshchina* contains a paper on 'Counter-revolutionary Sabotage in Agriculture' delivered by V. P. Milyutin (at that time head of the Central Statistical Office) at the Agrarian Institute of the Communist Party on 1 October 1930, followed by a lengthy discussion; this was a good supplement to Krylenko's speeches at the trial.

It is of considerable interest that, as previously stated, Milyutin said nothing about foreign intervention, which was apparently a later embellishment of the indictment of the Mensheviks. The 'sabotage' by Kondrat'ev and the others consisted of deliberately preparing wrong programmes and plans, according to Milyutin.[1] The latter was particularly incensed at Kondrat'ev's idea of limiting the number of quantitative targets which he believed the neo-narodniks advocated. He contended that the 'general regulatory principles' advocated by Kondrat'ev, Makarov, Chelintsev and Chayanov were a feature of capitalist planning and were the opposite of quantitative targets, which were a feature of socialist planning.

As we saw previously, Kondrat'ev figured as the star witness in the Menshevik trial, where he testified (p. 208) that he had had time to think the situation over (presumably while imprisoned)[2] and now

---

[1] *Kondrat'evshchina*, pp. 15–16. Absurdly, even Groman was included by him in the list of those guilty of this crime.

[2] Kondrat'ev seems to have been in prison fully a year by the time the Menshevik trial took place. According to *Kondrat'evshchina*, pp. 115 and 118, the arrest took place two or three months after the purge of the Narkomzem, which, like that of the Narkomfin, took place in December 1929. This places the arrest in February or March 1930. The Menshevik trial was in early March 1931. The statement on the arrest related directly to Makarov, but it seems very unlikely that he was arrested

thought his previous position criminal. He had come to accept not only Stalin's general line *in toto* (*op. cit.* p. 209), but also the famous Stalin formula of 'annihilation of the kulaks as a class' (*ibid.*); At that time 'annihilation as a class' involved extensive physical liquidation.

According to Kondrat'ev's testimony, until the end of 1928 the organisation he represented was wholly opposed to foreign intervention. Then information came from Ramzin, through Chayanov, that intervention was inevitable. This is supposed to have caused a change in the organisation's attitude, which in his testimony Kondrat'ev defined as 'forming a silent bloc with the intervention' (*Trial*, p. 198). While in the Menshevik trial all accusations of assistance to, or even sympathy with, foreign intervention were clearly inventions, the statement with regard to Kondrat'ev was particularly absurd. Possibly the formula chosen was a compromise between Krylenko and the somewhat reluctant Kondrat'ev.

A careful reading of Kondrat'ev's testimony in *Trial* reveals very small differences between statements of the defendants, other than the slight difference in wording as regards acceptance of intervention. It seems that Kondrat'ev was not anxious to mention the names of the other members of his organisation; thus Makarov's name seems not to have been mentioned by him at all. Yet Kondrat'ev mentioned the names of Yurovsky and Chayanov (*Trial*, p. 199). Chayanov's name was even brought up in such a manner as to connect him with the intervention. One should also note the persistence with which Kondrat'ev used the first name and patronymic when referring to three of the defendants, viz. Groman, Finn-Enotaevsky and Sukhanov.[1] This courtesy on his part may have been intentional.

earlier than Kondrat'ev or Chayanov. In this connection an interesting question was directed by Krylenko, the prosecutor, to Groman: 'You were originally arrested in connection with the affairs of the TKP?' Groman, the first to be arrested among the Mensheviks, was arrested only in July 1930, months after the neo-narodniks. Even in *Kondrat'evshchina*, prepared a little later, Groman is not adequately separated from Kondrat'ev, while Bazarov seems not to have been mentioned at all. The decision to have a Menshevik trial was apparently not made before some time in the second half of 1930.

[1] To call a man by his surname, even when preceded by 'Mr' or 'Professor' etc., is not very polite in the USSR; this was also the case in pre-revolutionary times.

On the whole, the substance of Kondrat'ev's testimony was no different from that of the defendants or of Ramzin and Larichev, who had already been convicted in the trial of the Industrial Party at the end of 1930. Somehow Kondrat'ev's testimony makes a somewhat less distressing impression. Perhaps, in spite of his far-reaching 'confessions', he was less completely broken than all or most of the defendants in the Menshevik trial, or Ramzin and Larichev at the earlier trial.

CONCLUSION

Nikolai Dmitrievich Kondrat'ev disappeared from view after the Menshevik trial. As far as I know, he did not reappear after Stalin's death as did Makarov, Weinstein and apparently Chelintsev. He may of course have died of natural causes during the intervening twenty-odd years, but he and Chayanov may also have been murdered in 1937, together with Bazarov and many others. In any case, the career of a man of the highest ability ended when he was only 39 years old. Clearly the Stalin régime did not need brilliant economists.

10

OTHER MENSHEVIKS

Special sketches have been devoted to Groman, Bazarov, Ginzburg, and Kondrat'ev. In this and the next chapter an attempt is made to give – at least in a few words – their due to others who fall within the very broad category of having been nonconformists to the right of the Bolsheviks and to the left of the Kadet Party.[1] Almost all the persons considered were socialists, although the neo-narodniks were actually doubtful socialists and there are three persons included of whose political affiliation nothing is known to the present writer. The remaining Mensheviks are dealt with in this chapter and the neo-narodniks in the next. The former are better represented, partly because the 'stenographic report' on the trial provides material on many of them. The availability of Valentinov's Memoirs also favours the Mensheviks. Again, the Mensheviks were mainly active in planning, the subject which has interested this writer most. And, finally, being myself a Menshevik, though not in a strict sense, I naturally know more about them than about the neo-narodniks.

I have felt reluctance to include people whom I could not visualise at least vaguely. Even a cursory acquaintance with a person helped in such visualisation. Sometimes a good picture may serve. Unfortunately, reasonably good photographs were found only of Groman and Bazarov. The omission of those of whom I could form no mental image eliminated a number even of defendants in the trial, although such as Salkind or Yakubovich may have deserved inclusion as much as, if not more than, others considered in this book.

SUKHANOV

Nikolai Nikolaevich Sukhanov (born Gimmer), both as a person and in view of his importance in the Menshevik group during the last decisive years, would actually have deserved a special sketch. Born on 10 December 1882, he was a very able man with a questing

---

[1] At least one Kadet, L. N. Litoshenko, has also been included.

intellect and, possibly because of this, somewhat unstable politically and otherwise, he was also a brilliant writer.[1] Groman said during the trial (p. 31) that 'Sukhanov liked to express himself intricately, in season and out of season'. He was hardly much of a leader, although the indictment included him among the five Menshevik leaders (*Trial*, pp. 46–7).[2] But 'leader' may have meant simply spokesman or one who stimulates others.

Anyone who can read Russian will be greatly interested to read Sukhanov's autobiography, dated January 1929, which appeared in Granat's *Prominent Men and Women of the USSR and the October Revolution*[3] (pp. 129–33). His father was a minor railway official heavily addicted to drink. The son, a delicate child, never had any home life. The divorce of his parents and his mother's imprisonment gave Tolstoy the idea for *Zhivoy Trup* (*The Living Corpse*). From the age of 14, Sukhanov was on his own, living on earnings from private teaching. Towards the end of his schooldays he became a follower of Tolstoy, who taught him his hostile attitude towards government. The non-resisting part of Tolstoy's teachings Sukhanov ceased to accept a few years later, as a result of listening to revolutionaries in Paris. The autobiography also tells us that he was always bad at mathematics.

The combination of Tolstoyan ideas with the doctrines of the revolutionaries brought Sukhanov to the extreme left in politics, where he remained for about a quarter of a century, until Stalin's activities taught him a lesson on the dangers of extremism. He was a member of the Socialist-Revolutionary Party in 1903–4, but left it because it was too moderate for him (*Trial*, pp. 378–85). While contributing in subsequent years mainly to populist journals, he leant more and more toward Marxism. 'By 1908–9 I considered myself an accomplished Marxist', he declared. As regards his position during World War I and the early years after the Revolution, he says in his autobiography, pp. 132–3: 'Since the beginning

---

As an editor he once said to me, one of his contributors 'You, Jasny, you write about such boring things. [At that time I was writing exclusively on the world grain market.] At least make a proper introduction. Take the reader by the throat, tell him that he will miss a great deal if he does not read your stuff.'

[2] The verdict, pp. 469–70, speaks of four leaders including Sukhanov.

[3] *Deyateli SSSR i Oktyabr'skoy Revolyutsii*, Vol. 3, Moscow, pp. 129–33.

of World War I, in questions of the international labour movement I agreed first with the Third International and later with the communists. As regards domestic economic policies of socialist construction, I shared the views of the ruling Party after the proclamation of the NEP.' In 1917–20 he was member of the Martov left-wing faction of Mensheviks (*Trial*, p. 385). He was aggressively hostile to War Communism. In his testimony (pp. 387–8) he repeatedly said, 'For me War Communism was nonsense ...War Communism I viewed with animosity...I held War Communism to be the greatest evil'. But also, 'within a year of the start of the NEP I was in my own eyes a Communist'. In 1923 he applied for membership of the Communist Party, but was not accepted (*Trial*, p. 388). He was apparently a member of the German Communist Party at that time. None the less, he had serious reservations and, when in Moscow, probably continued to mingle with the Mensheviks and other non-Communists. From 1923 to 1928 he did not formally belong to any Party, nor was he a member of the Group of Observers described by Valentinov.

In Lenin's time, even to be disparaged by Lenin was a distinction. Lenin wrote about or at least mentioned Sukhanov frequently in his writings, not always in terms of abuse. In Volume XVII (1913–14), p. 576, we find: 'Gimmer is not just anybody...but one of the most prominent economists who represent the most democratic, most left-wing bourgeois [everything not communist was bourgeois to Lenin] mode of thought in Russia and Europe.' And in Volume XXI (1917), p. 12:

If we consider the writer N. Sukhanov from *Novaya zhizn'*, all certainly will agree that he is not the worst but one of the best representatives of petit bourgeois democracy. He shows a sincere tendency toward internationalism, demonstrated in the most difficult times, in the midst of Tsarist reaction and chauvinism. He is educated and has shown a wish to understand independently the serious problems of the day. He proved this by his prolonged evolution from the ideas of the socialist-revolutionaries to revolutionary Marxism.

For several years Sukhanov, in contrast to Kondrat'ev, advocated the *obshchina*, the peasant land commune introduced into legislation in 1861, in its extreme form as the proper transition to the socialisation of agriculture.[1] He insisted that many institutions of pre-Revolutionary days had changed their roles since the Revolution and that this was true of the *obshchina*. It would seem, however, that the preservation, for example, of compulsory redistribution prescribed by the *obshchina* would have been an obstacle to the development of agriculture, and would have speeded up Stalin's forceful collectivisation. When this came, Sukhanov could not stomach it. His advocacy of the *obshchina* would alone have sufficed to exclude him from leadership, if he had been adapted to this role anyway. The neo-narodniks had not displayed any enthusiasm for the idea, and the Communists objected to it because the 'kulaks' were also members of the *obshchina*.

'I felt Communist leanings for about five years,' Sukhanov said at the trial (p. 388); this would have been the period 1921-6. His defence speech shows that the end of the NEP had a tremendous effect on him. His connection with Groman became close only during 1928. 'At the very beginning of 1929 Groman invited me to join an organisation based not on mine, but on a bourgeois-democratic platform' (*Trial*, p. 290).

In 1928 and 1929, Sukhanov held a kind of 'at home' on Sundays (*Trial*, p. 171). Since the topic is not touched on anywhere else in the *Trial*,[2] it seems appropriate to give at least the names of the frequent guests on those Sundays. According to the source, they fell into three main groups. First, Galov, Groman, Cherevanin, Ermansky, Kan, Rubin, Sandomirsky (all Mensheviks) and Maslov (a Social-Democrat), second, Kondrat'ev (a Socialist Revolutionary) and Aneev (a former Socialist Revolutionary), Bukhshpan, Weinstein, Kluchkov (who ranged from Socialist Revolutionary to vague populism), and third, Gorfinkel, Bissel, Kalamanovich (73 years old), and Malyantovich, who had been a minister of the Provisional Government. This group were attached neither to the Mensheviks nor to the Socialist Revolutionaries, but probably more to the Kadets.

[1] See especially *Na agrarnom fronte*, No. 11, 1926, pp. 97-110.
[2] It is worth recalling, especially in view of the huge subsidies allegedly received by the Menshevik organisation according to the Trial, that according to Sukhanov (*Trial*, p. 257) the drawing-room had three chairs and tea was served without sugar. cf. p. 82 above.

Kondrat'evshchina states indignantly that 'at the very end of 1928 Sukhanov defended a thesis which basically did not differ from Kondrat'ev's thesis' [i.e. the opinions expressed by Kondrat'ev in 1922]. The reference was to a paper read by Sukhanov to the Agrarian Institute of the Communist Academy 'On Economic Conditions for a Rise in Agriculture' on 4 December 1928.[1] In this paper Sukhanov insisted that all efforts to increase farm production were utopian, 'if the peasants do not get a proportionate quantity of industrial goods in return'. These opinions were certainly not new, but courage was needed to proclaim them to the Communist Academy as late as the end of 1928.

Sukhanov still participated as a discussion speaker in the conference of Marxist–Leninist Scientific Research Organisations in April 1929, devoted to L. Kritsman's paper 'Analysis of a Peasant Household'.[2] Not a single neo-narodnik took the floor. In his concluding remarks Kritsman called Sukhanov a corpse.[3] It was an honour to be abused by such as Kritsman.

In his testimony Sukhanov insisted that when he joined the Menshevik organisation in 1929 he did not accept the Menshevik programme, only the tactics. Probably since his Socialist-Revolutionary days or even earlier, he had been interested in peasant problems and this brought him into contact with the narodniks of all shades. This is why he was frequently mentioned together with the neo-narodniks, but there is no reason to doubt that he had been a Marxist for a long time before 1931, and in 1929–31 he was for practical purposes a Menshevik.

When one studies the period of the first Five-Year Plan, the years 1931 and especially 1932 appear the most disastrous. As compared with them, 1930, and even more 1929, seem almost normal. It is therefore of interest that Sukhanov said about the winter of 1929–30: 'This winter had cost the national economy as much as a good-sized war might have done' (*Trial*, p. 452).

Sukhanov was arrested on 20 July 1930 (*Trial*, p. 456). Thus his participation in the Menshevik organisation called by the GPU the

---

[1] *Kondrat'evshchina*, p. 111.
[2] See *Na agrarnom fronte*, Nos. 7 and 8, 1929. Sukhanov's speech is in No. 7, pp. 101–2.
[3] *Ibid.* No. 8, 1929, p. 101.

'United Bureau', if this existed at all, can have lasted for little more than one year. Rumour has it that, after serving his prison sentence after the Menshevik trial, he was exiled to a town in north-western Russia, where he committed suicide soon afterwards. Thus Russia lost another of its best thinkers.

SHTERN

Alexander Borisovich Shtern was the Menshevik 'conspirator' next after Ginzburg in influence in the VSNKh. Valentinov describes him as an ascetic, a man with a sensitive conscience and great tenderness (his eyes were always sad). He received a relatively high salary but spent almost nothing on himself (wearing a summer shirt instead of a jacket in the winter) and sent the bulk of it to relatives. In the past he had been an out-and-out Menshevik, but, as he said: 'I was always ashamed to hear about the dictatorship of the proletariat.'

Shtern was against the October Revolution, but he accepted it as 'a kind of divine judgement'. Once the crime was committed, everyone must do his utmost to reduce the bad consequences to the population – a more honourable attitude than to run away and castigate as a traitor everyone who stayed behind and worked in the Soviet State apparatus. (This attitude was adopted by many even towards those who were active in the Soviet machine before Stalin gained full power over it.)

With this near-religious attitude toward life and work, Shtern worked in the Ukrainian Commissariat of Food, whence he transferred to the Commissariat of Finance in Moscow. Dzerzhinsky, then head of the VSNKh, fought hard with his colleagues in the Bolshevik leadership to get Shtern transferred to his staff (this occurred at the end of 1925 or early in 1926, according to Valentinov). If Dzerzhinsky did not include Shtern among his four 'highly esteemed Mensheviks', this was only because he used this phrase before Shtern's transfer to the VSNKh.

In the VSNKh, Shtern was in charge of finance. But, in 1926 at least, he apparently also looked after short-range planning (yearly and quarterly plans), Ginzburg being fully occupied with the preparation of what became the Ginzburg draft of the Five-Year Plan. In that connection, Shtern prepared a detailed report to Gosplan on the plan for State industry in 1926–7.[1]

SOKOLOVSKY

Aron L'vovich Sokolovsky, 47 years old in 1931, was the founder and a member of the central committee of the Socialist-Zionist Party (abbreviated to SS and otherwise known as the 'territorialists'). After this he was a member of the central committee of the United Jewish Socialist Party, and with the leaders of that Party, joined the Bund and then the Communist Party. He joined the VSNKh in 1921, but played only a minor role for more than two years. In 1923, however, he became one of the most important VSNKh workers. According to Valentinov, he was much abler than Ginzburg: 'His mind was faster and more acute.'

In 1923 the VSNKh made an absurd attempt to boost industry by raising greatly the sale prices of industrial products (Pyatakov's idea). As the head of the section on trade policies and chairman of the Bureau of Prices, Sokolovsky was in charge of undoing the ill effects of this measure. In 1924 a symposium on *The Problems of Raw Materials*, edited by Sokolovsky was published, and he published in 1926 an article, 'Production Costs in State Industry', in *Sotsialistichesky khozyaistvo*. Sokolovsky's activities were in full agreement with the views of Dzerzhinsky, the chairman of the VSNKh. He was indeed one of the four Mensheviks whom Dzerzhinsky singled out for praise.

In *Trial* (p. 467) he was specifically accused of setting low targets for raw materials, especially for cotton, in the Five-Year Plan. This must have happened as far back as 1926. Moreover, supplies of raw materials, and specifically cotton, depended then as now on farm output, and this was planned by analysts other than Sokolovsky; none of them, however, was among the defendants in the trial. Illogical, but nobody at a high level cared for logic in 1931.

Verdict – eight years.

[1] Seventy-four pages in *Planovoe khozyaistvo*, Nos. 1 and 2, 1927; see also *Sotsialisticheskoe khozyaistvo*, No. 6, 1926, pp. 3–60.

GROMANITES

V. G. Groman in his testimony prior to the trial gave the names of those working with him on economic affairs. In addition to Bazarov, the following were mentioned:[1] (V. I.) Zeilinger, (B. A.) Gukhman, (G. V.) Shub, (G. M.) Pistrak, (R. Ya.) Broitman, all former Mensheviks, and (N. M.) Vishnevsky, a non-party man (*Trial*, p. 36).[2] Of all these, Gukhman was apparently the ablest. He was chief of the Conjuncture Bureau of Gosplan, a creation of Groman's, but also played a considerable role in the economic-statistical section of Gosplan (S. G. Strumilin was apparently more of a figurehead). G. V. Shub was *inter alia* chief editor of *Narodnoe khozyaistvo v 1921 godu* (*The National Economy in 1921*), the yearbook of *Economicheskaya zhizn'*. In the same publication he was mentioned as head of the economic-statistical section of 'Economic Life' (the organisation, not the journal). Shub, Gukhman and especially Zeilinger, and occasionally also Broitman, worked on the balance of the national economy, Groman's pet subject. Zeilinger also became co-editor, with Groman, of *Vestnik statistiki*, when this journal was brought into life by the CSO after Groman had gained a great influence there. Vishnevsky specialised in farm problems. He had apparently worked with Groman already at Penza. In 1920 he published, under Groman's editorship, *Principles and Methods of Distribution of Food and Products of Primary Necessity*.[3]

All persons enumerated by Groman, except Zeilinger, were included in the list of important contributors to Control Figures for 1926–7, Gukhman having been assigned a more important role in this along with Groman, Bazarov and Strumilin. Vishnevsky (along with Oganovsky, a narodnik) is mentioned among the chief workers on Gosplan's draft of the first Five-Year Plan for 1926–7 to 1930–1,

---

[1] The document does not give the initials.
[2] There were two Shubs, and both were listed as part-authors of *Kontrol'nye tsifry na 1926/27g*: but Groman must have meant D. V. Shub, a collaborator of his from Penza days. See, for example, Groman's paper on the balance of the national economy in *Ekonomicheskoe obozrenie*, No. 1, 1927, p. 46, where below Groman's name one may read 'with the participation of R. Ya. Broitman and D. V. Shub'; only I. V. Shub was listed among the authors of the first Five-Year Plan, which was not in Groman's hands.
[3] *Printsipy i metody organizovannogo raspredeleniya produktov prodovol'stviya i premetov pervoy neobkhodimosti*, Moscow, 1920.

here called *Perspektivy*. Both are also included among the chief authors of the first Five-Year Plan (for agriculture), but it is made clear that M. M. Volf (a Communist) was the responsible author. Even the granting of permission to use their names was a compromise, however. Gukhman and S. V. Ryvkind were stated as having been responsible for setting up the detailed statistical tables for the first Five-Year Plan. This was a gruelling task, but they can hardly be made responsible for the targets of the Five-Year Plan.

There was a dearth of 'wrecking activities' in those years: nobody but the present Head of the Central Statistical Office, V. Starovsky, was successful in concocting an important accusation of this type.[1] He did so at a meeting of Marxist statisticians on 12 November 1930, presided over by M. Smit, who, as already noted, had worked in the same office as the present writer, ostensibly as a 'statistician' but in fact as a research analyst, then headed by Groman. According to Starovsky, N. M. Vishnevsky was guilty of falsifying statistics. His crime consisted in calculating the total value of the hay and straw produced at the average price of the quantities sold, a procedure which has been followed in the USSR ever since the Revolution and perhaps before.[2] In any case, the selection of statistical procedures to be used was the responsibility of the Central Statistical Office rather than of Gosplan. That a 'Gromanite should falsify statistics was an idea such as could be mooted only in times as demented as the thirties.

Articles by Gukhman and Vishnevsky (both men published rather extensively; Vishnevsky also did some teaching) ceased to appear in *Planovoe khozaistvo* or *Ekonomicheskoe obozrenie* a few months after those of Groman and Bazarov were discontinued. R. E. Vaisberg, a Communist who had played a considerable role in Gosplan and in any case had observed its proceedings at close range, said at a meeting of Gosplan specialists on 15 December 1929 (*Planovoe khozyaistvo*, No. 1, 1930, p. 22):

[1] Editor's note: For a description of Starovsky's career – the longest ministerial tenure in Soviet history (31 years by 1971) – see M. Kaser, 'The Publication of Soviet Statistics', in V. Treml (ed.), *Soviet Statistics*, Durham, N. Carolina, 1971.

[2] For its continuing use see S. V. Shol'ts, *Kurs sel'skokhozyaistvennoy statistiki*, Moscow, 1945, p. 162. On the meeting referred to see *Pravda*, 28 November 1930; *Ekonomicheskaya zhizn'*, 29 November 1930; and *Planovoe khozyaistvo*, No. 10–11, 1930.

I shall not speak of the others [other than Groman]. We have, for example, such men as Vishnevsky and Gukhman, who sometimes try to sit between two chairs, to support the one and the other camp, but basically they side with Groman, being his pupils and his mouthpieces. Neither of them was heard in the great debate with those who criticised Groman; pupils do not go against their teachers.[1]

RUBIN

Isaak Il'ich Rubin, 45 years old in 1931, was a member of the Bund and a Menshevik from the age of eighteen right up to the trial. Rubin's 'crime' was that he taught Marxism as interpreted by Kautsky and other recognised authorities, rather than according to the latest Bolshevik interpretation, and in the last years especially that of Stalin. Those in power were particularly angry with Rubin because many Bolsheviks accepted his teachings as true Marxism.

No. 2 of *Bolshevik* for 1930 and *Planovoe khozyaistvo*, No. 1, 1930, contained a militant article against Rubin by V. Milyutin and B. Borilin, entitled 'On the Disagreements in Political Economy'. They wrote:

I. I. Rubin is the ideologist and representative of the ideology of the theoreticians of the Second International in political economy[2]....

It is a great error to describe I. I. Rubin as a fighter for orthodox Marxism against the revisionism of the mechanists and against the 'social school', or to accept uncritically and with negligible reservations a number of his theoretical assertions as strictly Marxist (see the articles of comrades Greblis, Korovai, Stepanov and G. Deborin in the collection *Against 'Mechanist Tendencies'*, under the editorship of Borilin and Leontiev.[3]

To this article was appended a statement from the editors of *Bolshevik* announcing the complete cessation of press discussions of Rubin's views or those of his followers (*Rubinshchina*). Shortly before the trial (*Pravda*, 13 January 1931), the same Borilin launched a diatribe entitled 'Let us tear out *Rubinshchina* by the roots'.

---

[1] *Planovoe khozyaistvo*, No. 10–11, 1930, p. 38. The same Vaisberg wrote 'One of those who proudly called themselves representatives of the Groman school, the statistician Vishnevsky'.

[2] *Planovoe khozyaistvo*, No. 1, 1930, p. 127.   [3] *Ibid.* p. 132.

Under almost the same title, an article ('Let us eradicate *Rubin-shchina* root and branch') was published in the same paper during the trial itself (*Pravda*, 7 March 1931).

Rubin ended up as an actor in the trial and got five years. Unfortunately his forced testimony included a disclosure that the Communist Ryazanov, head of the Marx–Engels Institute, had hidden some illegal papers for him. Ryazanov was called a traitor in the press and relegated to solitary confinement.

LOSITSKY

Alexander Emelyanovich Lositsky was a man of middle age and in poor health when I knew him in 1916–17. In spite of this he remained conscientiously and efficiently at his post as an expert of the CSO dealing with the statistics of personal consumption. In the grave years of starvation this concerned mainly food, especially grain; later some other consumer goods were added. For some time he covered also statistics of livestock and statistics of grain stocks in the hands of the peasantry. His work was based on workers' and peasants' budgets obtained by surveys. Chayanov said of it:[1] 'But the greatest importance, of course, attached to the statistical work of our whole statistical network, directed by the division for statistics of the CSO headed by A. E. Lositsky'.

Lositsky regularly reported on his work in professional journals and taught at Moscow University. For years everybody used his findings. His last economic article seems to have been 'Peasant Grain Stocks According to the Surveys', in *Vestnik statistiki*, No. 2, 1927, and 'Perspectives of Consumption of Food in the Union (during the period of the general plan)', in *Planovoe khozyaistvo*, No. 4, 1927. His projections in the second article were very moderate by Khrushchev's standards. For example, *per capita* meat consumption in 1940–1 was planned at 1.87 puds (almost 30 kilograms), but none of the targets suggested by him was achieved even remotely, for reasons for which Lositsky was of course not responsible. Development in the subsequent years was

[1] A. V. Chayanov, *Byudzhetnye issledovaniya, istoriya i metody* (*Budget Investigations, History and Methods*), Moscow, 1929.

not along lines suggested by the Mensheviks (with the workers participating in the increasing wealth) but along those suggested by Preobrazhensky (ruthless exploitation of the masses for rapid industrialisation).

Lositsky's last word in print may have been an obituary notice of P. A. Vikhlyaev, one of the Socialist-Revolutionary leaders and a noted statistician, in *Vestnik statistiki*, No. 2, 1928. He may have died himself soon after. Such people are unlikely to retire.

MASLOV

Peter Pavlovich Maslov (1867–1946) was author of *The Agrarian Problem in Russia* – by far the most important book on the subject written by a Russian Social-Democrat,[1] published also several times in Germany – and father of the rather unsuccessful Menshevik agrarian programme (this writer always believed it stillborn).

Maslov remained fully active during the twenties. The Civil War had taken him to Eastern Siberia, where he wrote an important book, *A Theory of Co-operation*, based on accounts of Buryat live-stock and arable farms.[2] Back in Moscow, he became also chairman of the general economic section of the high-ranking Institute of Economics of the Russian Association of Research Institutes in Social Sciences (RANION) and a member of the Academy of Sciences of the USSR.

As the chairmanship referred to indicates, Maslov had a taste for theroetical problems. We may cite his papers 'Problems of Distribution of Productive Forces', *Ekonomicheskoe obozrenie*, No. 11, 1924, and 'Have Industrial Crises Been Eliminated?', in another issue of the same journal and these he presented in 1926 to the Institute of Economics of RANION: 'The Influence of Natural and Social Conditions On Labour Productivity', and 'The effect of Distance on the Distribution of Productive Forces'. His speech in the important discussion on the general (fifteen-year) plan in

---

[1] *Agrarny vopros v Rossii*, 6th edn. Moscow–Leningrad, 1926. The first volume was apparently published before 1901. The second edition of Vol. II appeared in 1905. Whether the pre-revolutionary editions are included in the count to the 6th edition is unknown to the present writer.

[2] *Teoriya kooperatsii*, Chita, 1922.

1928 showed insufficient familiarity with the planning work (see *Planovoe khozyaistvo*, No. 6, 1928).

One of his publications warrants some discussion. Early in October 1924, he delivered to the *Torgovo-Promyshlennaya Gazeta*, the VSNKh daily, an article on 'The Reproduction of Fixed Capital'. It expressed enthusiastic support of Pyatakov's position, and, through him, of Preobrazhensky's. Maslov insisted that more capital was used than was reproduced, and that the principal means to remedy this situation was to reduce private consumption. Valentinov, the editor, was enraged – see his Memoirs, pp. 257–8. According to him, the attitude of the Group of Observers to the article was also negative. Valentinov even used very abusive language against Maslov. 'We refuse to go in for "expanded reproduction" at the cost of reducing consumption' – such, he claimed, was the attitude of the 'Group of Observers'. According to him, he induced Maslov to make some changes, after which the article was published in the 10 October 1924 issue of the paper. I hope that Groman's attitude toward Maslov's article was not so violently negative as Valentinov's; in any case he would certainly not have used abusive language against such a distinguished scholar as Peter Pavlovich Maslov.

In later years Preobrazhensky's recipes were realised by Stalin in a way which no one could have foreseen in 1924. Whether it was due to this article by Maslov, the fact that he was severely criticised by Lenin (even such criticism conveyed a degree of distinction at that time), or some other reason, e.g. because he did no work on problems which led to prosecutions – at all events, the fact is that he was treated less harshly than other Mensheviks. Indeed he became an Academician in 1929, when times were already bad for anyone in opposition, especially non-party opposition.

Again in contrast with the attitude toward members of the opposition of any kind, both editions of the *Great Soviet Encyclopedia* devoted space to Maslov (1st edn. Vol. 38, 1938, pp. 326–7; 2nd edn. Vol. 26, 1954, pp. 430–1). He was branded a Menshevik and his opinions were characterised as harmful (much room was of course devoted to Lenin's criticism of him), but he was not wholly neglected. The second edition of the *Encyclopedia* says nothing about his career between the October Revolution and his death in 1946, but the brief article on him is quite compatible with his having spent several years in exile after 1930. If this distinguished scholar had ever jumped, or tried to jump, on the band-wagon, as some writers abroad insist, the *Encyclopedia* would certainly have mentioned the fact.

CHEREVANIN

Fedor Andreyevich Cherevanin (real name Lipkin) was an exceptionally likeable man.[1] A Social-Democrat and Menshevik of long standing, he did some economic research in addition to his Party activities, which came first. At the time of the 1917 Revolution he was already past his prime. All or most of the time between 1918 and 1929 he lived in exile. *Trial* (p. 13) mentions that he returned to Russia in 1929. Thereafter he at once went back to his normal haunts, which in the first place meant connection with Groman, an old friend of his.[2]

Kondrat'ev testified that he met Cherevanin as one of the members of the counter-revolutionary Menshevik organisation (*Trial*, p. 195). The words were obviously put into his mouth. He was unlikely to have known Cherevanin at all. Those preparing the trial badly wanted a prominent member of the Menshevik party among the defendants, but obviously failed to extract a confession from Cherevanin, his age and fondness for drink notwithstanding. In 1931 Cherevanin was already in the Verkhne Uralsk 'isolator':[3] so his freedom did not last long.

FINN-ENOTAEVSKY

Alexander Yul'evich Finn-Enotaevsky was 58 years old at the time of the trial, a professor of economics, and a great expert on the world economy. He was a Bolshevik, when politically active, for

---

[1] There is no evidence that he was directly connected with the fight against Stalinism on the economic front, to which this essay is primarily devoted.

[2] In 1916–17 he was Groman's deputy in the statistical office in Petrograd, where this writer also worked (see the section on Groman); but he had known Groman much earlier than this.

[3] According to the Yugoslav Communist, A. Ciliga: see *Sotsialistichesky vestnik*, 27 March 1936.

many years until 1915. After 1915 he devoted himself entirely to study, teaching and writing on economic problems. In spite of his testimony to the contrary, he may never have been a Menshevik, even in the sense in which Groman or Ginzburg were. Apparently he was simply a personal friend of Groman's, whom the latter consulted on the status of the world economy. He paid for a few dinners at Groman's and Kondrat'ev's houses (see *Trial*, p. 189 and elsewhere) with ten years in jail. (See also Chapter 4.)

KAFENGAUZ

Lev Borisovich Kafengauz was a professor at the Moscow State University and the Moscow Industrial-Economic Institute named after Rykov. He was among those named by Dzerzhinsky, the head of the VSNKh, as the Mensheviks of whom he was particularly proud (Valentinov's information): there was sufficient reason. For about a decade Kafengauz was in charge of the statistics of the industry controlled by the VSNKh and editor of the yearbook *Promyshlennost' SSSR* and *Ezhemesyachny statichesky byulleten'* (*Monthly Statistical Bulletin*). Difficulties occurred with the 1927–8 yearbook, which was delayed for several months and signed by the editorial board instead of by Kafengauz. He retained the editorship of the *Bulletin* somewhat longer; the last issue signed by him was that of March 1930.

The statistics compiled under Kafengauz were certainly excellent material for that time. They were of considerable help in directing the economy and planning for the future. The work of the OSVOK (Special Conference on Restoring of the Fixed Capital), the Ginzburg draft of the Five-Year Plan, and the subsequent drafts of the Five-Year Plans for industry would have been impossible without the Kafengauz statistics; later, Five-Year Plans were to be largely drafted in disregard of statistics. Even the OGPU could not find in Kafengauz's industrial statistics sufficient proof of 'crime' to make him an actor in the trial. Since his name disappeared from the list of regular contributors of *Planovoe khozyaistvo* in 1930, together with those of the other 'criminals', it is to be assumed that he was one of those who went into exile.

OTHER DEFENDANTS

Other defendants in the trial were: Sher, Vasilii Vladimirovich (47 years old);[1] Yakubovich, Mikhail Petrovich (39); Salkind, Lazar Borisovich (45); Volkov, Ivan Grigorievich (47); Petunin, Kirill Gavrilovich (46); Berlatsky, Boris Markovich (41); and Teitelbaum, Moisei Isaevich (54). (Vladimir Konstantinovich Ikov, still another defendant, is omitted here as he had no connection with the economic field.) The fact that all these persons were among the defendants proves that for more than twelve years they refused to become followers of the Party line, and specifically of the Stalin line. However false their enforced testimony was at the trial, and to whatever non-existent crimes they may have confessed, they deserve our respect.

VALENTINOV

Nikolai Vladislavovich Valentinov (real name Volsky, another pen name E. Yurevsky), died in 1964 at the age of 86 or older. His first love was philosophy. Politics probably came next. He was a very able journalist, and the years from 1922 to 1927, when he was officially assistant editor but actually chief editor of the VSNKh daily, were, according to him, the happiest time of his life. In his memoirs he relates how he transformed it from a mediocre paper, which did not even appear on time, into a responsible organ which was of real help to the VSNKh. For most of this period Dzerzhinsky, on the extreme right wing of the Bolshevik party, with whose policies Valentinov was in substantial agreement, was head of the VSNKh. Valentinov was one of the four Mensheviks whose presence on his staff so delighted Dzherzhinsky.

Fortunately for himself and posterity, Valentinov was transferred at the end of 1928 from Moscow to Paris to edit a Soviet journal there. This enabled him to burn his boats in 1930, when it became clear that there was no room within the Soviet machine for a sensible and conscientious person. Valentinov was the only one among those dealt with in this essay who escaped and lived long enough to lift the veil from developments some of which would otherwise have

---

[1] The ages are in all cases those at the time of the trial.

remained quite unknown. His prolific literary activities for more than thirty years after he left Russia do not concern us here, except for his *Vstrechi s Leninym*, published in 1953 in New York by the Chekhov publishing house.[1] The book makes good reading, and gives a vivid picture of the man who led Russia to the catastrophe of War Communism. Lenin is here presented in the very last years of his life, when he could see the disastrous results of his deeds, better perhaps than any other Communist.

In 1956 Valentinov wrote another extensive section of his Memoirs, covering a large part of the period dealt with in this book. This material remains unpublished, but can be consulted. Thanks to the fact that Valentinov became an *émigré* and was previously an eye-witness of the developments dealt with in this book, I was able both to read the Memoirs and to have a lively correspondence with him. I am still glad that I did so after an extensive study of other literary material.

[1] Since translated into English by P. Rosta and B. Pearce: *Encounters with Lenin*, London, 1968.

OTHER NEO-NARODNIKS AND A FEW
OTHER NAMES TO BE REMEMBERED

The neo-narodniks were almost completely dominant in the teaching of agricultural subjects and in writing about them, especially the peasant economy, until 1928 and even somewhat later. They also played a great role in agricultural planning. If any names other than those of the neo-narodniks were prominent in the field of agricultural economy, these seem to have been L. N. Litoshenko and N. M. Vishnevsky. Litoshenko was for some time in charge of CSO research concerning peasant budgets, and he published excellent material on the subject. He played a great role in preparing the important 1923–4 report by the CSO on the balance of the national economy. Politically and ideologically, he was considerably to the right of Kondrat'ev, but frequently was lumped together with him by critics.[1] Vishnevsky was a Gromanite, as has already been shown.

How those in power rated their enemies in the neo-narodnik camp can be seen from the following quotation, taken from an article by I. Vermenichev, who ranks high among Communist agricultural economists: 'A group of bourgeois and petit bourgeois scholars of the type of Kondrat'ev, Yurovsky, Doyarenko, Oganovsky, Makarov, Chayanov, Chelintsev, etc., who were joined by Groman, Sukhanov, Bazarov, etc....'[2] Kondrat'ev's leadership among the neo-narodniks is apparent from the fact that several books or booklets emanating from those who joined the bandwagon were published under such titles as *Kondrat'evshchina* and *Against Kondrat'evshchina*.[3] In the cited article Vermenichev

---

[1] I. D. Vermenichev, in *Protiv Kondrat'evshchiny, klassovaya borba v ekonomicheskoi teorii* (*Against Kondrat'evshchina, the Class War in Economic Theory*), here abbreviated to *Against Kondrat'evshchina*, Moscow, 1931, p. 12, called Litoshenko a Kondrat'evite pure and simple.

[2] *Ibid.* p. 3. Karatygin, condemned in another trial, gave a list which was certainly dictated to him by the OGPU and which included the same names except Yurovsky: *ibid.* p. 58.

[3] *Kondrat'evshchina* was published by the Agrarian Institute of the Communist Party and *Against Kondrat'evshchina* by the Young Guard Library of the Young Communist League (Komsomol).

(*op. cit.* p. 11) called Chayanov and Chelintsev *petit bourgeois* utopians; Kondrat'ev, Makarov, Yurovsky etc. were in his opinion 'open defenders of the kulaks'. On the next page of the article, Litoshenko was added to the latter group.

Yurovsky and Doyarenko, named after Kondrat'ev in the above quotation, are discussed in the second section of this chapter. In Verminichev's list four names follow: Oganovsky, Makarov, Chayanov and Chelintsev, and these head our list of neo-narodniks (in a slightly different order) after Kondrat'ev. Apart from them, only Panteleimon Vikhlyaev and Albert Weinstein are given space here. At least A. D. Rybnikov and G. A. Studentsky, the latter a pupil of Chayanov, probably deserved a mention, but were left out for reasons similar to those indicated in the introduction to the preceding chapter.

In the chapter devoted to the trial and elsewhere, the articles and book by the Yugoslav Communist Ciliga have been quoted. He seems to have been well informed and also reliable. He mentions a large number of groups and even more names (his statements related to 1931–3). It may be for some good reason that he does not mention any neo-narodniks. Should we infer that the latter were treated less harshly and suffered exile instead of jail?

MAKAROV

Together with Chayanov (see below), Nikolai Pavlovich Makarov was the chief member of the neo-narodnik group after Kondrat'ev. He was born in 1886 and became well-known after 1912 when he joined Chayanov, Oganovsky, P. P. Maslov the Marxist and S. L. Maslov the Social-Revolutionary, on the board of the Agrarian Reform League,[1] and published a notable study on the dairy industry. His *Peasant Economy and its Interests*, a book of 392 pages, appeared five years later.[2]

In the early twenties he spent some time in the United States and Germany. Although offered a good position by Professor Warren of

[1] See introduction to Chayanov's pamphlet, *Chto takoe agrarny vopros?* (*What is the Agrarian Problem?*), Moscow, 1917.
[2] *Krest'yanskoe khozyaistvo i ego interesy*, Moscow, 1917.

Cornell University (personal information from Makarov), he went back to Russia around 1923. As well as teaching, he published several works, mostly on Soviet agriculture as a whole, especially the peasant economy but also a 406-page analysis of American farmers.[1]

In 1927 his 568-page volume, the *Organization of Agriculture* was published by *Ekonomicheskaya zhizn'* with a lengthy introduction by the editors, on p. 3 of which we read:

The present book was written by an author who has published many works and is known as belonging to the work-consumption school – seeing the peasant economy as being directed in the first place toward producing as much as is required to cover the needs of the family for food and some cash; the economy expands when the number of persons in the family is enlarged and *vice versa*: i.e., the school now appropriately called neo-narodniks.[2]

The introduction goes on to explain at great length the 'erroneous' position of this group. In spite of this, Makarov's book is described as useful both in the middle (p. viii) and at the end (p. xix) of the editors' introduction. Makarov was prominent also as a planner, partly in opposition to the planning of agricultural production by Gosplan.

For more than twenty-five years this writer was greatly impressed by the fact that Makarov as well as Chelintsev voluntarily returned to the USSR from abroad. Until a short time ago, I continued to regard this action as a heroic sacrifice. However, work on the present essay has made me think that both of them may have been to a large extent influenced by the idea that the NEP was going to last indefinitely. Possibly they even thought that the USSR was heading back to capitalism – such opinions were widely held. Very few of those who believed this in fact emigrated back to the Soviet Union.

A few years later – but already in a different epoch – at the time of the purge of the Narkomzem (Commissariat of Agriculture) in December 1929, Makarov was intimidated into making statements which are not a pleasure to reproduce. There is not the smallest

[1] *Amerikanskie farmery organizovali svoe khozyaistvo*, New York, 1921.
[2] *Organizatsiya sel'skogo khozyaistva*, Moscow, 1927.

indication that any of those who 'confessed', including Makarov, really changed their opinions, nor was this expected of them. On this occasion he is supposed to have declared:[1] 'It is necessary to take measures in order that the rate of collectivisation be brought up to 100 per cent at once...' He knew very well that at that particular time the 'measures' consisted in driving the peasants into collective farms with bayonets.

Makarov is further alleged to have declared on the same occasion (*Kondrat'evshchina*, p. 116): 'Two years ago I warned frankly that the attack [on the kulaks] was unnecessary because we needed the marketable produce of these groups. Now the situation has completely changed. They do not have any marketable produce. All that comes from them is social-political unrest. And therefore it is necessary to conclude the process of socialist construction.' This smells even more of murder.

Makarov knew very well that 'the kulaks' were only a pretext, that every peasant who did not want to join a collective farm was proclaimed a 'kulak'. Yet what made peasants into 'kulaks' if they produced only enough for their own needs and nothing for the market? Makarov's words do not really matter; he obviously lost his head. It may be some excuse that he was not the first neo-narodnik to lay down his arms.

As already stated, the apologists for Stalin's general line did not even pretend to believe in the sincerity of Makarov's change of position. In his discussion speech delivered a year later and included in *Kondrat'evshchina*, p. 116, D. P. Davydov called him an 'ideologist of the kulaks' and 'leader of the kulaks', and described his statements quoted above as examples of double-dealing.

Nothing was heard of Makarov after December 1929 for nearly thirty years. We can only guess what he as well as the others might have accomplished, if we consider the amount of work he achieved in only four to five years after his return from the United States. He was only 43 years old when his career was cut short some time in 1928.

In 1957 he came back into view with a book on the economy and

---

[1] *Kondrat'evshchina*, p. 118. This and similar reproductions of declarations of the neo-narodniks must be accepted as substantially true, however deplorable they may be. No claim seems to have been made that a Menshevik made any serious concessions before imprisonment.

organisation of the agriculture of the Donbass.[1] The preface indicates that the book was substantially ready in 1954. Every Soviet
agricultural economist was graciously permitted to praise, and
elaborate on, Khrushchev's farm policies. The pardoned 'criminals'
of the twenties must have been particularly careful not to step
beyond the limits set for them. One must feel sorry for Makarov, in
spite of the fact that the death of Stalin at least brought his physical
sufferings to an end.

CHAYANOV

Alexander Vasil'evich Chayanov was born in 1888. Together with
Makarov, he is usually listed next after Kondrat'ev as the leader of
the Working-Peasant Party.[2] Chayanov showed his great abilities
early. In 1911, at the age of 23, he read an important paper at a
Moscow regional agricultural conference, with such well-known
scholars as A. N. Chelintsev and B. D. Brutskus participating in
the discussion. Next year he published his first book *Ocherki po
teorii trudovogo khozaistva* (*Essays on the Theory of Working Enterprise*), Moscow, 1912–13 (later translated into German).

His work on the optimum size of farms, first published in 1922,
became a standard work on the problem and gained him an international reputation.[3] His calculations favoured the large farm, but
he believed that these findings did not apply to the peasant family
farm guided by other motives besides that of profit. In spite of the
findings in question Chayanov, together with Makarov and Chelintsev, was known as a pure representative of the working-peasant
philosophy (individual production by the peasants, co-operative
sales and purchases). While not accepting the need for production
co-operatives he favoured other forms of rural co-operation which
would help the peasant to enjoy the advantages of a large farm.

Russia was ahead of other countries as regards studies of peasant
economy and peasant life by the survey method. This type of
research dates back to the early 1890s, F. A. Shcherbina having

---

[1] *Ekonomika i organizatsiya sel'skogo khozyaistva Donbassa*, Moscow, 1957.
[2] See *Kondrat'evshchina*, pp. 5, 7 and elsewhere.
[3] *Optimal'nye razmery sel'skokhozyaistvennykh predpriyatii* (Optimum Sizes of Farm
Enterprises), Moscow, 1922; 2nd edn., 1924, 3rd edn., 1928. The latest edition was
also published in German in 1930.

been the greatest name in this field.[1] Chayanov was greatly interested in this type of research from his earliest days as an analyst, his first publications of 1912 and 1913 having been devoted to this subject. He continued this work after the Revolution and apparently played an important role in it. In his Budget Investigations, he gave *inter alia* the history of this type of research and an extensive bibliography. The book was acknowledged as the only work of its kind.

At least after 1920, Chayanov was director of the Scientific-Research Institute for Agricultural Economics, in which capacity he developed great activity. The institute seems to have brought out such good scholars as Albert Weinstein, G. A. Studentsky and S. Klepikov. A long series of studies was published with Chayanov's active participation. As an example may be quoted the publication of *Methods of Quantitative Calculation of the Effectiveness of Land*.[2] Its authors were given as B. Bruk, A. Weinstein, S. Platova, K. Sazonov and A. Chayanov (ed.). With full justification the Institute was known as the Chayanov Institute.[3] In 1924 Chayanov published a volume in German under the title *Sozialekonomie* (it also appeared in Russian).

If this writer has a feeling other than deep pity for any one of those who capitulated to superior force, it is for Chayanov, all his talents notwithstanding. He laid down his arms at the same time as Chelintsev. He was years younger than Chelintsev but certainly considered himself much more prominent; moreover, his climb-down was much more abrupt. Early in 1929, he published an article in *Ekonomicheskaya Zhizn'* (15 February 1929): its title 'From Class Peasant Co-operative to the Socialist Reconstruction of Agriculture' tells the whole story.

Actually, given the findings of *Optimal'nye razmery*, the shift from his former working-peasant philosophy to a favourable attitude towards large-scale farms, including the kolkhozes, should have been easier for Chayanov than for other representatives of the same philosophy; but such a shift fell far short of what he wrote in the above-mentioned article and others published at about the same

---

[1] See her *Krest'yanskie byudzhety* (Peasant Budgets), Voronezh, 1900.

[2] *Metody kolichestvennogo ucheta effekta Zemleustroistva*, Moscow, 1925.

[3] *Kondrat'evshchina*, p. 41. Also of interest is the author's remark that 'the Institute of Economics of the Communist Academy, where the Communists put in rare and timid appearances, was the arena of the enemies' work of sabotage'.

time. In the article, Chayanov declared that to defend his old positions now would be crude and reactionary. Most important, he stressed that his new positions 'fully coincide with the general line of socialist reconstruction of our national economy'. 'General line' at that time meant of course the Stalin line. Chayanov seems to have even gone beyond Stalin when he declared in the same article: 'The future organisation of agriculture is to be visualised not as a conglomerate of state and collective farms, co-operatives and remaining individual enterprises, but as single socialist economies of whole districts (*volosti*).' This seems to imply that Chayanov wanted in 1929 a rate of socialisation which has not been reached by agriculture even today. Chayanov moreover had something good to say about War Communism.

The editors of *Ekonomicheskaya zhizn'* pretended to believe in his sincerity (see addendum to the cited article), but in an article by M. Sulkovsky, 'Evolution and disintegration of the neo-narodnik philosophy' in *Na agrarnom fronte*, No. 11–12, 1929, they let fly at him.[1]

Giving up his old positions with reference to the peasant economy was not a reason for him to compete with ignorant Communists, indeed to outdo them, in unbounded admiration for the super-large 'factory farm'. In two articles on State grain farms,[2] Chayanov argued that the American machinery triad – tractor, combine and truck – made possible the operation of pure grain factories of immense, practically unlimited, dimensions, and, moreover, he believed that the advantage of such huge farms was not limited to grain production. Whether on his advice or otherwise, the Bolsheviks tried out the huge grain factories, but these turned out a failure in only two to three years (difficulties of management; highly seasonal labour requirements; allowing weeds to get out of hand; total loss of by-products).[3]

[1] See also the earlier article by Vermenichev, 'A Neo-narodnik Creeps Out', in *Na agrarnom fronte*, No. 10, 1928.
[2] Cited and discussed in the present writer, *The Socialized Agriculture of the USSR*, pp. 27–8. Enthusiasm for the giant grain farms was displayed by Chayanov already in an article or articles in the journal *Sovkhoz*, Nos. 9 and 10 of 1928.
[3] See my work, just cited, Ch. XI. The German edition of Chayanov's *Optimal'nye razmery* was not published before 1930. In a special preface, he tried to work in his new views in a few paragraphs. This was nothing but an insult to scholarship.

Once on the slippery slope, there was no stopping. A certain D. P. Davydov quoted Chayanov as having put the question to his audience in a session of the seminar of the National Institute for Agricultural Economic Organisation (NIOSKhE), 'Why should not you Communists, who are a small but united army, drive the peasants into the kolkhozes by military force?'[1] All this smacks very much of climbing on the band-wagon. It did not help him a bit, however; on the contrary, the trial of the neo-narodniks which was scheduled to take place in March 1931 (in the end it was replaced by secret verdicts of the OGPU) bore the name of Chayanov along with that of Kondrat'ev as the chief two defendants (*Trial*, p. 53). Nothing seems to be known of what happened to Chayanov after the Menshevik trial in March 1931.[2]

CHELINTSEV

Alexander Nikolaevich Chelintsev was born in 1874 and was known as a good agricultural economist long before World War I. As early as 1901 he published an article in the monthly *Mysl* on the daily wages of a farm worker in European Russia. He had already become particularly interested in surveys of the peasant economy before World War I. In 1919 his *Study of the Organisation of the Peasant Economy* was published at Khar'kov.[3] About this time he went to Prague, where he continued his teaching and research. He returned to Russia about 1923. Everything said above about Makarov's return applies to Chelintsev as well. The more honour is due to him for this act because he was so much older than Makarov.

Chelintsev was one of the strongest advocates of the 'family consumption theory'. He continued stressing the advantages of the peasant household as late as 1927.[4] While interested in all major

---

[1] *Kondrat'evshchina*, p. 119. The date of the memorable oration was not stated.
[2] At the time of the Menshevik trial Chayanov must be assumed to have been in prison, expecting the trial of his Party, together with Kondrat'ev and others. [Editor's note: A fuller survey of Chayanov's life and work may be found in introductions by Kerblay and Thorner in A. M. Chayanov, *The Theory of Peasant Economy* (trans. D. Thorner, B. Kerblay and R. E. F. Smith), Homewood, Illinois, 1966.]
[3] *Opyt izucheniya organizatsii krest'yanskogo sel'skokhozyaistva*, Khar'kov, 1919.
[4] See especially 'On the Problem of Differentiation of Peasant Enterprises', *Puti sel'skogo khozyaistva*, No. 4, 1927, pp. 124–5.

problems of agriculture, particularly those of peasant farming, including planning for the future, Chelintsev was a great expert on the regional differences in agriculture. He had already started these researches before World War I.

Chelintsev may have been the first to begin the retreat after the end of the NEP, but so far as the sources in my possession indicate, he did not go nearly as far as Makarov and especially as Chayanov. Nevertheless his decisive statement went quite a long way: 'Despite its appearance of "political progressiveness" this theory (the family-consumption theory to which Chelintsev held all his life) is very reactionary in substance...'[1] The novel feature of Chelintsev's views was the acceptance of the productive co-operative as the principal form for transition of agriculture into socialism. He thought of it, however, as a very prolonged process. It may have been a renewed retreat when, in his last article (*Puti sel'skogo khozyaistva*, No. 11, 1928), he insisted that the TOZ, the loosest form of the collective farm,[2] should be the principal form of co-operation in peasant farming for a long time ahead.

Chelintsev's name seems to have reappeared lately. But the gap of almost thirty years is of course irreparable for a man of his age. The end of his research career must be placed in 1928, the date of his articles in *Puti sel'skogo khozyaistva*, 1928, the last being in No. 11.

OGANOVSKY

Nikolai Petrovich Oganovsky, born in 1874, was already known as an expert in agricultural economy prior to World War I. He was a member of the Constituent Assembly representing the Socialist-Revolutionary Party (information from M. Vishnyak, who was Secretary of the Assembly), although he was actually a member of the People's Socialists, a less prominent party than the Socialist-Revolutionaries, but substantially of the same way of thinking.

In addition to teaching, Oganovsky did a great deal of agricultural planning. He also published extensively, possibly too much so for

[1] *Ibid.* No. 8, 1928.
[2] Three forms of co-operative farm were distinguished: the commune, the *artel'*, and the TOZ (common cultivation of the land, livestock remaining privately raised).

very careful work. At least a minor catastrophe occurred when a number of arithmetical errors were discovered in an important article of his.[1] The volume *Prominent Scholars of the USSR*, published by the Academy of Sciences, Vol. IV, Moscow, 1930, gave as Oganovsky's address a dormitory room, N. 44. We must hope that he did not have to share the room with anybody (except for his wife if he had one) but his quarters cannot have been very conducive to research.

In the winter 1926–7, Oganovsky, Vishnevsky and Lositsky (who dealt with livestock) worked out on Gosplan's instructions a fifteen-year plan for agriculture from 1926–7 to 1940–1.[2] They expected an average increase in gross agricultural production of 4.6 per cent per year. The rates of growth scheduled by the authors were sharply criticised by Kondrat'ev, Makarov and Chelintsev as too high.[3] The same rates were, on the other hand, denounced as far too low by Ya. Nikulikhin (a great 'star' at that dark time).[4] 4.6 per cent per year for fifteen years in succession would have almost doubled the initial production level. As it was, farm output actually declined in the fifteen years in question.[5]

Oganovsky may have disagreed with Kondrat'ev and the other neo-narodniks; he may have tried to make some concessions, but all these differences were not visible from the exalted heights occupied by the Bolsheviks at the time of the all-out drive. R. E. Vaisberg, who must have known Oganovsky well for years, wrote in his 'Bourgeois Distortions in the Field of Planning' (*Planovoe khozyaistvo*, 1930, No. 1, p. 17):

If one takes his [Oganovsky's] work on the plan, an interesting picture is obtained. The man starts, for example, from some miserable rates of growth of acreages, but, if pressed hard enough, he would go up another ½ per cent, another 1 per cent etc. His attitude toward yields is no better. I would recall his article in *Agricultural Gazette* in connection with the

---

[1] See L. Kritsman in *Na agrarnom fronte*, No. 1, 1925, and I. Fyodorovich, *ibid*. No. 3, 1925.
[2] See N. Oganovsky in *Sotsialisticheskoe khozyaistvo*, No. 2, 1927.
[3] See Makarov's article in *Puti sel'skogo khozyaistva*, No. 2, 1927, pp. 39 ff.
[4] *Against Kondrat'evshchina*, p. 141.
[5] *Narodnoe khozyaistvo SSSR v 1958g.* p. 350, shows an increase of 11 per cent in the fourteen years from 1926 to 1940, but this increase is more than cancelled out by the accretion of territory after the outbreak of World War II.

idea of raising yields by 35 per cent.[1] There he reached 13 per cent – a figure which he mentioned in Gosplan and above which nobody could push him... Thus we have a gap between 13 per cent and 35 per cent. This clearly shows the direct lines which lead... from Kondrat'ev to Oganovsky.

The Party's decision to raise the per hectare yields of grain by at least 30–35 per cent was made in December 1928. Oganovsky's article cited by Vaisberg must have been published after this (unfortunately, as was quite common at that time, Vaisberg did not give the date of the article). So Oganovsky stuck to his guns at a time when some other neo-narodniks were already retreating or preparing a retreat.

WEINSTEIN

Albert L. Weinstein was relatively rarely mentioned in the voluminous literature of the late twenties abusing the neo-narodniks, although his work was considerably in evidence in the literature of the preceding years. The name of Weinstein, born in 1892, appeared for the first time (to the knowledge of this writer) in a publication of the Chayanov Institute in 1920. Soon after this he became a permanent senior member of the Kondrat'ev Conjuncture Institute and remained there as long as the Institute remained in Kondrat'ev's hands. But he also contributed to other publications, including those of the Chayanov Institute, its weekly *Finansy i narodnoe khozyaistvo* (*Finance and the National Economy*), the monthly *Sotsialisticheskoe khozyaistvo* (*Socialist Economy*) etc.

On the assignment of the Scientific-Research Institute of Agricultural Economics (the Chayanov Institute), which acted for the agricultural sections of Gosplan RSFSR and Gosplan USSR, Weinstein worked on a great project 'The Development of Yields per Hectare of Grain in Russia before the War and Prospects of Development in the Future' (published in abbreviated form in *Planovoe khozyaistvo*, No. 7, 1927, pp. 81–100 and No. 8, pp. 57–89). The ultimate object was to forecast the development of the yields per hectare in the next ten to fifteen years.

[1] In accordance with the decision of the 11th session of the Central Executive Committee of the USSR in December 1928. This decision involved raising the yield of grain per hectare by at least 30–35 per cent in five years; the optimum variant of the first Five-Year Plan which had become law was actually based on a 35 per cent rise.

The long-range trend in yield per hectare of grain had been tackled repeatedly and efficiently before, but an important step forward seems to have been made by Weinstein. He concluded (*ibid.* No. 8, p. 87) that under favourable conditions the yields per hectare of grain might rise by 30–33 per cent in fifteen years. Whether he was influenced by the desire to make the estimate more acceptable to the Bolsheviks we do not know; but the favourable conditions on which the forecast was based never materialised, and the yield of grain per hectare did not increase at all in the next twenty-five years.[1]

In *Finansy i narodnoe khozyaistvo*, Weinstein discussed the important fact that in the early draft of the Five-Year Plan, which had been in the hands of S. G. Strumilin (a Communist, formerly a Menshevik), the income of the rural population was to rise, from 1925–6 to 1930–1, only by 4.4 per cent, while the income of the urban population was to increase by 43.6 per cent per working person in each case.[2]

In the great debate on the general plan in the Krzhizhanovsky Club of Planning Staffs in 1928 (*Planovoe khozyaistvo*, No. 6, 1928, pp. 155–8), Weinstein argued that 'for the general plan we have to eschew statistical calculations of the components of the total national economy'; but the same opinion was advocated before him by P. S. Osadchy, who was in charge of work on the general plan in Gosplan until about 1926, as well as by Kondrat'ev, Weinstein himself and possibly others. It was natural for Weinstein as a staff member of the Kondrat'ev Conjuncture Institute to bring Kondrat'ev's long cycles into the appraisal of prospects for the next 10–15 years, but he seems not to have convinced many. The rest of what he said in the debate seems to have been sensible but without much drive. Like Kondrat'ev, Weinstein was only 31–35 years old during the most intensive scholarly activities of the neo-narodniks. Another good man almost wasted.

The Academy of Sciences of the USSR, in *Nauchnye trudy po*

---

[1] It is not clear why the assignment for this project was not given to V. M. Obukhov, the established authority on the subject. Did they hope to get more favourable results from Weinstein? There is of course no harm in such a vital problem being dealt with by two good men independently.

[2] *Finansy i narodnoe khozyaistvo*, issue dated 10 July 1927, p. 3.

statistike (*Scientific Works on Statistics*) Vol. III, Moscow, 1957, published a treatise by Weinstein, 'Methods of Statistical Calculation of National Wealth in Relation to its Calculation for Pre-Revolutionary Russia'.[1] A note by the editor states that the treatise, which occupies sixty-two large pages, is only a small part of the total.

Weinstein could be expected to argue that, in pre-revolutionary Russia, almost all wealth was in the hands of the capitalists and large land-owners, which would have been substantially true, so there was no danger of getting into trouble by doing the work. Still, he chose the subject possibly in order to avoid more contemporary topics. This may be an indication that in spite of everything he had had to suffer during the twenty-five years of non-existence, he preserved in himself something worthy of admiration. Apart from this, Weinstein has been in evidence as a writer and a discussion speaker in important debates in recent years.[2]

VIKHLYAEV

Panteleimon Alexeevich Vikhlyaev certainly never thought of himself as a neo-narodnik. He was one of the leaders of the Socialist-Revolutionaries for many years before the October Revolution, and probably considered himself to be one until his death in 1928. If he is here included with the neo-narodniks, it is because there is no other more suitable group to put him in.[3]

Vikhlyaev was born in 1869 and was an agronomist by training. The first twenty years of his active life were devoted to work in the zemstvos, first as an agronomist and statistician and later as an economist. He was always deeply interested in problems of the peasantry. The direction of his thoughts is clear from the title of his important pamphlet, *Agrarny vopros s pravovi tochki zreniya*,

[1] Weinstein is the only case, as far as this essay is concerned, where the identity of a person reappearing from the 'dead' is absolutely certain. On p. 127 he quotes his own article published in 1929 and calls it 'mine'. However, Makarov's identity may also be regarded as virtually certain.

[2] Editor's note: Weinstein died in 1970; an official obituary appeared in *Voprosy ekonomiki*, No. 5, 1970, p. 160.

[3] How remote his position was from the neo-narodniks is obvious from the fact that Makarov did not mention him in his book of 1926.

Moscow, 1906 (*The Agrarian Problem from the Legal Viewpoint*).
According to A. E. Lositsky's eulogy at his funeral (*Ekonomicheskoe obozrenie*, No. 2, 1928, p. 31), Vikhlyaev's publications on the peasant economy of the Moscow guberniya from 1903 to 1915 were of great value.

World War I drew him away from regional to all-Russian problems. In the Provisional Government he was actually in charge of agrarian problems in the Ministry of Agriculture; V. Chernov, the Minister, being mainly busy with other matters (information from M. V. Vishnyak). The work involved was of course that of preparing to carry out 'socialisation of the land' – the cornerstone of the agrarian programme of the Socialist-Revolutionaries. The long delay in working out the details of 'socialisation of the land' (so as to make it as fair as possible) was a factor, probably a major one, in enabling Lenin to seize power by calling on the peasants to take the land themselves and handle it according to their wishes. Vikhlyaev cannot be made solely responsible for this unstatesmanlike delay, but much of the blame certainly falls on him.

After 1919 he concentrated on teaching and writing on statistics. He organised Russia's first statistical faculty at Moscow University, and was its chairman for several years. At the same time he was active in the Central Statistical Office as head of the section of Statistical Training. He died on 23 February 1928.

OTHERS

Three others must be discussed separately, in view of uncertainty as to their political affiliations. One of them actually belongs to a preceding epoch; the fact that he was subjected to a vicious attack in 1931 is a good illustration of the unstable mentality of the time: madmen rushing toward a precipice and shouting, 'Join us, everybody (including the dead) – anyone who does not march in step with us is liable to destruction!'

Leonid Naumovich Yurovsky, born in 1884, was one of the most brilliant of the men dealt with here. V. P. Milyutin, in his speech in the Agrarian Institute of the Communist Academy on 1 October 1930, when listing 'the agents of world bourgeoisie inside the

USSR', said 'Yurovsky played an outstanding role and was a member of the collegium of the Peoples' Commissariat of Finance', in which he remained for many years. M. Bronsky, a Communist, wrote in 1924 about a small book published by Yurovsky early in the same year: 'The small book by L. N. Yurovsky, a great expert on finance problems, is a valuable contribution on Soviet economy from the financial point of view. Professor Yurovsky...writes clearly and formulates his thoughts distinctly. He has managed to present one of the most difficult economic problems in a fascinating and readable booklet.'[1] The same Bronsky, in the same journal, attacked Yurovsky only four years later in a lengthy article entitled 'Neo-capitalist Ideology in Soviet Economic Literature'.[2] Yurovsky is generally believed to have played a great role in the creation of the chervonets, the rouble introduced in 1922 after the collapse of the currency inherited from the previous régime. He taught several economic subjects at the Moscow Industrial Economic Institute named after Rykov, and also published extensively. He called himself a member of the TKP (Worker-Peasant Party) at the trial of the Industrial Party at the end of 1930, in which he functioned as a witness.[3] In the late 1920s Soviet sources also frequently ranked him with this group. But *Against Kondrat'evshchina*, p. 85, was more correct, it seems, when it called him a Kadet. 'Left-wing Kadet' would have been a correct designation for him, at least up till the Stalin 'all-out drive'. Like most neo-narodniks, he conceded defeat as early as 1929.

Doyarenko was frequently included among the leaders of the Worker-Peasant Party. In *Against Kondrat'evshchina*[4] a special article is devoted to 'Doyarenkovshchina'. He was not an economist, having been professor of general agronomy at the Timiryazev Academy of Agricultural Sciences and in charge of experimental work there. The most explicit charge against him was that 'all his teaching and scientific activities in the field of agriculture and experimental work until his arrest in 1930 was based on the kulak

[1] *Sotsialisticheskoe khozyaistvo*, No. 2, 1924, pp. 383-4.
[2] *Sotsialisticheskoe khozyaistvo*, No. 3, 1928.
[3] *Pravda*, 2 December 1930.
[4] Pp. 93-111. All evidence on Doyarenko is from this source.

[read: individual-peasant] economy.'[1] Doyarenko was apparently particularly recalcitrant in the face of attempts to make him conform to a mould, especially the Communist one. In 1928 the Timiryazev Academy announced re-election of the professors, but the most honoured among them were approved without re-election. Among these was A. N. Chelintsev, but not the still more prominent Doyarenko. The alleged reasons were that he was not a member of the trade union, did not participate in social life etc., and was the ideologist of individual-peasant economy.[2]

The Soviet authorities surpassed themselves by bringing up the celebrated Alexandr Fedorovich Fortunatov, who was born, I believe, in 1856, started teaching at the Timiryazev Academy as far back as 1884, i.e. thirty-three years before the October Revolution, and died in 1925. A whole article is devoted to him in *Kondrat'ev-shchina*, entitled 'The Wreckers' Ideologist'. The author exclaims (p. 59): 'All his life, Fortunatov worked in the Timiryazev Academy. One generation of agronomists after another came under his influence.' Did they think he ought to have changed his teaching in anticipation of Lenin's coming to power, or that he was likely to change his opinions at or after the ripe age of 67 because the Bolsheviks seized power in October 1917? Evidently he had to be made to share the guilt of his pupil Doyarenko – a penal philosophy worthy of Alice in Wonderland.

[1] *Ibid.* p. 15.
[2] *Puti sel'skogo khozyaistva*, No. 4, 1929, p. 143.

INDEX

Abramovich, R. A., 13n, 65, 75, 76, 78, 79
Abramovich, S. D., 156
Agrarian Reform League, 197
agriculture: under War Communism, 11, 12; during NEP, 13, 16, 17, 19–21, 26–8; collectivisation of, 1, 21, 37, 38–41; co-operatives in, 17, 20, 200, 204; Five-Year Plan for, 167–72, 187; production of, 12, 27, 41; products of, compared with those of industry, (prices) 18–19, 22, 25, 104, (sales) 112–14; mentioned in trial, 70, 71; *see also* grain
Aneev, 182
Arkus, Ya. S., 156
Astrov, N. I., 95
Atlas, Z., 160n

banks, 10, 11, 71
Bazarov, V. A. (Rudnev), 3, 68, 123; early years of, 17n, 124–5; in Gosplan, 34, 97, 104, 109–10, 115, 120, 123, 125–8, 174; on Ginzburg, 139–40; on Groman, 117; and long-term plan, 56, 128–34, 146, 150, 170; and declining growth rate, 24, 49; dropped from list of planners, 55; attacks on, 109, 119; mentioned in trial, 65, 69, 70, 81, 177n, 186; in alleged groups, 72, 136–7; disappears, 83, 137
Belotsvetov, V. A., 156
Berlatsky, B. M., 63, 69, 77, 83, 194
Bernstein, E., 77
Birlrauer, M., 107
Bissel, 182
Black Hundreds, 32
Bogdanov, A., 110n, 124, 125
Bolshakov, I., 33
Bolsheviks, 10, 68, 91, 102–3, 124; trials of, 61
Borilin, B., 188
Broitman, R. Ya., 69, 70, 96, 123, 186
Bronsky, M., 210
Brounstein, M. A., 67, 68, 75, 78–9
Bruk, B., 201
Brutskus, B. D., 200

building materials, output of, 51
Bukharin, N., 2, 20, 61, 173
Bukharinists, 49
Bukhshpan, Y. A., 97, 182
Burns, A. F., 162
Bushinsky, V., 169

Central Statistical Office (CSO), 12, 104, 187, 189; Groman on Council of, 108, 123
Charnovsky, N., 73
Chayanov, A. V., 5, 35, 158, 200–3; in TKP, 174, 196, 197; on Lositsky, 189; submits, 55, 66, 201–2; mentioned in trial, 66, 73, 74, 177; disappears, 203
Chelintsev, A. N., 35, 198, 200, 203–4, 211; on planning, 129n, 170n, 172, 205; in TKP, 174; attacks on, 176, 196, 197; submits, 55, 175, 201; reappears, 178, 204
Cherevanin, F. A. (Lipkin), 5, 65, 99, 182, 192
Chernobaev, N. G., 156
Chernov, V., 209
Chuprov, A. I., 93
Ciliga, A., 38n, 83–5, 122, 192n, 197
Cities, Union of, 93, 94, 95, 96, 98, 119
Clemence, R. V., 162n
collectivisation of agriculture, *see under* agriculture
Communist Party, German, 181
Communist Party Conferences: (1924), 20; (1926), 21, 24
Communist Party Congresses: VIII (1919), 11; X (1921), 12–13, 16; XII (1923), 19; XIII (1924), 16n; XV (1927), 7, 21, 37–9, 61, 123; XVI (1930), 42, 44n; XX (1956), 61; XXII (1961), 129
Congress of Soviets, VI (1931), 38n, 42, 44n, 146
Conjuncture Council and Bureau of Gosplan (founded 1923), 105, 186
Conjuncture Institute (organised by Kondrat'ev, 1920), 163–4, 206
conjuncture reviews, 103

Index

Constitutional-Democratic Party, *see* Kadets

consumer goods, output of, 51-2, 131, 173; prices of, 26-8, 53

Control Figures: Groman and, 34, 96-7, 105-20 *passim*; change in targets of, 147; Weinstein on, 171; Chelintsev on, 172

co-operatives: agricultural, 17, 20, 200, 204; consumer, 14, 34

cotton, 130-1, 185

dairy products, price index for, 166, 167

Dallin, D., 76

Dan, T., 74n, 76, 77, 78

Davidov, O. P., 175n

Davydov, D. P., 199, 203

Demosthenov, S. S., 94n

Denike, Yu. P., 76

Deutscher, I., 55

Dolinsky, N. V., 94n

Doyarenko, 196, 197, 210-11

Dubovikov, F. G., 156

Dubrovsky, S. M. 169

Duma, 92

Dzerzhinsky, F, E.: head of VSNKh, 33, 122; and Mensheviks on his staff, 140, 184, 185, 193, 194

Eason, W., 52n

economic equilibrium, Groman on, 110-11

electrification, *see* GOELRO Engineer-Industrial Centre, *see* Industrial Party

engineers: political attitudes 29; trials of, 54, 61

Erlich, A., 124n

Ermansky, O. A., 182

Fabrikant, 35

Falkner, S. A., 4, 34, 56

famine: (1920-1), 1, 12, 163; (1932-3), 1, 41, 71, 135, 153

Fedorov, A, 14, 32

Feldman, G. A. 135n, 136

fibres, production of, 168; *see also* flax

finance, of alleged Menshevik groups, 66, 80-2

Finn-Enotaevsky, A. Yu., 34n, 192-3; trial of, 63, 77, 80-2, 121, 137, 177; in alleged groups, 72; verdict on, 38, 193

Five-Year Plan: for agriculture (1923-4), 167-72, 187; Gosplan draft for, 24, 40,

41-4, 69, 71, 99, 128-9; VSNKh (Ginzburg) draft for (industry), 41-4, 69, 71, 133, 141-5; raising of targets of, 42, 47, 145-8; fulfilment of, 44-53, 148-57

flax, 130-1, 166, 168

Food, Special Committee on (1915), 93, 94, 96

Food Commission (1917), 97, 98

foreign intervention, allegations at trial about, 65, 66, 73, 74, 75, 78, 176, 177

Fortunatov, A. F., 211

Galov, 182

Galperin, M. B., 156

Garvy, G., 158n, 162n

Garvy, A. P., 77

Gertsenshtein, A. G., 162n

Ginzburg, A. M., 5, 14, 33, 36, 139-42; Valentinov on, 65-6; and Five-Year Plan for industry under VSNKh, 3-4, 71, 122, 141-2, 146, 184-5 (*see also under* Five-Year Plan); and declining growth rate, 49; in USA and Germany, 76-7; dropped from list of planners, 56; trial of, 62, 63, 69, 71, 121, 122; in alleged groups, 66-7, 72, 73, 74; verdict, on 83

Gladkov, I., 49, 132-3, 134n

GOELRO (electrification) plan, 4, 169n-170n; and industrialisation, 15, 20; staff of, 9, 34, 73n

Gordon, A. S., 135

Gorfinkel, 182

Gorky, M., 30, 125

Gorlunov, 118

Gosplan: founded (1921), 9; Mensheviks in, 17n, 33-4, 69 (*see also under* Bazarov, Groman, Gukhman); Five-Year Plan drafted by, *see under* Five-Year Plan

GPU, 74, 75, 84, 85, 137

grain: government monopoly of, 97-8, 100; requisitioning of, 102; in collectivisation programme, 39, 202; production of, 27, 93, 168; forecasting of crops of, 120; price of, 28; yields per hectare of, 206-7; *see also* wheat

Granat, A. N., 180

Grinevetsky, E., 100

Grinko, G. F., 48n

Grinzer, M., 156, 157

Groman, E. P., 123

Groman, V. G., 3, 12n, 30, 89-90; early years of, 91-2; in World War I, 92-7; in

214

Index

kulaks, 10; during NEP, 20, 21, 22; campaign against, 7, 38, 39, 175, 177, 199, 203

Kutler, N. N., Finance Minister under Tsar, 36

labour force and productivity: in industry, 11, 50n, 54, 140–1, 151–3, 155; Stalin on, 116

land, socialisation of, 10

Lange, O., 37

Laptev, I. D., 173

Larichev, V. A., 63, 73, 82, 178

Larin (Yu. Lur), 9n, 99

Lavrov, V. I., 156

Lenin, V. I., 1, 9–11, 100, 195; and planning, 9, 169; and NEP, 13; and Stalin, 62; and Groman, 103; similarity between Groman and, 101–2; and Sukhanov, 181; and Maslov, 191

Levitsky, V. O., wife of, 95

Lezhnev, A. I., 67

Liberman, Ye. G., 130

Litoshenko, L. N., 31–2, 174, 175n, 196

livestock, 1, 17, 40, 41, 71; production figures for, 168

Lorimer, F., 12n

Lositsky, A. E., 5, 170, 189–90, 205; during NEP, 35, 36; and Vikhlyaev, 209

Löwenstein, Communist member of Reichstag, 65

Mach-Avenarius school of philosophy, 125, 137

Makarov, N. P., 5, 35, 197–200; and Five-Year Plan for agriculture, 167–78 *passim*, 205; attacks on, 196; submits, 55; and alleged groups, 66, 73; reappears, 199–200

Malafeev, A. N., 18, 53, 54, 57n, 153n, 154

Malyantovich, P. N., 182

Martov, Yu. O., 181; sister-in-law, 95

Marx, K., 104, 114, 125, 139

Marxism, Marxists, 34, 91, 114, 137, 180, 188

Maslov, P. P., Marxist, 65, 66, 135, 190–2, 197

Maslov, S. L., Social Revolutionary, 182, 197

mathematics, in planning, 128

Mekk, N. K. von, 32

Mendelson, A., 34, 136

Mensheviks, 2–3, 13, 91, 179; in VSNKh, 33, 122, 134; in Gosplan, 17n, 33–4, 69; Programme of, 109–16; Groman as leader of, 158; trial of, 2, 57, 61, 62–71, 84, 85, 176, 177; alleged 'United Bureau' and foreign centre of, 72, 75–82, 121, 136–7, 184; verdict on, 83

Milling, Central Bureau of, 95n, 96

Milyutin, V. P., 9n, 75; attacks by, on Mensheviks, 32–3, on Kondrat'ev, 107, 164, 176, on Rubin, 188, and on Yurovsky, 209–10

Mitchell, W. C., 162

Mullin, V. S., 175n

Nekrasov, N. V., 64

neo-narodniks, *see* TKP

NEP (New Economic Policy), 7, 15, 16–36, 77, 101, 126, 172, 198; end of, 7, 117, 182

Nikolaevsky, B., 77

Nikulikhin, Ya. P., 173, 205

Nutter, W., 45–6, 48, 52

obschchina (peasant land commune), 181–2

Observers, League (Group) of, 30, 101, 181, 191

Obukhov, V. M., 207n

Oganovsky, N. P., 27n, 186, 196, 197, 204–6

Oparin, D. I., 161

opposition (nonconformists): economic, 2; under War Communism, 13–15; during NEP, 28–36; after NEP, 37, 55–7; Trotskyist, 78

Osadchy, P. S., 73, 105, 119, 134n, 207

Ozerov, I. N., 165n

Pervushin, S. A., 4, 34, 56

Peshekhonov, A., 30

Petrov, A., 96

Petunin, K. G.; trial of, 63, 69, 194; in alleged groups, 72, 74n, 78, 80, 81; verdict on, 83

Pistrak, G. M., 69, 70, 123, 186

planning: Lenin and, 9, 169; Groman and, 98, 99, 103, 104, 110; Bazarov and, 128–34; genetic and teleological approach, 70–1, 127–8, 170–1; *see also* Five-Year Plan

Platova, S., 201

Pollock, F., 10n, 11n, 17, 29n

216

Index